Encyclopaedia of
MEDICAL &
PSYCHOLOGICAL
ASTROLOGY

How to find
Health Patterns in the chart.

Leoni Hodgson

ISBN: 978-0-6483012-2-6

About the Author

Leoni Hodgson has worked professionally as a practitioner and teacher in several specialist areas in the esoteric arts - Astrology (DMNZAS - Diploma Member of the NZ Astrological Society 1982, and the PMAFA - Professional Member of the American Federation of Astrologers 1983), Esoteric Psychology (MA in Esoteric Psychology and Ph.De in Esoteric Philosophy), Raja Yoga, and Esoteric Healing (INEH Certificate).

About this Book

The author is very grateful to all astrologers who have contributed their knowledge and wisdom to Medical and Psychological Astrology. To build on this body of knowledge - after investigating the books currently available, the author saw a need for a book such as this:

A Medical/ Psychological Encyclopaedia that includes medical definitions.

Acknowledgment of the psychology - body connection; of an emotional disturbance (primarily) - and the appearance of a related physical disease.

The presentation of health formulas, in which signs and planets that represent a disease, are clearly distinguished from those that represent the mind and body parts affected.

To demonstrate how the formulas work, disease patterns from charts have been included - and associated birth chart data, so readers can erect charts and see for themselves what is being explained.

The inclusion of Esoteric and Eastern spiritual notions and terms. This expands exoteric astrology into wider fields of knowledge.

The ideas presented in this book, the health formulas, the chakras, rays, planets, and signs representing the various diseases and mental troubles; these need to be subjected to rigorous scrutiny. More research is required, so that the information is fine-tuned, corrected, changed, added to, improved and enhanced. This, so that the astrology of medicine and psychology is placed upon a more accurate scientific footing, and can gain the respect it deserves in mainstream psychology and medicine. This is the long-term goal of this book.

Leoni Hodgson

Acknowledgments

This book is dedicated to the world service work of Master Djwhal Khul.

My loving thanks to Jeanni Monks and Paula Villano for courage, strength and inspiring optimism in the face of major health challenges.

Grateful thanks also for the website astro.com, from where most birthchart and disease data was sourced.

Other Books Written by the Author

Journey of the Soul.
A Handbook for Esoteric Psychology and Astrology.
Published 2018.

Medical Astrology.
Discover the Psychology of Disease using Triangles.
Published February 2018.

Astrology of Spirit, Soul and Body.
A Handbook for Esoteric Astrology.
Published November 2018.

Learn Astrology.
A Guide for Absolute Beginners.
Published February 2020.

The Spiritual Evolution of Nations.
Astrology Eclipses, Stars & Planet Transits.
Published April 2021.

Foreword

Every astrologer has their standard repertoire of delineations when a client comes for a session. The questions from clients usually run along the lines of work, family, home, economics, partnerships and then the big one – love. But often toward the end of a consult the question arises, often as an afterthought: "Do you see any concerns for my health in the near future?" Good question, but how to answer raises another dilemma for the astrologer, because questions of health are multifaceted and often require extra time to examine. Sometimes the answers are clear enough, if the client is otherwise in good health. This is where Leoni's book comes in very handy, and for which I am very pleased to give this introduction.

Many books have been written on medical astrology. So what makes An Encyclopaedia of Medical & Psychological Astrology, different from all the others? Leoni's approach is direct, easy to follow and – more to the point – enables the astrologer to quickly zero in on whatever ails a person, as well as the potential for illness as shown in the natal chart. To begin, she points out that most illness is the result of prevailing disharmony between one's personal life and one's own soul, summarized in the following words from her introduction:

> "So, philosophically, the effect of disease is purificatory. It is Nature's way of forcing us to change the trajectory of our lives, how we engage with ourselves and with others so that we are in harmony with divine flow. Astrology enables us to map that process."

What follows in the pages of this book, then, is the 'roadmap' to astrological diagnoses of illnesses. Her approach is formulaic. There are no case studies. Instead, this is a reference book, much as one would see in Rex Bills' The Rulership Book and H. L. Cornell's Encyclopaedia of Medical Astrology – in fact, a cross in style between the two works just mentioned.

The book is arranged in alphabetical order, cross-referencing between illnesses and factors. Where specific illnesses are catalogued most often chart details are listed for the person where the illness manifested, so astrologers can erect the chart and look for themselves if the need arises or in the process of learning the method.

The introductory chapter gives all the factors used in the delineations, with a brief explanation and then the formula is outlined. The alphabetical chapters are comprehensive, from the esoteric to the orthodox, from the sublime to the mundane. This is a reference book that should grace every astrologer's bookshelf. It will certainly be added to my own.

With the preceding in mind, it should be noted that astrological diagnoses in matters of health should always be confirmed by one's own health care provider and should complement one's own regular health care.

Leoni's book complements her earlier book, MEDICAL ASTROLOGY: Discovering the Psychology of Disease using Triangles and is an adjunct to it. We welcome this, Leoni's further contribution to the study and practice of medical astrology, nicely summarizing her 40+ years of astrological practice and consultations. This book, paired with her other book on medical astrology just mentioned, takes us further on the journey to explore the complexities and wonders of the human energy system and its secrets.

Leoni also has a Facebook group where these matters are openly explored and discussed and one is invited to join in and actually practice the techniques in this book. She is a long-time colleague in the esoteric community and fellow astrologer. In a world undergoing tremendous changes and with all the attendant stresses, this is a book those times have called forth.

Thank you, Leoni

Malvin Artley
May 2023
www.malvinartley.com

Contents

Chapter I.
Introduction.

In a general sense the cause of disease is disharmony with life. Clashing energies and conflicts cause disease. In man, the immediate problem is disharmony with his core-centre, the soul. This means that prior to enlightenment, which is that advanced state when consciousness is fully illumined with the light and love of the soul; illness is inevitable. The body may not break down until life's end but the rule holds good. Disease is simply nature's way of letting us know that its flow is blocked and that an adjustment or easing of that blockage is required.

So, philosophically, the effect of disease is purificatory. It is Nature's way of forcing us to change the trajectory of our lives, how we engage with ourselves and with others so that we are in harmony with divine flow. Astrology enables us to map that process - the psychological causes that underlie individual diseases, and remedial actions we can take to circumvent those causes from manifesting as a physical disease.

Introduction

The primary cause of disease is disharmony with life - nature's way of letting us know that its life-flow is blocked and that an adjustment or easing of that blockage is required.

This disharmony that leads to disease, is due mainly to our troubled emotions. Mainstream medicine is just beginning to make the link between psychology and disease. But esoteric healers and astrologers have known of this connection for centuries. Here is a quote.

> If our thoughts and emotions are violent, disturbed or repressed, this causes disruption in the etheric body and the glandular release of toxic chemicals in the physical that eventually lead to disease. If our thoughts and emotions are positive and filled with joy, then energy flow will be smoother and the result will be more wholesome and health benefiting. [1]

Consequently, when looking for the cause of a disease in the chart, an examination of the planets and signs that represent the emotions should be made. These are the Moon, Mars and Neptune; and the water signs Cancer, Scorpio and Pisces.

If they link into planets you are studying for a disease, it is a clue to the troubled psychology which is behind the appearance of the physical trouble.

The esoteric factor in psychology and health.

Because esoteric concepts have been included in this book, this section has been added to assist those who have not yet delved into the esoteric side of astrology. The author recommends that all astrologers interested in medical astrology should do such an investigation. This, because esotericism addresses the realm of the superhuman - the higher powers and energies of the soul, our true self. The soul uses the process of reincarnation to *force* its personality aspect to evolve and grow spiritually. Disease is an *avoidable* part of that forcing process.

Here is a definition for soul.

> Soul is the manifestation of spirit, in time and space. Soul, consciousness and awareness are synonymous terms. To be conscious is to be aware of our surroundings. To be self-conscious is to be aware of ourselves as human beings. To be soul conscious is to be aware of ourselves as both human and divine, as beings functioning in time and space with the purpose of becoming more spiritually aware. [2]

---

1   Hodgson, Leoni; Medical Astrology, 96.
2   Hodgson, Leoni, Astrology of Spirit, Soul and Body, 3.

Our astrology charts, natal and progressed, map this developmental process - the psychological causes that underlie individual diseases, and remedial actions we can take to circumvent those causes from manifesting as a physical disease.

a. "Higher powers and Energies" refers to the Seven Rays.

Refer to the Ray sections in the book for more information on the rays.

> The Seven Rays are the seven basic energies of the universe from which all things are made. Originating from the heart of our galaxy, they reach us via the signs and planets. They are seven different forces, vibrations, colours and characteristics that condition human nature on all levels. [1]

b. The developmental aspect of the signs and planets.

Together, the signs form a school of learning for man. Each sign is a class, with three levels to bring about the necessary developments. These levels can be compared to the primary, secondary and tertiary levels in modern schools. They develop the three levels of consciousness we commonly call Spirit, Soul and Body.

- The 1st *exoteric* level of planet rulers, develop *personality* consciousness.
- The 2nd *esoteric* level of planet rulers, develop soul consciousness.
- The 3rd *hierarchy* level of planet rulers, develop *spiritual* awareness.

Consequently, there are two or more planet rulers or 'teachers' for each sign, and each ruler is responsible for developing a level of consciousness in its class (sign). More information on the signs and planets are given in the alphabet sections.

Astrology Signs and Planet Rulers

Signs	Exoteric Ruler	Esoteric Ruler	Hierarchy ruler
	Personality ruler	*Soul purpose ruler*	*Spiritual ruler*
Aries	Mars	Mercury	Uranus
Taurus	Venus	Vulcan	Vulcan
Gemini	Mercury	Venus	Earth
Cancer	Moon	Neptune	Neptune
Leo	Sun	Sun v. Neptune	Sun v. Uranus
Virgo	Mercury	Moon v. Vulcan	Jupiter
Libra	Venus	Uranus	Saturn
Scorpio	Mars, Pluto	Mars	Mercury
Sagittarius	Jupiter	Earth	Mars
Aquarius	Uranus, Saturn	Jupiter	Moon v. Uranus
Capricorn	Saturn	Saturn	Venus
Pisces	Jupiter, Neptune	Pluto	Pluto v = veiling

For those who wish to study Esoteric Astrology, Hodgson's books Journey of the Soul and Astrology of Spirit, Soul and Body, are comprehensive guides on the subject.

---

1 Hodgson, Leoni; Astrology of Spirit, Soul and Body, 19.

A. Planet/ Sign Basics in Health and Disease.

This section includes some astrology basics and information to help readers navigate this book.

a. The signs and planets govern different parts of our nature - spiritual, psychological and physical. Every body organ, every process, every function is represented by at least one planet, sometimes more than one.

b. The personal planets represent our personal bodies of expression.
    The Sun: the personality consciousness.
    The Moon: emotional patterns and the physical form.
    Mercury: the mind.
    Venus: expression of personal love and affection.
    Mars: expression of desire, passion, sex.

c. Good physical health is an important life goal and generally, a strong and well-placed Sun supported by Mars, Jupiter and some easy aspects is a good start. It indicates abundant vitality, which is crucial for good physical health.

1. Afflicted Planets and Stress.

Potential ill health is found in the natal chart by finding and analysing afflicted planets. This because their forces have been compromised in some way. Their vitalising functions have become toxic. The forces may be repressed, may flow too powerfully, or be otherwise expressed in a manner that is undermining health.

> A general rule to remember is that a well aspected planet is conducive to good health; a poorly aspected or *afflicted* planet indicates the potential for malfunction and disease.

When afflicted planets link up with other planets and points in the chart, they form a 'stress pattern', also called a health or disease pattern in this book.

> Generally, a stress pattern consists of 2 or more planets in aspect to each other (usually a hard aspect), especially if it connects to the health houses - the 6th (acute illnesses) and 12th (chronic illnesses).

Stress patterns in the chart represent shortcomings and limitations in our psychology. Unregenerated, they cause inner conflict, and eventually - a physical or mental illness.

Planet stresses and afflictions in a chart do not necessarily mean disease is imminent. Everyone has them. Charts of highly successful people have many planet afflictions. What makes the difference is how we deal with stress. If we learn from our disappointments and challenges to be wiser and make better choices in the future, if we make lifestyle changes to alleviate the stress, if we go forward with positivity rather than succumb to bitterness; potentially we can neutralise a potential health crisis. When stress is removed so that energies can flow freely and healthily, it benefits health.

2. Planets afflicted by sign.

A planet is considered afflicted if it is in a sign that is hostile to its force - a sign in which it *falls* or is in *detriment*. When this occurs, its energy is distorted in some way, has become toxic, which means potential trouble for health. The following chart shows the signs in which planet forces are positively strengthened, or are distorted and toxic.

Planet Dignities, Detriments, Exaltations and Fall.

Signs	Dignified *strengthened*	Detriment *energy distorted*	Exalted *strengthened*	Falls *energy distorted*
Sun	Leo	Aquarius	Aries	Libra
Moon	Cancer	Capricorn	Taurus	Scorpio
Mercury	Gemini-Virgo	Sagittarius-Pisces	Aquarius	Leo
Venus	Taurus-Libra	Scorpio-Aries	Pisces	Virgo
Mars	Aries-Scorpio	Libra-Taurus	Capricorn	Cancer
Jupiter	Sagittarius-Pisces	Gemini-Virgo	Cancer	Capricorn
Saturn	Capricorn-Aquarius	Cancer-Leo	Libra	Aries
Uranus	Aquarius	Leo	Scorpio	Taurus
Neptune	Pisces	Virgo	Cancer	Capricorn
Pluto	Scorpio	Taurus	Aries	Libra

This information is critical when analysing the inherent health of the body. Afflictions by sign are probably the most important indicators of potential trouble. Note them carefully.

3. Planets afflicted by aspect.

A planet is considered afflicted if it has many *hard* aspects. Such aspects represent disruptive energies - of the nature of the planets involved.

a. The major hard aspects:

They represent the most disruptive forces:

- The square (□, 90°).
- The opposition (☍, 180°).
- The conjunction (☌, 0°) when it is made by a 'malefic' planet to a 'personal planet,' or to the ascendant.
- Midpoints that contain malefics.

b. Minor hard aspects

The forces these aspects represent, are not usually considered to be as disruptive as the major hard aspects. But do not be fooled. A *minor* negative habit in character (which minor aspects supposedly represent), if it endures across the years will turn into a chronic negative attitude and eventually cause havoc with health. While major planet patterns with hard aspects - such as the t-square, tend to predominate with major health issues; minor aspects are also numerous.

The minor aspects used in this book are:
- The semi-square ($\angle$, 45°).
- The quincunx (π, 150°).
- The sesquiquadrate ($\mathbb{Q}$, 135°).
- The quindecile (qd, 165°).

c. Easy aspects.
- The trine ($\triangle$, 120°).
- The sextile ($\star$, 60°).

Do not dismiss easy aspects when looking for disease patterns. Normally considered to be beneficial, technically they simply indicate an easy flow of energy. If a malefic is involved or a planet is afflicted, an easy aspect can represent the easy flow of toxic energy.

Here are 3 examples.
- *Mars is in Taurus, sextile Saturn in Cancer.* Both planets are in detriment which means - though their forces flow relatively well; this force is toxic.
- *Saturn is in Cancer trine the Sun in the 6H.* Saturn is in detriment and the Sun is in the 6H. This easy flow of toxic force from Saturn will potentially affect heart health.
- *Retrograde Mars in Aries, sextile Mercury in Aquarius.* Retrograde planets also indicate an affliction, toxic flow.

Keep this in mind and use the trine or sextile aspects in a disease pattern if it seems appropriate to do so.

4. Planets afflicted in other ways.

a. Unaspected or retrograde planets. They are considered afflicted. Especially retrograde Mercury, Venus and Mars; and the unaspected Sun, Moon, Mercury, Venus and Mars. The latter are not integrated into the psyche and that is a major problem.

b. 6th - 12th houses. Healthwise, a planet is potentially afflicted if it is located in the 12th house of hospitals or in the 6th house of health.

c. Jupiter and Venus. These are considered to be beneficial and helpful planets - and they are. But in a stress pattern, they can also represent disease effects in the body. Venus can corrupt and weaken, and Jupiter represents over-growth and over-building.

d. The Sun, Moon and Mercury are considered neutral planets. But when afflicted their forces can be toxic. The Sun inflames and over-builds, Mercury spreads airborne germs, and the Moon can represent corruption, decay and the breeding of germs.

5. Malefic Planets.

The term *malefic* was used by ancient astrologers for planets which they believed had an evil effect - originally, for Mars and Saturn. Later Uranus, Neptune and Pluto were added. Obviously, all planets have their positive side. But this malefic/ evil concept remains valid today, because negative and evil forces in nature do exist. The planets are simply the representatives of all the forces in nature - both positive and negative, good and evil.

Where health is concerned: Mars inflames. Saturn blocks, hardens and degrades. Uranus causes aberrations and fosters the breeding of germs. Neptune is insidious, it perverts and poisons. Pluto is malignant, it destroys and kills.

B. Finding Planets to Represent an Organ

Organ-planet rulerships are given in the book.

a. Look for that organ in the alphabet section of the book.

b. Look to see if a suggested planet, aspects a planet that could represent the disease.

c. If it does, you have a candidate. If not, continue searching for an alternative.

While it is handy to have a book such as this, which gives planet-organ suggestions, it is important to know how to conduct a search to find these connections. This - because sometimes, the main rulers of the organs are not implicated in the chart. Then, lateral thinking is required to find an alternative ruler. Here is a guide.

1. Find a prime planet ruler for an organ, by sign rulership.

Identify the sign that rules the part of the body, which the organ is in. The ruler of that sign is a prime ruler of the organ. See if it makes a connection to a disease planet.

2. Find an alternative prime planet ruler for the organ.

Sometimes, a prime ruler of an organ has no connection to the sign ruling the organ.

> EG. While Cancer and the Moon are the prime rulers of digestion, Jupiter is the prime ruler of the liver making the Moon a secondary or substitute ruler. While reproductive organs are ruled generally by Scorpio and Mars, the Moon has prime rulership over female reproduction organs.

Acquiring this knowledge comes with practice and experience. Search through the various rulers (given in this book). If none of them are suitable, then go to the next step.

3. Look further afield for an alternative ruler.

a. In the chart, see if there is a planet *in the sign, ruling the organ*. If so, it can be used.

> EG. The problem is the heart, which is ruled by Leo. You have checked the Sun and it seems uninvolved. Then look to see if there is a planet in Leo and if it makes the desired connection. If so, use that planet. The planet itself will explain more about the problem. For instance, if it is Mars then inflammation is a problem. If it is Saturn, chronic aging and hardening has occurred.

b. Look for planets in polar-opposite signs. Paired signs are counter-balancing forces, and because of this, are related to each other's organs and systems.

> EG: There is trouble in the testes. But Mars, the prime ruler of the testes is uninvolved, and there are no planets in Scorpio which rules the testes. Then check Scorpio's polar-opposite - Taurus. If there is a planet in Taurus, it could represent the organ.

In the following alphabet sections, when a planet is selected to represent a problem in a polar-opposite sign - it will be written like this: ♂ ♉/♏. The sign the planet is in, is written first (♉). The target sign (in this case Scorpio), is written second (/♏).

c. Look to see if a planet is in a decanate ruled by the prime sign and organ.

> EG: You are looking for a ruler of the heart, and you see a planet in the 2nd decanate of Aries, which is ruled by Leo. That planet could be used.

d. Planets are connected if one planet falls in the other's sign. The ruler of a sign disposits (has power over), all planets located in its sign.

C. Finding the Energy, the Planets and Signs, to Represent a Disease

The Seven Rays are the seven basic energies of nature, from which all things are made. Medical Astrologers should become familiar with these energies and the seven groups of diseases they produce. The rays flow through the signs and planets.

1. Is a prime ruler for the disease or trouble, connecting to the organ?

Sometimes just one planet is favoured to represent a disease. For instance, Mars for inflammation and Saturn for arthritis. In the book, find the planet-sign rulers for a disease. If there is more than one planet, usually the first one given is the prime ruler. Look to see if it - or any of the other suggested planets, make a connection to the troubled organ.

EG. The problem is inflammation.
  a. If Mars connects to the troubled organ, you have found the disease planet.
  b. If not, look to see if any the Sun, or planets in fire signs are making the connection. If for instance, the troubled organ squares Uranus, or Pluto in fiery Leo; either of those planets could represent the inflammatory problem because Uranus wields electrical fire that burns, and fire signs are naturally related to heat and burning problems.

EG. The problem is a viral infection.
  a. You see that Neptune, the prime ruler for viruses, is not involved.
  b. But Mars rules infections generally, and Uranus is the prime ruler for bacterial infections, and either of those planets could substitute for Neptune.
  c. Alternatively, a planet is located in Neptune's sign Pisces, or in a Cancer or Scorpio decanate ruled by Pisces. Then that planet could represent the virus.

2. When none of the favoured planets seem implicated in the disease.

If an organ is chronically diseased, but none of the favoured planets or signs for the disease seem involved, then carefully scrutinise all aspects to the planet/s representing the organ.

EG. The problem is cirrhosis of the liver, where scar tissue replaces healthy liver tissue.
In your search you find that Jupiter, the favoured ruler for the liver has no links to either Capricorn or Saturn for scarring. But Jupiter squares one of the other malefics, which is located in a health house. Use that planet for the problem and *make it fit*. For example:
  • If Mars is the malefic involved, it can indicate there is serious inflammation. This fits, inflammation precedes scarring, and Mars could indicate surgery is likely.
  • Uranus can represent tissue aberrations are occurring in the liver.
  • Neptune insidious and poisonous changes.
  • Pluto malignant tissue and a looming disease that could kill.

Go with what the chart presents, remembering you are dealing with disruptive energy and all afflicted planets represent different forms of that disruption.

3. The message is, be flexible in your search.

Lateral thinking is required. Keep this in mind as you work with the following alphabet sections. This rule applies to disease patterns in charts. Sometimes there may be several patterns in a birth chart, which could suit. In this book, suggestions have been kept brief to avoid confusion.

D. About the entries in this book.

Each disease is accompanied by a Definition, a Key, and a Health Formula.

The definition is a crucial part when searching for a disease pattern, because it gives the clue to the planets and signs involved. For example, here is a definition for a heart attack.

> *Heart attack (myocardial infarction):* Sudden blockage of blood to the heart. Rapid intervention is required to avoid death, actual or to a part of the heart.

This definition is translated into the language of astrology.

> *Heart attack (myocardial infarction):* Sudden (♂♅) blockage (♄) of blood flow (♒♅♆) to the heart (♌☉). Unless intervention is made quickly (♂♅), it will result in death (♏♇, 8♏), of a part of the heart or of life.

From the definition, a Key and Health Formula are assembled.

The Key and Health Formula.

1. The Key.

a. First, a Key to the construction of the formula is given.

b. The Key has two parts. (i) The body part/s affected, and (ii) [the disease].

Square brackets. To differentiate between the organ affected and the disease, square brackets are used to contain the disease planets. Although this is the general rule, sometimes in complicated patterns, organ planets will be pulled into the brackets.

c. For a heart attack the Key is: Link the heart > blood flow [blockage/ attack].

> Before the brackets (i) the heart > blood flow.
> Inside the brackets (ii) the disease [blockage/ attack].

2. The Health Formula.

From this Key, an astrology Health Formula is assembled.

The formula for a heart attack is: ☉♌ / ♒♅♆ [♄♇/♃ > ♂♅].

a. The heart / and blood flow: ♌☉ / ♒♅♆.

Sun and Leo for the heart, and Aquarius, Uranus, Neptune for blood flow are suggested. These are not the only rulers that could represent blood flow; but they are the prime rulers.

Rounded brackets. Planets or signs in rounded brackets are alternative options. For instance, Mars could be added to the heart organ planets (as an optional extra), because it rules the heart muscle - like this: ☉♌ (♂).

Angle brackets **(>).** Are used to show clear divisions between different parts of the formula.

The slash (/). In a formula it indicates either/ or, a choice. For example, it is used in the formula for a heart attack: [♄♇/♂♅]. Saturn and Pluto for the blockage, Mars and Uranus for the attack. Any of these planets - alone or with others, could represent the trouble afflicting the heart. So for instance, ☉ [□♂]. or ☉ [∠♇/ □♅].

The slash is also used for midpoint (mp) aspects. For instance (♅ mp ♆/♂), means Uranus is midpoint Neptune and Mars.

b. The disease: [♄ ♇/♃ > ♂ ♅].

For 'blockage' Saturn, Pluto / and Jupiter are suggested. For the 'attack', Mars and Uranus. In the chart, look to see if a representative of the heart or blood flow, has a connection to one of these.

3. Planets that appear more than once.

Sometimes the same planet or sign may appear on both sides of a formula. This because it can represent both the organ and the disease.

EG. the Key and Formula for Irritable Bowel Syndrome (IBS) is:

Link large intestines (bowel) [diarrhoea, pain, irritation]. ♏ ♂ ♇ (♍ ☿) [♂ ♅].

Because Mars can represent both the bowel and inflammation, it appears on both the organ and disease sides of the formula. In such a case, when diagnosing, you use Mars just once. - to represent either the organ, the disease, or both the organ and disease.

For example:

a. Mars representing just the organ. ♂ for the bowel [□ ♅].

b. Mars representing the disease. ♇ [☍ ♂] for diarrhoea, pain, irritation.

c. Mars representing both the organ and disease. EG. ♂ ♉6 [□ ♄]. You see that heavily afflicted Mars has only one aspect - to Saturn. Even though Saturn does not appear in the formula, you use what the chart presents. So in this case, Mars can represent both the bowel and disease (diarrhoea, pain, irritation) - and Saturn, the afflicting planet, will represent a subsidiary problem associated with IBS. Perhaps IBS is in danger of becoming a chronic condition. Or it is responsible for the appearance of a skin (♄), rash (♂). You respect what the chart presents (and as said in C.2); make the extra planet fit.

4. Example disease patterns.

For many of the entries in the book, example disease patterns have been given - and associated birth chart data. When a birth time is not known, charts have been set up for 12 noon, Equal House system, 0 Aries rising, at the birth location.

<u>The Key and Health Formula for a Heart Attack - and Examples.</u>

The Key: Link the heart / blood flow [blockage > attack].

The Formula: ☉ ♌ / ♒ ♅ ♆ [♄ ♇/♃ > ♂ ♅].

All these men died from a heart attack.

(1) Jean Carmet (25 Apr 1920, 12:00, Tours, Fr).

In Jean's chart we find: ☉ > [□ ♃ ♌1 > ☍ ♂].

- The heart (☉).
- Blockage [□ ♃ ♌1]
- Attack [☍ ♂].

Readers will notice that a sign - Leo, has been included (♃ ♌). This is because Leo, as a ruler of the cardiovascular system, is directly related to the problem.

(2) Michel Berger (28 Nov 1947, 17:15, Neuilly sur Seine, Fr).

In Michael's chart we find: ☉6 [☌ ♃ > □ ♂ ♌].

- The heart (☉6).
- Blockage [☌ ♃].
- Attack [□ ♂ ♌].

E. Miscellaneous

1. Planets in Houses.

"H" is an abbreviation for 'house'. Sometimes it is used to indicate the house a planet is in, sometimes it is not used. These are the two ways planets in houses are indicated.

☿6 or ☿6H, for Mercury in the 6th house.

♃1, or ♃1H, for Jupiter in the 1st house.

2. Rulers of Houses.

The small letter "r" is used as an abbreviation for "rule," "rules, or "ruler." Like this:

♃ r6, or ♃ r6H; for Jupiter ruling the 6th house.

♏ r9, or ♏ r9H; for Scorpio ruling the 9th house.

If one sign spans the entire width of a house, that sign alone rules the house's affairs. But if a second or even a third sign (including an intercepted sign), rule sections of a house; they are secondary rulers. They corule the house.

For example: 25 Scorpio is on the 6H cusp and 28 Sagittarius is on the 7H cusp.

This means that Scorpio is the prime ruler of the 6H because it is on the cusp, and Sagittarius (which actually rules most of the house - 28 degrees of it) corules it.

- Scorpio's abbreviated rulership is written like this: ♏ r6H.
- Because Mars and Pluto rule Scorpio, they also rule the 6th house: ♂ ♇ r6H.
- Sagittarius' corulership is written like this: ♐ corules the 6H.
- Because Jupiter rules Sagittarius, it corules the 6th house: ♃ corules the 6H.

3. Abbreviations used in the book.

Asc	Ascendant	Cwn	Crown chakra
Dec	Descendant	Disp	Disposited
G.cross	Grand cross	H	House
Hrt	Heart chakra	IC	Imum Coeli, or under-sky.
MC	Medium Coeli, midheaven	mp	Midpoint
n	natal	p	Progressed
qd	Quindecile, 165 degrees	r	Rule, rules, ruler
R	Ray	Sac	Sacral chakra
s.arc	Solar Arc directions	Spx	Solar plexus chakra
Thr	Throat chakra	t	Transit
Tsq	T-square		

Chapter 2. The Encyclopaedia A - Z

Aries...............................head

Taurus...........................throat

Gemini..................lungs, arms, hands

Cancer......................breasts

Leo.........................heart, spine

Cancer........................stomach

Libra.........................kidneys

Virgo..........................intestines

Scorpio........................genitals

Sagittarius...........hips   thighs

Capricorn....................knees

Aquarius......................ankles

Pisces.....................feet

A

Abdomen: The part of the body between the chest and the hips that contains the digestion organs. Spx. ♋ ☽, ♍ ☿.

Abduction: Taking someone away by force and deception. [♇].

Aberration: Deviates from the normal type. [♅].

Abnormal, Abnormalities: Different from what is considered normal. [♅ ♆].

Abnormal Growth - see Acromegaly.

Abortion: Termination of a pregnancy. The ruler of the 5H, or planets in it, may be involved. Link foetus [and abortion]. Sac. ♋ ☽, 5H [♏♂♇].
(1) French writer Anais Nin (21 Feb 1903, 20:25, Neuilly sur Seine, Fr). In 1934, she had the first of several aborted pregnancies. ☽ ♑ [☌ ♅ r5H].

Abrasions: Surface layers of the skin are broken. Link skin [broken]. ♑ ♄ (♋ ☽) [♂ ♅].

Abscess: A painful collection of pus (dead white cells), usually caused by a bacterial infection. Examine the position of Cancer and the Moon since they rule white cells and the Moon rules pus and decay. Link the body part [and abscess - ♋ ☽].
(1) President Gerald Ford (14 Jul 1913, 00:43, Omaha, NB), had surgery in 2000, to drain a mouth (♀) abscess. ♀ coruler 6H [☍ ☽].

Accidents: These are mostly caused by explosions of force, generated by hatred, jealousy or vindictiveness, which are R6, Mars' traits. This force turns back upon the individual concerned like a boomerang [1]. True accidents happen when innocent people get caught up in violence created by others. Link to Mercury for transport accidents. [♂ (♅)].
(1) Jayne Mansfield (19 Apr 1933, 09:11, Lower Merion, PA). A car in which the actress was being transported was in an accident and she was killed. ☿ ♈ [⚻♂3 > ∠♄8].

Aches: Pain. Chronic, continuous dull pain [♄]. Sharp acute pain [♂].

Achondroplasia: see Dwarfism - Disproportionate.

Acid, Acidity, Acidosis: Caused by an overproduction of acid that builds up in the blood. Excess acid in the body is a result of criticism, violent dislike and hatred. [2] [♂].

- Acid Reflux, GERD: (Gastroesophageal reflux disease). Gastric acid flows back into the food pipe, irritating the lining. Link digestion [and acid]. Spx. ♋ ☽ [♂].

Acne: Often associated with puberty, hair follicles plug with oil and dead cells causing blackheads, pus-filled pimples and red bumps. Link face/ skin [acne]. ♈ ♂/ ♑ ♄ (♋) [♂].

Acoustic Neuroma: A non-cancerous tumour on the main nerve leading from the inner ear to the brain. Affects balance and hearing. Venus or Libra may link in for balance. Link ears [benign tumour]. Cwn. ♊ ☿ [♃].

1 Bailey, Alice. Esoteric Psychology II, 548.
2 Bailey, Alice: Esoteric Healing, 38.

Acquired Immunodeficiency Syndrome, AIDS: (See HIV). AIDS is caused by a virus that destroys the body's immune system. Look first for attacks on the Sun and Leo that represent the vitality of the immune system. When vitality drops, so does immunity. Link immune system [virus > destruction]. Hrt. ♌☉ (♂) [♂♅♆ >♄♇].
These examples all died from the disease.
(1) Astro.com 11083 (20 Oct 1948, 13:30, Havana, Cuba). ☉ [♇♌ mp ☉/ ☽ ♉/♏ r6H].
(2) Astro.com 11146 (14 Jan 1949, 21:31, San Mateo, CA). ☉♑5 [⚻♅ r6H].
(3) Astro.com 11189 (8 Mar 1949, 18:05, Bronx, New York). ☉6 [☌♂ r8H > qd ♄12℞].
(4) Astro.com 11362 (16 Sep 1949, 09:54, San Pedro, CA). ☉ [♇♌ mp ☉/♅♋8].

Acromegaly, Gigantism: Abnormal growth caused by an overproduction of pituitary growth hormone. Link pituitary [aberration / over-growth]. Ajna. ♀ [♅ / ♐♃].
(1) Andre the Giant (19 May 1946, 15:10, Coulommiers, France). ♀ [☌♅ / △♃℞].
(2) Tony Robbins (29 Feb 1960, 20:10, Los Angeles, CA). ♀♒ [☍♅].

Acromicria: Abnormal smallness of the head and extremities caused by a deficiency in pituitary growth hormone. Link pituitary [deficiency, smallness]. Ajna. ♀ [♄].

Acupuncture: Oriental medical technique of inserting needles through the skin. ♂.

Acute Diseases: These are diseases that come on rapidly and are of short duration. [♂♅].

Adam's Apple: Cartilage that sticks out at the front of the throat. ♉♀.

ADD, ADHD - see Attention Deficit Hyperactivity Disorder.

Addictive, Addiction: (See Drug Addiction). An inability to stop using a substance or engage in a behaviour even though it is causing psychological or/ and physical harm. Compelling desire is a 6th ray trait. Taurus is the sign of desire. Spx. [♓♆, ♉♀].

Addison's Disease: A disorder in which the adrenal glands do not produce adequate *cortisol* (and sometimes *aldosterone*). Symptoms are extreme fatigue, nausea, darkening of the skin and dizziness. Link adrenal-cortex [and under-production]. Base. ♎♀ (♏♂) [♄♇].
(1) President John Kennedy (29 May 1917, 15:00, Brookline, MA) suffered from Addison's disease. His problem was life-threatening, requiring regular doses of cortisone. He was in pain most of the time. ♂ ♉/♏ coruler 6H [∠♇♋].

Adenoids: Tissue at the very back of the nasal passage. ♉♀.

Adenoma - see Tumours - Benign; Brain Tumour, Benign; Pituitary Tumour.

Adipose Tissue: Fatty (Jupiter), connective tissue (Cancer, Moon). ♃ > ♋☽.

Adrenals: The physical anchorages for the forces of the base chakra. The glands of combat.

- **Adrenal Cortex:** The outer part of the gland. It produces *cortisol*, the body's main stress hormone, which regulates salt-water balance in the body; and *aldosterone*, which regulates salt-water balance and blood pressure. Base. ♎♀ (♏♂).

- **Adrenal Medulla:** It is the inner part of the adrenal gland. Its main hormones are *adrenaline* and *noradrenaline*, which are involved in the fight or flight syndrome. Base. ♏♂♇.

- **Adrenal Cancer:** Most adrenal cancers start in the cortex. Link adrenals [and cancer formula]. ♎♀ (♏♂♇) [(♋☽ >♄♇) > ♃☉].
(1) Brian Keith (14 Nov 1921, 14:00, Bayonne, NJ). ♀♏ [(☍☽8 > ⚻♄♎) > ♄☌♃].

- Adrenaline: Adrenal medulla hormone that helps quick defensive reactions. ♏♂.

Ageing: Normal process of becoming older. R1, ♄.

- Ageing Unnaturally - see Progeria.

Aggression: Feelings of anger resulting in hostile or violent behaviour. R6. Spx. [♂].

Agoraphobia: (See Phobias, Panic Attacks). An anxiety disorder. A persistent and excessive fear of open or crowded spaces. Pluto on an angle often appears with phobias and nightmares. The 8H of trauma, or 12H of undoing may be involved. Link emotions [and phobia]. Spx. ♋ ☽ ♂ [♏♇♄].
(1) Olivia Hussey (17 Apr 1951, 06:40, Buenos Aires, Arg.). ☽ [wide ☌♇]. Dec [☌♆].
(2) Terry Buske (16 Nov 1952, 23:37, Freeport, IL). ☽♏ [□♇12]. Asc [☌♇12].

Ageusia: (See Hypogeusia). Permanent loss of taste. It is commonly caused by a head injury, which damages related nerves. Link nerves, taste [injury/ loss]. ♊ ☿ [♂♅/ ♄].
(1) Jim Hodgson (8 Sep 1947, 01:55, Hawkwell, UK). ☿ r12H [□♅♊12].

AIDS - see Acquired Immunodeficiency Syndrome.

Air Pollutants: Material in the air (Gemini, Mercury, air signs), that can have adverse effects on health. Link air [germs]. ♊ ☿ [♂♅♆ (♇)].

Airplane Incidents: Link air planes [accidents, crashes]. ♒♅ [♂].
(1) Kobe Bryant (23 Aug 1978, no time). He died in a helicopter crash. The pilot flew into clouds and became confused (♆), while travelling (♐). ♅♏ [mp ♆♐ /♂].

Airways: These consist of the nasal passages, mouth, pharynx (throat tube), the trachea (windpipe connecting the throat and lungs), the bronchial tubes (at the bottom of the windpipe connecting to each lung), and the lungs. Generally ruled by Gemini and Mercury; the other air signs and rulers could substitute. The airways in the throat region are coruled by Taurus and Venus. Thr. ♊ ☿.

AJNA CHAKRA: (See Chakras and Etheric web).
Consciousness: The mind works through this centre. When developed, it focalises the forces of the advanced, intelligent and fully integrated personality.
Ray and Astrology energies: The primary ray is the 5th of Concrete Mind and Science, which flows via Venus. Ray 4 via Mercury is also associated.
Body rulership: The ajna enters the body through the front of the head just above the eyebrows, anchoring in the pituitary gland. It has 96 petals which divide into 2 wings - like that of an aeroplane. It vitalises the lower brain, the central nervous system, the third eye, the front of the head, the eyes (particularly the left eye), the ears and nose.
Disease: Modern psychological disorders, and diseases of the pituitary gland, the nervous system, and the senses.

Albinism: The congenital absence of melanin resulting in a white body. Such people are commonly called 'albinos.' The Moon and Saturn cause a pale appearance, but Saturn can also darken. Link the body, skin [albinism]. Asc, 1H, ♑♄ (♋) [☽♄].
(1) Astro.com 4887 (14 Dec 1914, 06:10, Edinburgh, Scot). Asc ♏ [♂1 ∠☽♏12, ☍♄].
(2) Astro.com 4943 (14 Nov 1915, 09:00, Edinburgh, Scot). Asc [□☽, ⚼♄♋℞].
(3) Astro.com 10451 (11 Jan 1947, 03:00, Cisco, MA). Asc ♏ [♇☌♄].

Albumin: A protein in blood plasma. Its important function is protective, to prevent blood leaking into the tissues. ♋ ☽.

Alcohol. Alcoholism: Alcohol [♆♓ (♂ firewater)]. Addiction to alcohol. Spx. [♓♆].

Aldosterone: Adrenal hormone that regulates salt-water balance and blood pressure. ♎♀.

Alimentary Canal - see Digestion System and Gastrointestinal Tract.

Allergies, Allergic Reaction: (See Asthma, Coeliac Disease, Food Allergies, and Hay Fever). An allergy is an immune reaction caused by a typically harmless substance that is breathed or eaten. Emotional hyper-sensitivity, a fear-based reaction to life - these are some inner causes related to the appearance of an allergy. Link body part affected [emotions > immune reaction]. Spx. Body part [♋ ☽ > ♂ (☉ ♅)].

Alopecia: (See Autoimmune Disease). The immune system attacks healthy hair cells, and hair falls out. Link hair [immune attack > loss]. Cwn. ♈♂ [♂☉ > ♄♇].
(1) May Calamawy (28 Oct 1986, 13:00, Manama, Bahrain). ♂12 [□☉ > □♇♏].
(2) Nina Hastie (19 May 1983, 01:00, Pretoria, S.Afr). ♂ [☌☉ > ⚻♄ r12℞].
(3) Ramon Campayo (22 Sep 1965, 00:30, Ayna, Spain). ♂♏ [□ ☽ ♌ > ☽ ⚻ ♄].

ALS - see Amyotrophic Lateral Sclerosis

Alta Major Chakra: The third head chakra. It is located in the medulla oblongata, which is at the bottom of the brain, where it connects to the spinal cord. Thr. ♊ ☿.

Alveoli: Tiny air sacs at the end of the bronchioles. Thr. ♊ ☿.

Alzheimer's: The most common type of dementia (see Dementia). It affects the part of the brain associated with learning, so early symptoms include changes in memory, thinking and reasoning skills. Planets for the intelligence (☿ ♀), or consciousness (☉), may connect in. Link the brain [to aging, atrophy]. Cwn. ♈♂, ♋☽ [♄♇].
(1) Ally Macleod (26 Feb 1931, 07:50, Glasgow, Scotland). ♅♈1 [□♄♑ r12H].
(2) Barry Goldwater (2 Jan 1909, 03:00, Phoenix, AZ). ☽ [∠♄♈]. ♈ r6H.
(3) Charlton Heston (4 Oct 1923, 07:55, Evanston, IL). ☽♋ [□♄12].

Ambidexterity: Ability to use either hand skilfully. ♊ ☿.

Amenorrhoea: No menstruation, often a consequence of great stress. Link menstruation [lack of]. Sac. ♏♂ (♋☽) [♄♇].
(1) Alexandra Cane (9 June 1991, no time). She reported on social media that her menstrual cycle "came back on Mother's Day in 2021". ☽ ♉/♏ [□♄♒℞].

Amino acids: They are the building blocks of proteins, which are needed for the growth and maintenance of our cells and tissues, to repair cells and make new ones. Ray 3, carried by Saturn rules cells, [1] protein and amino acids. ♑♄.

Amnesia: Refers to a temporary loss of memory, partial or full. Causes include head injuries, a bad reaction to some drugs, alcohol abuse and severe emotional trauma. Link consciousness / or cognizance [and loss]. Cwn. Ajna. ☉/☿ [♄♇].
(1) Astro.com 8168 (8 May 1938, 23:52, Los Angeles, CA). The subject is reported as being an incest victim who has "spent time in a mental hospital for amnesia." So, the cause is trauma, which is related more to Pluto. ☿ [□♇♋6].

1 Bailey, Alice: A Treatise on White Magic, 196.

Amputate: Cutting off a body appendage: a finger, arm, hand (Gemini); leg, thigh region (Sagittarius), lower leg (Aquarius); and toe, foot (Pisces). Link the body part amputated [and amputation, ♏♂].
These three examples had legs amputated.
(1) Guillaume Depardieu (7 Apr 1971, 11:35, Paris, FR). Lower leg. ♅ [□♂6].
(2) Rudiger von der Goltz (10 Jul 1894, 07:45, Berlin, Ger). ♅ corules 6H [⚻♂♈].
(3) Sarah Bernhardt (23 Oct 1844, 20:00, Pairs, FR). The famous French stage actress had her right leg amputated due to a shattered knee. ♅♈℞ [☍♂♎ r6H]. ☉ [□♄ for knee].

Amygdala: Cells near the base of the brain that help define and regulate emotions. Part of the Limbic system. Thr. ♉♀.

Amyloidosis: A blood plasma cell disorder. Abnormal (♅), proteins (♃♄), gather on the heart, kidney or other organs causing blockages and further trouble. There is currently no cure though treatment can help clear deposits before they build up again. Link blood plasma cells [and protein > blockages]. Additionally, the body part affected may link in. Hrt. ♋☽ [♃♄ > ♄♇].
(1) David Lange (4 Aug 1942, 03:30, Otahuhu, NZ). ☽ [♄12 mp ☽/♃♋].
(2) Jeanni Monks (22 Jun 1949, 05:11, Bulawayo, Zimbabwe). Kidneys. ♀♋ [∠♄. Yod: ♃8℞ ⚻☉♅♋, ⚻♄].
(3) Michael Cofer (7 Apr 1960, no time). ☽ [△♃♑ > ☌♇].

Amyotrophic Lateral Sclerosis, ALS: Also known as Lou Gehrig's and Motor Neurone Disease. Motor neurons gradually deteriorate and die, impairing physical function and mobility. Link the nervous system > muscles [harden, death]. Jupiter/ Sagittarius for impaired movement may also be involved. Ajna. ♊☿ (♀♒♅) > ♂ [♄♇].
(1) Catfish Hunter (8 Apr 1946, 08:00, Hertford, NC). ♅♊1 [mp ♀12 /♄♋ > ♄☌♂].
(2) David Niven (1 Mar 1910, no time). The charming British actor died from this disease's effects. ♅♑ > △♂♉ [♅⚻♇♊].
(3) Lou Gehrig (19 Jun 1903, no time). The disease was named after Gehrig, an American professional baseball player. ☿♊ > △♂♎ [☿ wide ☌♇♊].
(4) Steven Hawking (8 Jan 1942, no time). The famous scientist lived with this disease until 2018. ☿♑ > □♂♈ [☿☍♇].

Anaemia: (See Pernicious Anaemia). The haemoglobin concentration in red blood cells is lower than normal. This is mostly caused by an iron deficiency. People who follow vegan and vegetarian diets need to be extra careful to include iron-rich foods in their diet. Link haemoglobin [and reduction]. Hrt. ♂ [♄♇].

Anaesthetic: Medicine designed to stop/ decrease pain during surgery. ♓♆.

Anal Canal, Anus: Tube where the gastrointestinal tract ends and exits the body, through which body waste is discharged. Spx. ♏♂♇.

- Anal Cancer: The disease developing in the anus. Link anus [and the cancer formula]. ♏♂♇ [(♋☽ >♄♇) > ♃☉].
(1) Farrah Fawcett (2 Feb 1947, 15:10, Corpus Christi, TX). In 1976, the actress became a star in the TV hit series Charlie's Angels. She was diagnosed with the disease in 2006, and died from it in 2009. ♇ [(☍♂8) > ☍☉8].

- Anal Fissure: A tear in the anal lining. Link anus [and tear]. Spx. ♏♂♇ [♂♅].

- Anal Sphincter Muscles: They control the flow of faeces into the rectum. Spx. ♏♂♇.

Analgesics: Medications to relieve different types of pain. ♆.

Anaphylaxis Shock: The immune system releases excessive chemicals, which shocks the body. Airways tighten restricting breathing. Link airways [the cause of the shock > attack/ shock]. Hrt. Thr. ♊ ☿ [cause > ♂/♅].

(1) Clara Nunes (12 Aug 1942, 18:00, Paraopeba, Brazil). She died from anaphylaxis shock during surgery to treat varicose veins. ☿ [☌♂ > □♅♊].

(2) Jason Mantzoukas (18 Dec 1972, 16:40, Nahant, MA), was born with an egg allergy and has an attack if eggs are eaten. ☿ ♐6 [☍ ☽ ♊12 for food > ∠♅].

Aneurism, Aneurysm: An artery weakens and balloons. Pressure on the artery causes the trouble. Link arteries [pressure/ balloon]. Hrt. ♃♌♒ [♄♇/ ♃].

Add Mars or Uranus for a ruptured aneurysm and haemorrhage, which caused the death (♏♂♇, 8H), of the following individuals.

(1) Albert Einstein (14 Mar 1879, 11:30, Ulm, Ger). ♃♒ [Tsq. □♇♉, ☍♅].

(2) Betty Garrett (23 May 1919, 07:00, St. Joseph, MO). ♃ ♋/♑ [∠♂♉12].

(3) Lucille Ball (6 Aug 1911, 17:00, Jamestown, NY). ♃♏ [☍♄☌♂♉].

Anger: Strong feeling of annoyance, displeasure, or hostility. R6. Spx. [♂].

Angina: Chest pain caused by reduced blood flow to the heart. Link heart/ blood [blockage > pain]. Hrt. ♌☉/ ♂♃♒ [♄♇ > ♂].

(1) Sir Ernest Shackleton (15 Feb 1874, 05:00, Kildare, Ireland). ☉♒ [□♇♉ > ♇∠♂].

(2) Guglielmo Marconi (25 Apr 1874, 09:15, Bologna, Italy). ☉□♅♌ [♅☍♄♒].

Animal Attacks, Bites: (See Rabies). Such attacks have been identified as a major public health problem and most of these are bites. [♂].

(1) Steve Irwin (22 Feb 1962, 01:00, Melbourne, Australia). A stingray stinger pierced his chest, penetrating his thoracic wall and heart, causing massive trauma. ♅♌ (heart) [☍♃☌♂, for the sting and massive trauma].

(2) Taylor Mitchell (27 Aug 1990, no time). While out on a walk, he was attacked and killed by a coyote. ☉ (life) [□♂♉/♏].

Ankles: Joints that allow up-and-down movements of the foot. Base. ♒♅.

Ankylosing Spondylitis/ Axial Spondyloarthritis: Inflammatory arthritis affecting the spine and large joints. Jupiter and Sagittarius may link in for impaired movement. Link spine/ joints [inflame, pain > arthritis]. Spx. ♌☉/ ♑♄ [♂☉ > ♄(♇)].

(1) Dan Reynolds (14 Jul 1987, no time). ☉ [qd ♆♑ > ♆⚻♂♌].

(2) John Addey (15 Jun 1920, 08:15, Barnsley, Eng). ♄ r6H [∠♂♎].

(3) Joost Zwagerman (18 Nov 1963, 22:00, Alkmaar Neth). ☉ [mp ♄ r6H /♅☌♇].

(4) Zach Kornfeld (26 Jul 1990, no time). ☉♌ [☌♃ > ♃☍♄].

Anorexia: (See Body Dysmorphia). Eating disorder where body-image (Asc, 1H) is distorted. There is an obsessive desire to lose weight and this is achieved by refusing (Saturn), to eat (Cancer, Moon). But the true cause is a negative core-belief of self-loathing, such as 'I am vile,' or 'I am ugly.' Link emotions/ food, nutrition [and denial]. Spx. ♋☽♂,♍ [♄♇].

(1) Astro.com 1667 (18 Nov 1974, 20:00, London, Eng). ☽ ♑6 [☍ ♄ ♋12℞].
(2) Astro.com 11182 (24 Feb 1949, 17:48, Huntington Beach, CA). ☽ [⚻ ♄ ♍12].
(3) Astro.com 11706 (2 Oct 1950, 05:09, New York, NY). ☽ [□ ♄ ♍12℞].

Anosmia: (See Hyposmia). Permanent loss of the sense of smell. A common cause is a head injury, which damages related nerves. Link nerves, smell [injury/ loss]. ♊ ☿ [♂ ♅/ ♄].
(1) Jim Hodgson (8 Sep 1947, 01:55, Hawkwell, UK). ☿ [□ ♅ ♊12].

Antahkarana - see Consciousness Thread.

Anthrax: A serious bacterial infection. It occurs naturally in soil and people can get sick if they come in contact with infected animals. It affects the airways, causing severe lung problems, difficulty breathing, and shock. Link airways, [infection > shock]. ♊ ☿ [♅ ♂ ♆ > ♅].
(1) Robert Stevens (20 Jun 1938, no time). A journalist, located in Florida, who was killed in the 2001 anthrax terror attacks in the USA. He received a letter containing anthrax. ☉ ☌ ☿ ♊ for airways and the letter, [∠ ♅ ♉].

Antibiotics: Medicines that fight bacterial infections by either killing (Pluto), the bacteria or suppressing (Saturn) it. ♄ ♇.

Antibodies: Immune system proteins produced to protect the body against unwanted pathogens. Hrt. ♌ ☉ ♂.

Antigen: Is part of a germ - bacteria or virus, which the body's immune system can recognize and attack. [♂ ♅ ♆].

Antisocial Personality Disorder - see Sociopath.

Anus - see Anal Canal.

Anxiety: (See Panic Attack). Excessive and persistent worry about everyday situations. Spx. ☽ ♆ [♄]. an

Aorta: Largest artery carrying oxygen-rich blood from the heart, to vessels, to the body. Hrt. ♃ ♌ ♒.

Aphasia: A language disorder caused by brain damage, which affects the ability to express and understand written and spoken language. Damage is most often caused by a stroke, but can also be caused by an injury - both ruled by Mars. Link brain > communication [stroke, injury]. Cwn. ♊ ♈ ♂, ♋ ☽ / ♊ ☿ [♂(♅)].
(1) Hans-Hinrich Taeger (15 Oct 1944, 06:35, Gorlitz, Ger). He suffered a stroke, and developed aphasia as consequence. ☿ 12 [mp ☽ /♂1].
(2) Jean Stafford (1 Jul 1915, 23:50, Covina, CA). She also suffered a stroke and developed aphasia. ☿ ♋℞ [☌ ♇3 > ⚼ ♅ ♒℞].
(3) Terry Jones (1 Feb 1942, 11:00, Colwyn Bay, Wales). Lived for several years with degenerative aphasia and gradually lost the ability to speak. ☽ > qd ☿ ♒12 [☽ □ ♂ ♉ 1].

Apnoea - see Sleep Apnoea.

Apoplexy - see Stroke.

Appendix: Narrow, finger-shaped pouch that projects out from the colon. According to one theory, the appendix houses a collection of beneficial gut bacteria that can recolonize the gut after an infection. Spx. ♏ ♂ ♇, ♍ ☿ .

- Appendicitis: The appendix becomes inflamed, fills with pus, causing pain. Mars can represent inflammation and pain. Death can occur if the appendix bursts. Cancer-Moon may link in for pus. Link appendix [inflammation, pain, burst]. Spx. ♏︎♂︎♆, ♍︎☿ [♂︎☉ (♅♇)]. These two examples died from a burst appendix.

(1) Gabriel Miro (28 Jul 1879, 18:00, Alicante, Spain). ☿♍︎ r6H [♂︎♅8].

(2) Georges Rodenbach (29 Apr 1845, 02:00, Tournai, Belgium). ♂︎12 [□♆♈︎].

Appetite: Natural desire to satisfy a bodily need, especially food. ♉︎♀︎.

AQUARIUS. ♒︎.

Rulers: The exoteric ruler is Uranus, the esoteric ruler is Jupiter, the hierarchy ruler is the Moon unveiling Uranus. As spiritual development proceeds, as the form refines (the Moon), spiritual force represented by Uranus flows into consciousness.

Rays: Carries R5 of Concrete Mind and Science. Also, R2 via Jupiter, and R7 via Uranus. Energy is mental, airy and concentrated.

Body: Aquarius is related to the base chakra through its rulership of the lower legs, calves and ankles. It is also related to the heart centre via its opposite sign Leo, governing blood circulation and blood quality. Other areas it governs are the etheric body, DNA and via Uranus, it rules the electrochemical activity of the nervous system.

Disease: When planets are afflicted in Aquarius, or Aquarius rules the 6H, it can indicate trouble with nerves or the cardiovascular system which Aquarius rules with its opposite sign Leo. As an afflictor, its 5th ray negative traits (being too detached and separative in thought), can upset the interworking's of the nervous system and messaging. For instance, neural pathways may atrophy - a problem associated with autism. The endocrine glands may start to send incorrect messages so that glands malfunction and release toxic chemicals. Interference in the energy play between the pineal and pituitary glands can result in migraine.

Psychology: Separativeness is the main negative trait. In contrast, the evolutionary goal in Aquarius is to develop a sense of universal brotherliness and love, to give selfless service to the masses. This goal is enshrined in Aquarius' higher keynote - 'Water of life am I, poured forth for thirsty men.'

Arachnophobia: (See Phobias, Panic Attacks). Being smothered, suffocated, by an extreme or irrational fear of spiders. The fear of 'scary, creepy, crawly, bitey, germy, bloodsucking' things is particularly related to Scorpio and Pluto. Examine the emotions, look for Pluto on an angle, for planets in the 8H and 12H. Link the emotions [terror, phobias]. Spx. ♋︎☽♂︎ [♏︎♆♄].

(1) Henry Bowers (29 Jul 1883, 05:00, Greenock, Scot). The Sun and three other planets in the 12H, indicates a consciousness that is deeply introspective and susceptible to imagined fears, like spiders attacking. ♃♋︎12 [∠♆♂︎☽]. ♋︎ rules the 12H.

ARIES. ♈︎.

Rulers: Exoteric ruler is Mars, the esoteric ruler is Mercury, the hierarchy ruler is Uranus.

Rays: Aries carries R1 of Will and Power, and R7 of Ceremony, Order and Magic. It also carries R6 via Mars, and R4 via Mercury. Its energy is fiery, intensely hot and fast-moving. It carries power, a gift from the 1st and 7th 'power' rays.

Body: Aries rules the skull and the head - generally, the top part down to and including the upper jaw. This includes also the crown chakra, the brain, the pineal gland, the face and nose.

Disease: When planets are afflicted in Aries, or when Aries rules the 6H, it indicates trouble with the brain and head, and/ or with the kidneys, which are governed by its opposite sign Libra. As an afflictor, Aries fire is dangerous because it carries the power rays (1 and 7), which can strike suddenly. Strokes, brain meningitis and head injuries are examples.

Psychology: The high goal is to develop intelligent self-control and rein in reactive emotions and impulses. Its higher keynote is: ‘I come forth and from the plane of mind - I rule.’

Arms, Wrists and Hands: Upper body limbs used for reaching, touching, grasping - the wrist, palm, fingers and thumbs. Thr. ♊ ☿.

Arrested Psychological Development: Psychological (primarily emotional) development stops developing before adulthood. It can be the result of abuse, trauma, grief or neglect. Link the self/ the emotions [and arrested]. ☉/ ☽ [♑ ♄(♇)].

Arrhythmia - see Heart Arrhythmia.

Arrogance: Overbearing attitude of superiority. [♌ ☉].

Arrow Wounds: Injuries caused by arrows. [♐ ♃, ♂].

Arsenic: It is a metalloid chemical element, carcinogenic to humans. [♄ ♅♇ (♆)]

- Arsenic Poisoning: (See Poison - Mineral Kingdom). Arsenic is found naturally in soil or groundwater. When an excessive amount is ingested, it can kill quickly - there is vomiting, abdominal pain, bloody diarrhoea, and brain malfunction. Spx. [♄ ♅♇, ♆].

(1) Jane Austen (16 Dec 1775, 23:45, Steventon, Eng). Because it was suspected that Austen suffered from arsenic poisoning - mainly due to skin discolouration, a lock of her hair was tested for arsenic. It was positive. ☉ r12H [□♆♍1]. ☽ for ingested [☌ ♄].

Arteries, the Arterial System: Blood vessels that deliver oxygen-rich blood from the heart to body tissues. The overall rulers of the cardiovascular are Leo and the Sun. However, Jupiter is specifically the ruler of arteries and of arterial blood, and Aquarius-Uranus rule blood vessels and blood circulation. Hrt. ♃♒.

- Arteriosclerosis: This is a general term for a group of conditions that cause arteries to become thick and stiff due to aging. Link arteries [aging, hardening]. Hrt. ♃♒ [♄♇].

The following had arteriosclerosis and died of a heart attack. ♂♅ added for attack.

(1) Cecil Cunningham (2 Aug 1888, no time). ☉♌/♒ [☌ ♄♌ > □♂].

(2) Cecil Kellaway (22 Aug 1890, no time). ☉♌/♒ [☌ ♄ > ♄□♂].

(3) Chico Marx (22 Mar 1887, 14:45, New York, NY). ☉8 [☌ ♂♈ > ♂□♄♋].

(4) Evangeline Booth (25 Dec 1865, 15:00, London, Eng). ☉♃♑ [☍ ♅℞1].

Arthritis: A general term for age-related joint pain/ inflammation and stiffness. Osteoarthritis, is the most common form of arthritis. Gout is a common form of inflammatory arthritis. According to esoteric lore, the originating cause of arthritis is gluttony:

> [Arthritis is] the result of the satisfaction of physical desire as it expresses itself through food, either in this life or the previous one. There would be little or no arthritis if the race ate with correctness. [1]

This means it is karmic. Unsurprisingly, joints and arthritis are both governed by Saturn, the Lord of Karma. Jupiter may link in for impaired mobility and gluttony, even if this occurred in a past life. Link joints [arthritis > pain, inflamed]. Spx. ♑♄ [♑♄ > ♂☉].

1 Bailey, Alice: Esoteric Healing, 311.

(1) Elsie Wheeler (3 Sep 1887, 21:45, Norris City, IL), of Sabian Symbol fame was seriously crippled by arthritis at a very young age. This means the seeds of the condition were karmic, were inherited from a previous life. ♄ [☌ ♂ ♌ r12H].

Asbestos: Naturally occurring fibrous silicate mineral - long, thin fibrous crystals. ♄ ♅.

- Asbestosis/ Mesothelioma: (See Poison - Mineral Kingdom). Inhaling asbestos fibres causes lung disease. Link lungs [asbestosis/ poison]. Thr. ♊ ☿ [♄ ♅ / ♆].
(1) Christie Hennessy (19 Nov 1945, no time), singer, songwriter. ☿ ♐ [☍ ♅ ♊ ℞].
(2) Merlin Olson (15 Sep 1940, no time), American football player. ☿ [☌ ♆ ♍ 6].
(3) Paul Gleeson (4 May 1939, no time), American actor. ☿ 1 [☌ ♄, ♄ □ ♇].
(4) Steve McQueen (24 Mar 1930, 12:15, Indianapolis, IN). ♃ ♊ [⚻ ♄ ♑ 6].

Ascendant: (See Reincarnate). The degree of the zodiac rising over the Eastern horizon at the time of birth. It represents variously: our appearance, a new incarnation, the head (via Aries which qualifies this house), and with the 1H, the physical body type we are born with and through which we navigate life. Esoterically, it represents the purpose of the soul, those spiritual developments the soul wishes to bring about in our psychology and relationships.

Asperger's: (See Autism Spectrum Disorder - ASD). Asperger's is a high-functioning form of ASD - a brain developmental problem. It is related to the separative action of the 5th ray. Link brain > cognizance [under-development/ cleavage]. Ajna. ♈ ☽, ☿ ♀ [♄/ ♀ ♒].
(1) Andrea Negro (25 Aug 2001, 17:00, Nice, FR). ☽ [qd ♄]. ♀ ♋ [∠ ♄ ♊ 6].
(2) Nikki Bacharach (12 Jul 1966, 21:59, Los Angeles, CA), daughter of the famous music composer, Burt Bacharach. ☽ r6H > □ ☿ 6 [☽ ∠ ♄]. ♀ ♊ [□ ♅].
(3) Susan Boyle (1 Apr 1961, 09:50, Bangour Village, Scot). ☽ > ⚻ ☿ [∠ ♄]. ♀ ♈ [□ ♄].

Asphyxia: Suffocation. Vital organs are starved of oxygen. It can be caused by drowning, asthma, choking or breathing in poisonous gas. Link airways [suffocation]. There may also be interlinking planets for the cause. Thr. ♊ ☿ [♏ ☌ ♇].

The first two examples were brothers and criminals, found dead in a car, asphyxiated by petrol fumes (♓ ♆).
(1) Christian Saincene (3 Sep 1945, 05:20, Marseille, FR). ☿ [mp ♇/☉].
(2) Fernand Saincene (10 Feb 1942, 23:45, Marseille, FR). ☿ coruler 8 [qd ♇].
(3) Michael Hutchence (22 Jan 1960, 05:00, Sydney, Australia). The Australian rock star was suffocated by a belt attached to a door. Some said it was suicide. But his partner Paula Yates insisted that Michael's death was accidental auto-erotic asphyxiation. This could be so, with sexual Mars trine Pluto in the 8H. ☿ 12 [□ ☽ ♏ > ☽ ☌ ♆ ♏].

Assassination: Killing of a person, especially a public figure for ideological or political gain. Since most assassinations are political, Aquarius, Uranus, the 11H, may link in. Link self, life [assassination]. ☉, Asc [♏ ♂ ♇].
(1) Franz Ferdinand, Archduke (18 Dec 1863, 07:15, Graz, Austria). His assassination in 1914 was the immediate cause of World War I. ☉ r8H [⚼ ♇].
(2) John Kennedy, President (29 May 1917, 15:00, Brookline MA). He was assassinated by Lee Harvey Oswald, who was himself killed shortly after. ☉8 [mp ♂/♇].

Asthma: (See Allergies). An allergic/ immune reaction causing airways to become inflamed, narrow, swell and produce extra mucous. The inner cause is emotional hypersensitivity.

Saturn or Jupiter may link in to emphasise congestion/ difficulty breathing. Link airways [emotions/ mucous > immune reaction]. Thr. ♊ ☿ [♋ ☽, ♂ ♆ > ♂ (☉ ♅)].

These examples are from An Encyclopaedia of Psychological Astrology, Carter.

(1) EPA p37 (29 Dec 1876, 05:30, Belfast, Ireland). ☿ [⚹ ♂ ♏ 12 > ⚻ ♅].

(2) EPA p37 (26 May 1920, 02:50, Hastings, Eng). ☿ ♊ [□ ♅ ♓ 12 > ⚼ ♂ ♎ ℞].

(3) EPA p58 (2 Dec 1886, 01:00, Croydon, Eng). ☿ ♐ ℞ [qd ♆ > ☌ ☉].

(4) Jodie Forrest (8 Feb 1956, 14:07, Arlington, VA), in 1978 she almost died from a severe asthma attack. ☿ ♑ [□ ♆ ♏ ℞ > ♆ ∠ ♂ 6].

Astigmatism: A defect in the eye or lens, caused by a deviation from spherical curvature. Link eyes [and deviation]. Ajna. ☉ ☽ [♅].

Astral Body, Astral Plane: The astral plane is a finer energy plane, one step up (or in), from the Physical Plane. Our astral or emotional bodies of expression, are formed from its force. It is the plane of delusion, the repository of all our imaginary dreams, hopes, wishes, fears, nightmares, and dark imaginings, etc. The solar plexus chakra is the organ in the body, which astral force works through. Spx. R6, ♂ ♆ (♋ ☽).

- Astral Maniac: (See Serial Killers). A person with an uncontrollable astral-desire nature. The problem can be relatively harmless, but if desires are dark, it can produce very dangerous people. Spx. R6 [♏ ♂ ♇].

(1) Marquis De Sade (2 June 1740, 17:00, Paris, Fr). French nobleman whose perverse sexual preferences and erotic writings gave rise to the term sadism. Even though he was imprisoned and vilified by many, he persisted in his ways - his sexual appetites drove him. He is a good example of someone with this disorder. Asc ♏ [☌ ♇ ♏ 12 ℞, qd ♂ ♈ 6].

Astringent: Causes body tissues (such as skin) to tighten. ♄.

Asylum, Mental: Psychiatric hospital, specialised mental health care. ♓ ♆.

Asymmetry: Lack or absence of symmetry. [♅].

Ataxia: Poor muscle control that causes clumsy voluntary movements and difficulty with balance. It usually results from damage to the cerebellum. It is a progressive disease that unimpeded, will cripple and kill. Sagittarius or Jupiter representing gait or movement may also be implicated. Link cerebellum > balance [damage]. Thr. ♊ ☿ > ♀ ♎ [♂ ♅, ♄ ♇].

(1) Clinton Stewart (7 Jan 1984, no time). The former American major leaguer and historian died aged 36, after a 21-year battle with Friedreich's Ataxia. ☿ ℞ [⚹ ♂ ♎ > ♂ ☌ ♇ ♏].

Atherosclerosis: A form of arteriosclerosis. Plaque - a fatty, waxy build-up, clogs arteries and reduces blood flow. Link arteries [and plaque]. Hrt. ♃ ♒ [♄ ♃].

(1) Chris Farley (15 Feb 1964, 15:34, Madison, WI). The American actor and comedian, had advanced atherosclerosis. ☉ ♒ [☌ ♄ r6H].

Athlete's Foot - see Tinea.

Atlas Axis: The top-most bone of the cervical vertebrae, just below the skull. Thr. ♉ ♀.

Atoms: These single neutral particles are the smallest units of matter. Atomic fission/ reaction, involves a change in an atom's nucleus, usually producing a different element. ♇.

Atrial Fibrillation - see Heart Arrhythmia.

Atrophies, Attrition: Progressive degeneration or shrinkage of muscle/ nerve tissue. [♑ ♄].

Attention Deficit Hyperactivity Disorder, ADHD: ADD is essentially the same. The cause is an overactive emotional body. Link emotions [overactivity]. Spx. ♋ ☽ ♂ [♂ ♅].
(1) American TV star Howie Mandel (29 Nov 1955, 10:00, Toronto, Canada), was diagnosed with ADHD as an adult. He said it made him impulsive and unfocused. ♂ [□ ♅].

Aura, Health Aura: It is a subtle invisible essence or etheric energy [1] that emanates from all living beings. The ethers are governed by the 7th violet ray, carried by Uranus. ♅.

Autism Spectrum Disorder (ASD): (See Asperger's). A mind/ brain developmental problem - under-connectivity in important strategic areas that have to do with the emotions and relating. It results in great difficulty in communicating and forming relationships because of avoidance, dissociation, separativeness, introversion and anti-social tendencies. These are Ray 5 of Concrete Mind (carried mainly by ♒ ♀), 'cleavage' traits, bringing the condition under this ray.

> In the activity of the 5th ray will be found eventually the source of many psychological disorders and mental troubles. Cleavage is the outstanding characteristic - within the individual or between the individual and his group, rendering him anti-social. [2]

Scientists now believe autism is a genetic disorder, which is related to the notion of karma. Link the brain > cognizance [under-development/ cleavage]. Ajna. ♈ ☽, ☿ ♀ [♄, ♀ ♒].
(1) Astro.com 13740 (9 Jan 1962, 12:23, Honolulu, HI). ☿ r6H [☌ ♄ ♒].
(2) Jett Travolta (13 Apr 1992, 00:33, Daytona Beach FL). ☿ r6H ☌ ♀ ♈ [∠ ♄ ♒]. ☽ [qd ♄ ♒].
(3) Tagtrug Mukpo (9 Mar 1971, 18:50, Boulder, CO). Serious brain under-development/ damage from infancy ☿ ♓6 [∠ ♀ ♒ > ☍ ♇12].

- Autoimmune Disease, an Immune Attack: (See also Alopecia, Coeliac Disease, Grave's Disease, Guillain-Barre Syndrome**,** Hashimoto's Disease, Sjoren's Syndrome, Multiple Sclerosis, Pernicious Anaemia). The immune system goes rogue and attacks the body. At the root of autoimmune disease is misuse of the power of thought. Negative thoughts such as self-hatred and self-anger, are directed at the self with such intensity and fervour; the immune system thinks the body is under attack and it reacts. Mars is the primary representative for an immune attack, then the Sun, then fire signs - most autoimmune diseases are inflammatory. A chronic attack results in a loss of body function. At one end of the spectrum the loss is relatively mild, such as hair loss. At the other end, serious diseases can bring loss of life.

In the following sections, an immune attack will be presented as ♂ ☉. But Uranus, sometimes Pluto, or planets in any of the fire signs could substitute. Hrt. [♂ ☉ (♅)].

Autonomic Nervous System: The control system in the body that acts largely unconsciously, regulating vital functions such as heart rate, digestion, respiration etc. Ajna. ♊ ☿.

Autopsy: Medical examination of a body after death, looking for the cause of death. ♏ ♂ ♇, 8H.

Avian Flu: Is a bird flu caused by the influenza A virus. Symptoms are the same as regular influenza. (See Influenza).

1 Bailey, Alice: A Treatise on Cosmic Fire, 53.
2 Bailey, Alice: Esoteric Healing, 302.

B

Babies: New-born infants, usually up to about 2 months of age. Any type of trouble or disease in babies, the seeds of the trouble, are from a past life. All natal charts are karmic, containing the fruits of the past and new duties and possibilities for the present and for the future. ♋ ☽, 5H.

Back, the Dorsum: From the top of the buttocks to the back of the neck. ♑ ♄.

- **Back, Lower:** Lumbar region. ♎ ♀.

- **Back, Upper:** Vicinity of thoracic vertebrae. ♌ ☉.

Bacteria: A large group of single-cell microorganisms. Some are beneficial for the body, some cause disease. R7, ♅.

- **Bacterial Infection:** Infectious bacterial diseases are governed by the 7th ray. This force brings together life and matter upon the physical plane - including at the bacterial level. When imperfect it results in "the activity of all germs and bacteria." [1]. Ray 7 is carried by Uranus, and it is the primary ruler of a bacterial infection. The other rulers of infection are Mars and Neptune. [♅ ♂ ♆].

Bad Breath - see Halitosis.

Balance (Vestibular) System: (See Vertigo). Fluid canals and crystals in the inner ear help maintain balance. Balance problems can be caused by an ear infection or head injury. Gemini-Mercury for ears, Libra for balance. Ajna. ♊ ☿, ♎ ♀.

Baldness: Loss, or absence of hair. Look for Mars-Saturn, Aries-Capricorn, connections. Link hair [and loss]. Cwn. ♈ ♂ [♑ ♄].
Bruce Willis ♂ [☍ ♄], Dwayne Johnson ♂ [qd ♃ ♑ ℞], Ed Harris ♂ [♂ ♑], Floyd Mayweather ♂ [☍ ♄], Jason Statham [♄ ♈], Jeremy Meeks ♂ [☌ ♄], John Travolta ♂ [⚼ ♅ ♋/♑], Kelly Slater ♂ ♉ [△ ♃ ♑], Lonnie Rashid Lynn ♂ ♉ [⚼ ♃ ♑], Mark Strong ♂ [⚼ ♄], Patrick Stewart ♂ [□ ♄], Pitbull ♂ [△ ♄], Samuel Jackson ♂ [⚼ ♄], Staley Tucci ♂ [☍ ♄], Taye Diggs ♂ [☍ ♄], Tyrese Gibson ♂ [△ ♄], Tyson Beckford ♂ [☍ ♄], Vin Diesel ♂ [qd ♄ ♈], William Devaughn ♂ [☌ ♄], and William, the Prince of Wales ♂ [☌ ♄].

Barren: Incapable of producing offspring. The common cause in women is an ovulation problem. In men, degraded sperm quality or lack of sperm. It is a 1st ray problem, which when afflicted, 'denies.' The 5H that rules children, is often involved. Link reproduction [with denial]. Sac. ♋ ☽, 5H [♄ ♇].
(1) Princess Soraya Pahlavi (22 Jun 1932, 22:30, Isfahan, Iran), the second wife of the Shah of Iran (1941-1979). After seven years of marriage, they were still childless. So, she was divorced. The likely cause for her barren condition was a bacterial infection, which damaged her Fallopian tubes. ♇ ♋5 [□ ♅].

1 Bailey, Alice: Esoteric Healing, 304.

Basal Ganglia: Clusters of brain neurons that process information about movement. Ajna. ♊ ☿.

BASE CHAKRA: (See Chakras and Etheric Web).

Consciousness: Dictators who have very strong and selfish personal wills use the 1st ray power of the base chakra.

Ray and Astrology energies: Rays flowing through this chakra are rays 1 (carried by Pluto), and 3, 4 and 7. Astrology rulers (for the mainframe structure), are Capricorn and Saturn, Sagittarius, Aquarius and Pisces. Additionally, it is vitalised by the "Mother of the World" [1], a term for Mother Nature.

Body rulership: This 4-petal lotus enters at the base of the spine around S5 and the top of the coccyx, and anchors in the adrenal glands. The 1st ray, which anchors in the adrenals, empowers the survival instinct, the most powerful instinct in the body. The base governs the mainframe structure of the physical body, all substance, bones and tissue that surround and support the main organs ruled by the higher chakras. [2] Other organs vitalised are the urinary tract - kidneys, ureters and bladder. Physical fire - kundalini, which warms the body, is housed in the base chakra.

Diseases: Problems and diseases of the spine, with the body structure including the skeleton, bones, tissue, muscles and skin. Diseases of the adrenals and urinary tract.

Bedwetting: Involuntary urination while asleep. The inner cause in children is fear of a controlling carer. This fear is only released during sleep, which is when bedwetting occurs. Saturn is the prime controller, while Jupiter (the antithesis of Saturn) brings freedom. Sometimes there may be links to representatives of sleep (♆♓ ☽, 2H). Link urine/ bladder [with fear > and relaxing]. Base. ♎♀/ ♏♂♇ [♄ > ♃].

(1) JonBenet Ramsey (6 Aug 1990, 01:36, Atlanta, GA). Child beauty pageant winner who was murdered. ♀♋ r6H [☍ ♄ > ☌ ♃].

(2) Sarah Silverman (1 Dec 1970, 06:30, Bedford, NH). American stand-up comedian who struggled with bedwetting until well into her teens. ♀♏ [☍ ♄6℞ > ♄ ☍ ♃♏12].

Belch: Excess air from the upper digestive tract being released through the mouth. Spx. ♋.

Bell's Palsy: (See Paralysis). Sudden weakness in muscle nerves on one half of the face. Link nerves > muscles [weakness/ paralysis]. Ajna. ♊ ☿ (♀♒♅) > ♂ [♄♆/ ♄♇].

(1) Ralph Nader (27 Feb 1934, 04:52, Winstead, CT). The American presidential hopeful, in 1986 suddenly developed Bell's palsy. With his face frozen on one side, he withdrew from the spotlight for a while. ☿♓℞ > ☌ ♂ [☍ ♆♍].

Beneficial Influence: A positive influence beneficial to health. Jupiter is the greater benefic, Venus the lesser. Easy aspects to the Sun which represents 'life', are also helpful. ♃ ♀.

Benign Tumour, Adenoma - see Tumours, Benign.

Beriberi: A thiamine deficiency. Can be caused by a diet of mostly white rice. Link nutrition [deficient]. ♋ ☽, ♍, 6H [♄ (♇)].

Biceps: Muscle on the front part of the upper arm. Thr. ♊ ♂.

Bile: A digestive juice containing bile salts, which breaks down fats during digestion. 'Bile' has come to mean bitterness, anger, relating it to Saturn and Mars. Spx. ♄ ♂.

1 Bailey, Alice: Esoteric Healing, 45.
2 Bailey, Alice: Esoteric Healing, 203.

Biliousness - see Nausea.

Biology: Is the scientific (♅) study of life (☉), of living organisms. ♅ > ☉.

Biopsy: A medical procedure. The examination of tissue removed from a living body to discover the presence, cause, or extent of a disease. ♍ ☿ > ♅.

Bipolar: This psychological disorder is characterised by extremely excitable mood swings, and manic/ depressive episodes. It is a 4th ray condition (☽ ☿), the force that oscillates back and forth, or up and down. In this case the emotional swings are swinging out of control. Link emotions/ mental [manic > depressive]. Spx. ♋ ☽ ♂/ ☿ [♂ ♅ > ♄].

(1) Russell Brand (4 June 1975, 0:00, Grays, Eng). The British comedian was diagnosed bipolar. His Moon and Mars are in super-juice Aries, counter-fought by disciplinarian Saturn in the 6H of health. ☽ ☌ ♈ [♂ □ ♄ ♋6].

Birth: Emergence of a baby from the body of its mother. Sac. ♋ ☽ , Asc.

Birth Problems - see Barren, Miscarriage.

Birthmark: Discoloured skin apparent at birth or close to. Vascular birthmarks occur when blood vessels do not form correctly. Pigmented birthmarks are caused by an overgrowth of the cells that create pigment colour in the skin. Link skin [mark]. ♑ ♄ (♋ ☽) [♂].

(1) A. J. Croce (28 Sep 1971, 08:45, Bryn Mawr, Wales). Buttocks. ♄ [△ ♂ r6H > ☍ ♃].

(2) Franz Nissl (9 Sep 1860, 15:30, Frankenthal, Ger). On his face. 1H [♂ ♑].

Bizarre Growths: When the building of the body and its repair, departs chaotically from nature's intelligent design. [♅ > ♃].

Blackheads: Acne, bumps on the skin filled with excess oil and dead skin. [♈ ♂].

Bladder: It is part of the urinary system that removes waste from the blood. Kidneys make urine, the bladder stores it prior to urination. The kidneys and bladder are ruled by the base chakra, [1] Libra [2] and Scorpio. Base. ♎ ♀, ♏ ♂ ♇.

- **Bladder Cancer**: Link bladder [cancer formula]. ♎ ♀, ♏ ♂ ♇ [(♋ ☽ > ♄ ♇) > ♃ ☉].

(1) EPA, page 42 (30 Dec 1832, 22:49, London, Eng). ♂ ♉/♏ [∠♇ > ♇ □ ☉]

- **Bladder Infection** - see Urinary Tract Infection.

- **Bladder Weak:** Inability to hold urine or leaking urine. Link bladder [and weakness]. Base. ♎ ♀, ♏ ♂ ♇ [♓ ♆, ♃ ♀].

Bleeding: Loss of blood from the circulatory system. It can be external, such as with a cut. Or internal, caused by an injury to an internal organ. Hrt. [♂].

Blind: Complete or almost complete loss of vision in both eyes. The Sun rules vision generally, and the right eye. The Moon rules problems with the left eye. The eyes are in the Aries region. If eye nerves are involved, so may Mercury or Uranus be. Link vision [loss of]. Ajna. ♈ ☉ ☽ [♄ ♇].

These people were blind from birth.

(1) Earl of Arundel (7 Sep 1879, 08:00, London, Eng). ☉ [⚻ ♄ ♈ ℞].

(2) Infanta Margarita (6 Mar 1939, 03:25, Rome, Italy). ☉ [♄ ♈ mp ☉/♅ ♉].

(3) Stevie Wonder (13 May 1950, 16:15, Saginaw, MI). ☉ ☌ ☿ ℞ [☉ □ ♇ ♌].

1 Bailey, Alice: Light of the Soul, 309.
2 Heindel, Astro-Diagnosis, 21.

Blister: A raised, fluid-filled bubble on the skin. [♂> ☽ ♃].

Bloat: A build up of gas in the stomach and intestines. Stomach fullness. Spx. ♋ ☽ [♃].

Blockage: There are various types. EG. A cancer mass or blood clot. [♄ ♇/♃].

BLOOD: Body fluid in the circulatory system, which delivers nutrients and oxygen to the cells and removes waste products. Blood carries the life principle, which uses the heart as its central organ. [1] Mars is the primary ruler of blood. Here are some quotes:

> Mars vitalises the blood stream, vitalises, purifies and stimulates all aspects and organisms in the body, via the blood stream. [2]
>
> The colour assigned to Mars is red and this is a correspondence to the colour of the blood stream. [3]
>
> Mars is objective and full of blood. [4]

Other representatives of blood are Aquarius (its circulation), and Leo (the pumping of), and their rulers Uranus and the Sun. They are the overall rulers of the cardiovascular system, and as polar-opposite signs, can rule each other's organs. Jupiter rules arterial blood, Venus the venous system, and Neptune the bloodstream.
But to assist clarity, in all alphabet sections:

- the rulers for blood will be presented as ♂ ♃ ♒.
- the rulers for the arteries will be presented as ♃ ♒
- the blood system, blood circulation, blood stream, blood flow as ♒ ♅ ♆.

- Blood, Arterial System: Blood vessels, which deliver oxygen-rich blood from the heart to body tissues. Hrt. ♃ ♒.

- Blood Cancer - see Leukaemia, Hodgkin and Non-Hodgkin Lymphoma.

- Blood Cells, Red and White - see Red Blood Cells and White Blood Cells.

- Blood Circulation, the Blood System: The blood system and the circulation of blood and life-giving nutrients to all parts of the body, are governed by Aquarius, [5] and therefore by Uranus. Additionally, Neptune governs the blood stream. Hrt. ♒ ♅ ♆.

- Blood Clot: A portion of blood thickens, forming a gel-like, semisolid mass. Jupiter can represent arterial blockages. Link blood [and clot]. Hrt. ♂ ♃ ♒ [♄ ♇/♃].
(1) Frank Herbert (8 Oct 1920, 07:30, Tacoma, WA). ♂ r6H [□ ♄].
(2) Gene Roddenberry (19 Aug 1921, 01:35, El Paso, TX), died of a massive blood clot that caused a stroke. ♂ ♌ [∠ ♄ r8H].
(3) Steve Watt (26 Jan 1959, no time). Blood clot in the brain. ♂ ♉, ☍ ♃ 8 [♃ □ ♇].

- Blood Diseases, Blood Cancer - see sections under specific diseases.

- Blood Flow - see Blood Stream.

- Blood Oxygenation: The process where oxygen (the life-supporting component of the air) is transferred into the blood. Link blood [and oxygenation]. Hrt. Thr. ♂ ♃ ♒ > ♊ ☿.

- Blood Poisoned: A bacterial infection enters the bloodstream. Link blood [and bacterial poisoning]. Hrt. ♂ ♃ ♒ [♅(♂ ♆)].

1 Bailey, Alice: Education in the New Age, 26.
2 Bailey, Alice: Esoteric Astrology, 211.
3 Bailey, Alice: Esoteric Astrology, 212.
4 Bailey, Alice: Esoteric Astrology, 217.
5 Bailey, Alice: Esoteric Astrology, 142.

- **Blood Pressure, High (HBP), Hypertension:** The pressure of the blood against the artery walls is too high, usually due to vessel width being narrowed by plaque. Link blood/ arteries [and high pressure]. Hrt. ♂/ ♃♒ [♄♇, ♃].
These stars all had high blood pressure. White's led to kidney failure.
(1) Barry White (12 Sep 1944, 16:42, Galveston, TX). ♂♎ [□ ♄♋6].
(2) Monserrat Caballe (12 Apr 1933, 21:00, Barcelona, Spain). ♃♍℞ [⚻ ♄♒].
(3) Esther Williams (8 Aug 1921, 09:39, Los Angeles, CA). ♃12 [☌ ♄].

- **Blood Pressure Low/ Hypotension:** A sudden drop in blood pressure when standing from a sitting position or after lying down. Link blood [pressure]. Hrt. ♂♃♒ [♄].

- **Blood Quality:** Comes under the domain of Aquarius and its ruler. ♒♅.

- **Blood Stream:** The stream of blood circulating around the body. Neptune is the ruler of the bloodstream, [1] of liquid waterways that cycle around the body. Hrt. ♆ (♒♅).

- **Blood Sugar High** - see Hyperglycaemia.

- **Blood Sugar Low** - see Hypoglycaemia.

- **Blood Transfusion:** Medical procedure where blood is put into a patient's bloodstream through a vein. Link blood/ vein > transfusion. Hrt. ♂♃♒/ ♀> ♊☿♐.
(1) Laurent Gaudin (21 Jul 1980, 13:10, Echirolles, Fr). Got AIDS via a blood transfusion. ♀♊ > ☍♆ for AIDS. ♆ r6H, ♀ the 8H.

- **Blood, Venous:** Network of veins that send deoxygenated blood back to the heart. Hrt. ♀.

- **Blood Vessels.** Network of tubes through which blood is pumped around the body. ♒♅.

Blush: Redness of skin on the face. Sometimes on the neck and chest due to dilated capillaries. It is an involuntary nervous response often due to feeling embarrassed. The cause is emotional. Link emotions [and Mars for redness]. Spx. ♋☽♆ [♂].
(1) Katie Holmes (18 Dec 1978, 21:32, Toledo, OH). She reportedly blushed easily when pressed for details about her emotional life. ☽♌12 [⚼ ♂].

BODY, Physical Body: The Moon governs the physical body, [2] and so do the Asc or planets in the 1H. Secondary representatives are Saturn, which carries R3 - "the dense body is governed by the 3rd ray"; [3] and Mars which "rules and controls the physical vehicle." [4] ☽, Asc, 1H (♄♂).

- **Body Containers:** The tissue envelopes enclosing and protecting organs. ♋☽.

- **Body Dysmorphia**: (See Anorexia, Glamour, Negative Core Beliefs). Obsessive focus on a perceived flaw in the appearance - a problem that is often associated with eating disorders. Self-perception is distorted by negative core beliefs about being ugly, unloved, unworthy, etc. Link the appearance [glamour > obsessive]. Asc [♆ (☽♂) > ♇].
(1) Elissa Washuta (25 Nov 1984, Hackettstown, NJ). Asc ♈ [△♆♑ > ☍♇].
(2) Gabbie Hanna (7 Feb 1991, 03:30, New Castle, PA). Asc [□ ♀♓]. ☽12 [☌ ♇].
(3) Kitty (25 Feb 1993, 12:34, Plantation Acres, Fl). Asc [□ ☿♓, ⚻♆♑]. ☽ [⚻♇].
(4) Lili Reinhart (13 Sep 1996, 11:15, Cleveland, OH). Asc ♏ [♂☍♆]. ♇1 [⚹ ☽♆].

1 Bailey, Alice: Esoteric Healing, 143.
2 Bailey, Alice: Esoteric Astrology, 19.
3 Bailey, Alice: Destiny of the Nations, 118.
4 Bailey, Alice: Esoteric Astrology, 210.

- **Body Fat:** Is used as energy and it insulates and cushions the body. ♃.

- **Body Fluid Highways:** Such as the bloodstream and lymphatic system. ♓♆.

- **Body Fluids, White:** Are traditionally ruled by the Moon, white being the colour allocated to the Moon. ♋☽. (See Fluid in the Body).

- **Body Intelligence, Body Elemental:** The instinctive intelligence of the collective cell-life of the body. The 3rd ray (carried by Saturn), rules the intelligence of cells, of "intelligent substance." [1] Ray 3, ♄.

- **Body Warmth:** The Sun gives warmth to the body. Additionally, Mars is the ruler of kundalini, the fire of matter, which warms the body from the base chakra. ☉♂.

Boils, Carbuncles: A skin infection. A pus-filled bump under the skin that is usually caused by staph bacteria. Carbuncles are clusters of boils. The inner cause is repression of anger, of rage - boils represent that toxicity trying to find release. Link skin [infection > boil]. Spx. ♑♄ (♋) [♂♅♆ > ♋☽♃].

(1) J. P. Morgan Snr (17 Apr 1837, 03:00, Hartford, CT). The American financier and investment banker had "painful boils on his face and neck" (Astro.com). Psychological poison translates into blood poisoning. The inner cause is easy to see in his chart - he had huge (♃), anger issues (♂), which he would suppress. ♄ [□♂♃6].

Bones: The bones of the skeleton are made of connective tissue reinforced with calcium and specialised bone cells. Base. ♑♄.

- **Bones Brittle** - see Osteogenesis Imperfecta.

- **Bone Cancer:** Cell malignancy grows in the bones. Emotionally, there is a lack of trust in the structures of life. Link bones [and the cancer formula]. Spx. Base. ♑♄ [(♋☽ >♄♇) > ♃☉].

(1) Brenda Frazier (9 Jun 1921, 22:00, Montreal, Canada). Died from inoperable bone cancer. ♄8 [(□♂6) > ♄☌♃♍]. Saturn represents both the bones and repression.

- **Bone Deformities** - see Deformed.

- **Bone Fractures:** Bone breaks that occur for various reasons. Primarily by accidents, when bodies are healthy, such as in action sports (the 5H). Mars, the ruler of fractures also rules action and motor sports. Link bones [and fractures]. Signs and planets that rule the region of the body the bones are in, may be involved. Base. ♑♄ [♂♅].

(1) Fausto Coppi (15 Sep 1919, 21:30, Castellanza, Italy). Through his career, the champion motorcycle racer suffered numerous fractures in the arms, wrists, fingers (Mercury), knees, lower legs and ankles. ♄5 ☌☿ [☍♅].

- **Bone Marrow:** Soft tissue found in the centre of bones, which gives birth to stem cells - the body's raw materials from which all other specialized cells are made. Sac. Base. ♋☽.

Borderline Personality Disorder (BPD): A mental illness that severely impacts a person's ability to regulate their emotions. The wilfulness of Mars (also of ray 6, a dominant emotional body or desire nature), is central to the disorder. Look for its afflictions to the Sun (personality), or to Mercury or Venus, the reasoning, rationalising planets. Any malefics linking in will give further information. Link the self, mind [wilful selfishness]. Spx. ☉ Asc, ☿♀) [♂♅].

1 Bailey, Alice: Esoteric Astrology, 173.

(1) Ricky Williams (21 May 1977, 13:57, San Diego, CA). The American footballer has been open about his BPD diagnosis. The Sun is in Gemini 9H, a mutable sign and cadent house which in certain cases, can weaken the personality. In contrast, Mars is very strong in its own assertive sign Aries, and the 8H ruled by Scorpio; showing a wilful, impulsive nature. The 8H, rules emotional trauma, which could account for part of his trouble. Mars' conjunct to Venus (afflicted in Aries), adds narcissism to the mix. ⊙♊9 [∠♂♈8]. ♂☌♀♈.

Bowels, Large and Small - see Intestines Large and Small.

- Bowel Cancer, Rectal Cancer, Colon Cancer: It develops from the inner lining of the bowel and is usually preceded by growths called polyps. Link the bowel [and the cancer formula]. Spx. ♏♂♇ (♍☿) [(♋☽ >♄♇) > ♃⊙].

(1) Claude Debussy (22 Aug 1862, 04:30, St. Germain, Fr). His final years were plagued by rectal cancer. ♇♉℞ [☽♋ r12H, mp ♃♍℞ /♇].

(2) Elizabeth Montgomery (15 Apr 1933, 16:38, LA, CA). ♇♋ [(∠♆12) > ♆☌♃♍].

(3) Franco Fabrizi (15 Feb 1916, 08:00, Cortemaggiore, Italy). ♇♋ [(∠♂6) > ♇□♃].

(4) Robin Gibb (22 Dec 1949, 03:15, Douglas, Isle of Man), died of colon cancer. His chart shows he was an unforgiving perfectionist (♂♍), the root cause of what would grow into the physical disease. ♇ [(qd ☽) > ☽☌♃].

BPD - see Borderline Personality Disorder.

BRAIN, THE: Composed of the cerebrum, cerebellum and brainstem, the brain communicates with the body (and outer world), through the central nervous system (CNS).

Astrologically, the brain and CNS are divided. Brain substance is governed by the crown chakra, by Aries, and it is conditioned by the "third ray," [1] which flows through Cancer (the Moon), and Saturn. Thinking, messaging is ruled by the ajna, Gemini and Mercury.

The mind, the brain and the nervous system are the mediums through which both the personality and soul work, enabling them to interact externally. First the personality controls this intelligence system. Later, when soul contact is made, the soul takes control - via the crown chakra and pineal. "The pineal gland in the centre of the brain, is the home of the soul." [2]. Cwn. ♈♂, ☽♋ (♄).

- Brain Aneurysm: (See Aneurysm). A bulge or balloon developing in a brain artery. Link brain / arteries [ballooning]. Cwn. ♈♂, ☽♋/ ♃♒ [♃].

These three ladies died of ruptured (♂♅) aneurysms.

(1) Betty Clooney (12 Apr 1931, 13:30, Maysville, KY). ♅♈ [□♃♋ > ♃☌♇ for death].

(2) Jeanne-Claude (13 Jun 1935, 18:00, Casablanca, Morocco). ☽♏12 [☌♃℞].

(3) Pamela Harriman (20 Mar 1920, 04:30, Farnborough, Eng). ♂♏8℞ [□♃℞].

- Brain Atoms: The brain is composed of atoms that vibrate to the energy of the ray which controls the physical body. [3] Most physical bodies are governed by R3 ♄, or R7 ♅.

- Brain Cancer/ Malignant Tumour: (See Cancer the Disease, Glioblastoma, Pituitary Cancer). Link the brain [and the cancer formula]. ♈♂, ♋☽ [(♋☽ >♄♇) > ♃⊙].

(1) James Ingram (16 Feb 1952, 12:49, Akron, OH). The American singer, songwriter, died from brain cancer. Cwn. ♃♈ [(□♅♋/♑1 > ♃☍♄ r8H)].

1 Bailey, Alice: Esoteric Astrology, 222.
2 Bailey, Alice: Light of the Soul, 318.
3 Bailey, Alice: Discipleship in the New Age II, 494.

- **Brain Fag or Fog:** Trouble concentrating, staying focused, due to mental and physical exhaustion. Link the mind [weariness/ fog]. Ajna. Cwn. ♊ ☿ [♄/♆].

- **Brain Haemorrhage:** Too intense blood pressure in the brain ruptures artery walls, causing bleeding in the brain. A type of stroke. The psychology related to a brain vessel rupture, is a very stubborn and explosive will. Link brain > artery [rupture, bleeding, haemorrhage]. Cwn. ♈ ♂, ☽ ♋ > ♃ ♌ ♒ [♂ ♅ (♇)].

These three died from a brain haemorrhage. Pressure in the brain is represented by ♄ ♈.

(1) Django Reinhardt (23 Jan 1910, 15:00, Liberchies, Belgium). ♄ ♈ > ☍ ♃ r6H [□ ♅].

(2) Nico, birth name Christa Päffgen (16 Oct 1938, 17:30, Cologne, Ger). ♄ ♈ 12℞ [disposited by ♂6, ♂ ⚻ ♃ ♒℞].

(3) Phillipe Gaubert (5 Jul 1879, 06:00, Cahors, Fr). ♂ ♄ ♈ [mp ♇ ♉/♃ ♓8℞].

- **Brain Stem:** Consists of the midbrain, pons and medulla oblongata. A relay station, passing messages back and forth between the body and the cerebral cortex. Thr. ♊ ☿.

- **Brain Tissue Lesions:** Areas of damaged brain tissue due to injury or disease. They can be harmless or threaten life if they turn into malignant tumours. Virulent R5 energy (carried primarily by Venus and Aquarius), is given as a cause of brain lesions in Esoteric Healing (page 302). This is interesting because ray 5, the ray of science and medical procedures, governs surgery, radiation therapy and chemotherapy - which can cause a brain lesion. Psychologically, R5 as a cause indicates that chronic separativeness - the persistent thinking of hostile thoughts about others, may in time have a harmful effect on brain tissue.

The following examples selected at random were examined to see if Aquarius or Venus were in the lesion pattern. They were and are included to represent the brain lesion. The 1H is related to the brain, so lesion planets may link into that house. If Saturn or Pluto link into the pattern by hard aspect, the lesion could become malignant. Link brain [and lesion]. Cwn. ♈ ♂, ☽ ♋ [♒ ♅ (♀)].

(1) Arthur Shawcross (6 Jun 1945, 04:14, Kittery, ME). ♂ ☽ ♈ 12 [☌ ♀ > ♀ □ ♇ ♌].

(2) John McCain (29 Aug 1936, 18:25, Colon, Panama). Popular American politician and hero of the Vietnam War. ☽ ♒, wide ☍ ♂6 [♂, □ ♅ ♉].

(3) Lance Armstrong (18 Sep 1971, no time). Champion American cyclist and drug cheat. ♂ ♒ [⚼ ♇. ♇ ☌ ♀].

- **Brain Tumour, Benign.** (See Pituitary Tumour, Tumours - Benign). These are non-cancerous and only grow in one place. But they can be dangerous if they press on the brain or nerves. Uranus may link in for an abnormality. Link the brain > cells [overbuilding]. Cwn. ♈ ♂, ♋ ☽ > ☉ ☽ [♃].

(1) Scott Hamilton (28 Aug 1958, 09:00, Toledo, OH). The champion Olympic figure skater, since 2004 has been battling recurring non-cancerous brain tumours (adenomas). Previously he overcame testicular cancer. ♂ ♉ > □ ☽ [☽ △ ♃ ♎/♈].

Breasts: The mammary glands located on the chest. Spx. ♋ ☽ (♀).

- **Breast Cancer:** (See Cancer, The Disease). Breast cancer primarily affects women. Negative beliefs related to the condition are: 'Not being worthy to receive love or emotional nourishment', and 'not being feminine enough.' Cancer and the Moon rule the breasts and emotions, so in the formula can represent both. Venus which governs femininity may be included. Link the breasts [and the cancer formula]. Spx. ♋ ☽ [(♋ ☽ > ♄ ♇) > ♃ ☉].

These three ladies died from the disease.
(1) Jill Ireland (24 Apr 1936, 21:00, Hounslow, Eng). ☽ 8 [(□ ♄) > ☍ ♃ ♐ ℞].
(2) Linda McCartney (24 Sep 1941, 10:00, New York, NY). The Moon and Venus are conjunct so both can represent the breasts. ☽ ♀ ♏ 1 [(♀ □ ♇) > ♇ ∠ ♃ 8].
(3) Olivia Newton-John (26 Sep 1948, 06:00, Cambridge, Eng), died from the disease in 2022. ☽ ♋ [(∠ ♇) > □ ☉ 1].

Breath, Breathing, Respiration and Respiratory System: The respiration system includes the nose, mouth, throat, voice box, windpipe and the bronchi/ lungs. The breath, which carries life, is an expression of spirit, of deity:

> The 1st aspect, the Life, the Breath. [1]

Healthy lungs and healthy breathing are conducive to health and wholeness in the body.

> According to the wholeness of the breathing apparatus, and according to the ability of that apparatus to oxygenate and render pure the blood, so will be the health or wholeness of the dense physical body. [2]

Breathing apparatus, the bronchi, are controlled by the throat chakra.[3] Thr. ♊ ☿.

- Breathing Congestion: Mucous build up in the breathing passages and lungs. Link breathing [mucous > congestion]. Hrt. Thr. ♊ ☿ [♋ ☽ > ♄].

> Problems connected with breathing are related to the heart, and establishing right rhythm and right contact with the environment (with others). [4]

- Breathing Shallow: Rapid, shallow breathing. Hrt. Spx. ♊ ☿ [♂ ♅].

Bright's Disease - see Nephritis.

Broken: As in fractured bones. [♂ ♅].

Broken Back: A spinal fracture. A break in one or more vertebrae. There may or may not be damage to the spinal cord. Jupiter - Sagittarius will be involved if movement is impaired. Link the spine [and fracture]. Hrt. Base. ♌ ☉, ♑ ♄ [♂ ♅].
(1) John Warner (18 Feb 1927, 13:55, Washington, DC). ☉ ♒/♌ [□ ♂ > □ ♄ ♐. ♐ r6H].
(2) Raymond Palmer (1 Aug 1910, 17:00, Milwaukee, WI). ☉ ♌ [qd ♅ ♑ ℞ 1].
(3) Ted Kennedy (22 Feb 1932, 03:58, Dorchester, MA). ☉ [☌ ♂ > qd ♃ ♌ ℞ r12].

Broken Bones: (See Nose Broken). Afflictions from Mars (broken), and Capricorn-Saturn (bones), to rulers of the relevant area. EG. Mercury for arm bones, Jupiter for thigh bones. Base. ♑ ♄ [♂ ♅].

Bronchial Tract/ Tree: Tubes that connect the trachea/ windpipe to the lungs, for breathing. The bronchi are vitalised by the throat chakra. Thr. [5] ♊ ☿.

- Bronchitis: Virus causing inflamed bronchial tubes, thickened mucous and shortness of breath. Saturn may link in for congestion and shortness of breath. If the condition becomes chronic, it is included in the Chronic Obstructive Pulmonary Disease group. Link airways [virus, inflamed > mucous]. Thr. ♊ ☿ [♂ ♅ ♆ > ♋ ☽ (♓ ♆)].
These three examples are from Encyclopaedia of Psychological Astrology, Carter.

---

1 Bailey, Alice: The Rays and the Initiations, 103.
2 Bailey, Alice: Treatise on White Magic, 569.
3 Bailey, Alice: Esoteric Healing, 45.
4 Bailey, Alice: Esoteric Healing, 130.
5 Bailey, Alice: Esoteric Healing, 45.

(1) EPA page 45-1 (19 Oct 1916, 08:30, London, Eng). ☿ [⚹♆ > □♇♋8].

(2) EPA page 45-2 (6 Jan 1892, 02:20, London, ENG). ♇♊8 [☌♆].

(3) EPA page 45-3, Alfred Percy Sinnett (18 Jan 1840, 23:30, London, Eng). He died from the disease. ☿♑/♋ r12H , coruler 8H [∠♂].

Brow: The forehead. Ajna. ♈♂.

Bruise: Bleeding under the skin due to trauma of any kind. Hrt. Base. [♂].

Buboes: Swollen lymph nodes caused by a bacterial infection. Link lymph [infection > swollen]. Thr. ♓♆, ♋☽ [♅♂♆> ♃].

- Bubonic Plague: The Black Death, a virulent plague that decimated millions through the Middle Ages. It is characterized by painful swollen lymph nodes or 'buboes'.

Plagues are ruled by ray 7, carried primarily by Uranus (and therefore by its sign Aquarius), and by Cancer. As for the inner cause:

> The separative and maleficent thoughts of man are largely responsible for the destructive quality of some of nature's processes, including certain phenomena, such as plague and famine. [1]

The plague is spread by the bites of infected fleas (ruled by Mars). Link lymph [and infection]. ♓♆, ♋☽ [♅♂♆].

(1) Andrea del Sarto (16 Jul 1486, 13:30, Florence, Italy), died during a 16th century outbreak of bubonic plague. ☽♑ ∠ ♆ [♅♃℞ mp ♆/☽].

Buddhi, Mind Wisdom. Is ruled by Mercury. [2] Jupiter carries the wisdom ray (2). ☿♃.

Bulimia: An eating habit of binge-eating, gorging, then forced vomiting. The cause is emotional, 'feeling unloved', 'self-disgust.' Eating habits (Virgo, Mercury, 6H) may be included. Link emotions/ food [gorging > vomiting]. Spx. ♋☽ [♃ > ♂♅]

(1) Princess Diana (1 Jul 1961, 19:45, Sandringham, Eng) said in an interview: "I had bulimia. You inflict it upon yourself because your self-esteem is at a low ebb, and you don't think you're worthy or valuable. You fill your stomach up four or five times a day - and it gives you a feeling of comfort." ☽ [□♀♉ for gorging on sweet foods > ☍♂].

Bunions: A bony bump that forms on the joint at the base of the big toe. Link feet [and bony bump]. Base. ♓♆ [♄/♃].

Burns: Injuries to skin due to heat or fire. Link to skin. ♄♑ (♋☽) [♂☉, fire signs].

(1) Diane Barrière-Desseigne (9 Jan 1957, 12:25, Paris, FR). She survived a plane crash,but was left heavily burnt, badly disfigured and completely paralysed. She has 5 planets in fire signs including Moon-Mars in Aries (12H), conjunct an Aries ascendant. Mars on the Asc emphasises the disfigurement to her appearance. ☽♈12 [☌♂, Asc].

Bursitis: Inflammation of the fluid-filled pads (bursae) that act as cushions at the joints. Saturn may link in for joints, and Jupiter-Sagittarius for impaired movement. Link bursae [and inflammation]. Base. ♋☽ [♂☉].

(1) Barry Manilow (17 Jun 1943, 09:00, Brooklyn, NY). ☽ [△♂♈ > ☍♄ r6H].

(2) Jim Hodgson (8 Sep 1947, 01:55, Hawkwell, UK). ♂♋12 [♄♌ mp ☉/♂].

Buttocks: Round fleshy parts that form the bottom. ♃♐.

---

1 Bailey, Alice: Treatise of Cosmic Fire, 889.

2 Bailey, Alice: Esoteric Astrology, 649.

C

Cadaver: Dead human body. ♄.

Caesarean Birth: A surgical procedure where a baby is delivered through an incision made through the abdomen and uterus. Link birth [and caesarean]. Sac. ♋ ☽, 5H [♂ ♅].

Caesarean births used to occur when there were birth emergencies. But today, for pain or safety concerns surrounding natural birth, some women choose to have a caesarean. Allegedly, these two women chose caesareans because of these concerns.

(1) Christine Aguilera (18 Dec 1980, 10:46, Staten Is. NY). ☽ r5/ 6H [△ ♂].

(2) Victoria Beckham (17 Apr 1974, 10:07, Harlow, Eng), of Spice Girls fame, chose to have all her four children by caesarean section. ☽ [△ ♂12, coruler 5H].

Caffeine Induced Sleeplessness: (See Insomnia). Results from the overconsumption of the stimulant caffeine. Link sleep [to stimulant]. ☽ ♆, 12H [♂ ♅].

(1) Britney Spears (2 Dec 1981, 01:30, McComb, MS). In 2023, Spears said she "drinks so much caffeine she stays awake for three days in a row". ♆ [□ ♂♍/♓12].

Calcification: Calcium builds up in body tissue, causing the tissue to harden. [♄ ♑].

Calcium: Mineral important for healthy bones and teeth. Helps blood clot. ♑ ♄.

Calculus - see Plaque.

Calf: Back portion of the lower leg. Base. ♒ ♅.

Cancer (the Disease): (See cancer examples under their own names, or under the names of the organs affected). Cancer is a disease where cells divide and spread uncontrollably. It is related to the 1st and 2nd rays. The 1st ray, which in psychology can lead to the suppression of the emotions, and in disease, tends to age and harden.

Cancer is a subtle reaction to the energy of the first ray, the will-to-live. [1]

If the emotions or desires are violently repressed over an extended period, the *will-to-live* aspect innate in the body, in cells, may have a violent reaction. Sensing existence/ life is threatened, to survive, cells begin to overbuild wildly (R2: Jupiter, Sun). The result is cancer. In the formula, Cancer and the Moon represent the emotions. But Mars and Neptune, or Scorpio or Pisces (water signs), could substitute. Saturn or Pluto represent the repression aspect of the disease, Jupiter and the Sun the overbuilding aspect.

The *Key*: Link the body part affected [(emotional > repression) > cell over-building].
The *Formula*: The body part [(♋ ☽ > ♄ ♇) > ♃ ☉].

CANCER (the Sign). ♋.

Rulers: The exoteric ruler is the Moon, the esoteric and hierarchy ruler is Neptune.

Rays: Carries R3 of Intelligent Activity, and R7 of Ceremony, Order and Magic; R4 via the Moon, and R6 via Neptune. Energy is emotional, watery, moist, cold and fluid.

---

1 Bailey, Alice: *Esoteric Healing,* 383.

Body: Cancer governs the solar plexus chakra, which vitalises digestion, the stomach, pancreas, gallbladder and liver. Cancer carries the 3rd ray which rules matter, so is a ruler of the physical form, tissue and flesh. Cancer and the Moon represent the mother-producing production of stem cells, 'white' baby cells which then turn into specialized cells such as blood cells, brain cells, heart muscle cells and bone cells. Cancer (and the 3rd ray), rule reproduction - pregnancy, gestation, birth and female reproduction cycles. The protective quality of Cancer is seen in its rulership of all body 'containers' that enfold cells and organs such as the breasts and the womb. Cancer rules white body fluids such as lymph and mucous, and is a backup ruler for the lymphatic system.

Disease: Its diseases are seepy, watery, damp, lethargic and devitalising. When planets are afflicted in Cancer, or when Cancer rules the 6H, it mainly indicates trouble with digestion, and sometimes with the knees that are governed by opposite sign Capricorn. As an afflictor it can be virulent. This because - with the Moon, Cancer is a prime ruler of the emotions, and most individual diseases are caused by troubled emotions. Cancer also represents diseases we inherit genetically, through our family line or because we are part of the human kingdom.

Psychology: Cancer rules the emotional life and the need for emotional balancing and control. Its higher keynote is, 'I build a lighted house and therein dwell.' The 'lighted house' refers to a lighted consciousness.

Candida: (See Vaginal Thrush). Fungal/ yeast infection, typically on the skin or mucous membranes. Link skin/ mucous membranes [fungal]. Spx. ♑♄/ ♋☽ [♋☽, ♓♆ (♏♂)]. (1) Astro.com 438 (1 Aug 1955, 05:00, Lama SC), had a serious case of candida infection in the mouth (♉♀), prior to developing AIDS. Spx. Sac. ♀♋12 (mouth) [☌♅, □♆].

Capillaries: Smallest type of blood vessels that connect arteries and veins. Capillaries have thin walls that allow oxygen, nutrients, carbon dioxide and waste products to pass through, to and from tissue cells. Ruled traditionally by Gemini and Mercury, the normal blood vessel rulers could substitute. Hrt. ♊ ☿ ♒.

CAPRICORN. ♑:

Rulers: The exoteric and esoteric ruler is Saturn, the hierarchy ruler is Venus. Adversity leads to struggle, opportunity. Success results in love-wisdom (Venus).

Rays: Carries R1 of Will and Power, R3 of Intelligence and Activity, R7 of Ceremony, Order and Magi, and R5 via Venus. Its energy is earthy, cold and dry.

Body: Capricorn governs ray 3 of matter, and consequently governs the base chakra and the dense physical body as a whole. It governs the main-frame rigid skeleton and bony structure of the body, the joints (especially the knee-joints), the tendons, ligaments, cartilage and muscles that tie the body together and that give it its durability and strength. It also rules the skin, teeth and hair that protect the soft inner parts of the body. Because R3 also governs the throat chakra, Capricorn is related to that centre.

In disease: When planets are afflicted in Capricorn, or when Capricorn rules the 6H, it indicates trouble mainly with the knees, and/ or with digestion, which is governed by its opposite sign Cancer. As an afflictor - and working with its ruler Saturn, its force chills, it hardens and ages.

Psychology: Capricorn is the sign of initiation - of expanded understanding and wisdom. To achieve this, the Capricorn disciple has to learn to kneel in humility "with his knees upon the rocky mountain top and to offer his heart and life to the soul and to human service." [1]

1 Bailey, Alice; Esoteric Astrology, 169.

Capricorn's higher keynote refers to this - 'Lost am I in light supernal, yet on that light I turn my back.' It means turning away from all personal ambition and giving all in service.

Carbohydrates: Sugar molecules converted to energy to support body functions. ♀ ♃.

Carbuncle - see Boils, Carbuncles.

Carcinogenic: (See Cancer the Disease). Any substance/ radiation that promotes carcinogenesis, the formation of cancer, the overbuilding of cells. [Malefics].

Carcinoma: Most common cancer. See Cancer (the Disease).

Cardiovascular System: (See Heart). Made up of the heart and blood vessels, this system supplies the body cells with a continuous supply of blood, oxygen and nutrients while also removing carbon dioxide and other waste. Leo (and the Sun) and its opposite sign Aquarius (with Uranus), are the overall rulers of the cardiovascular system. Specifically, Leo and the Sun govern the heart and vitalisation; while Aquarius and Uranus govern "the blood system and its circulation." [1] Because they are opposite signs, Leo and Aquarius can represent each other's organs and functions.

There are sub-rulers within the system. Jupiter for arteries, Venus for the venous system, Neptune for the blood stream, and Mars for blood. Hrt. ♌☉,♒♅.

- Cardiac Arrest: The heart stops beating, usually due to a problem in the heart's electrical (♅) system that pumps blood. Link the heart/ beat [arrest]. Hrt. ♌☉ / ♂♅ [♇♄].
These three died from cardiac arrest.
(1) Bobby Layne, (19 Dec 1926, 09:20, Santa Anna, TX). ☉ □ ♅ [qd ♇6]. In this example, Pluto represents both the 'arrest' and death.
(2) Hank Gremminger (1 Sep 1933, 03:30, Windthorst, TX). ☉ ⚻ ♄ ♒℞ [∠♇12].
(3) Tony Curtis (3 Jun 1925, 09:00, New York, NY). ☉ [♂♇12, mp ☉/♆♌].

- Cardiac Arrhythmia - see Heart Arrhythmia.

- Cardiomyopathy: There are two main types. *Dilated* cardiomyopathy, the ventricles thin, grow larger. *Hypertrophic* cardiomyopathy, the heart muscle thickens. The latter is said to be the most common cause of sudden death in young athletes. Either way, blood-pumping is weakened. Link the heart muscle [to weakening, thickening]. Hrt. ☉♌♂ [♓♆/ ♃ ♄].
(1) Mitch Frerotte (30 Mar 1965, 02:12, Kittanning, PA). ☉♈ [∠♃ ♉ r12H]. The American football player died from a massive heart attack at age 43. ☉♈ [⚻♂8]

Carotid Arteries: Major blood vessels in the neck that supply blood to the brain, neck, and face. Hrt. ♉ ♀ > ♃♒.

Carotid Gland/ Bulb: It helps keep blood pressure healthy by regulating its flow from the aorta to the head and neck. Thr. ♉ ♀.

Carpal, Metacarpal Bones: These are bones of the wrist and palm. Thr. ♊ ☿.

- Carpal Tunnel Syndrome (CTS): (See Paralysis). Numbness, tingling in the hand and arm, and sometimes paralysis. It is caused by a pinched nerve in the wrist. Link arms, wrists/ nerves [with pinched, numbness > tingling]. Thr. ♊ ☿ [♄ > ♅].
(1) Leon Fleisher (23 Jul 1928, 22:20, San Francisco, CA), was a brilliant American pianist and conductor, who developed paralysis of his right hand. He had a deep fear of failure which would have contributed to the condition. ☿ coruler 6H [⚻ ♄ ♐℞ > □ ♅].

1 Bailey, Alice: Esoteric Astrology, 142.

(2) Ric Drasin (12 Jul 1944, 21:00, Bakersfield, CA). An American bodybuilder and professional wrestler, he had CTS in both hands. ☿ 6 [☌ ♇ for pinched > ♇ ⚹ ♅ ♊].

Cartilage: Flexible connective tissue. Base. ♑ ♄.

Castration: The removal or destruction of the penis. Scorpio and its rulers govern both the sex organs [and castration]. Sac. ♏ ♂ [♏ ♂ ♇].
(1) Astro.com. Scott (4 Sep 1948, 18:30, Buffalo, NY), a child victim who was kidnapped, stabbed, and castrated by a psychotic neighbour. Asc [☍ ♇. ♇ mp ♀ r3H neighbours / ☉]. ☉ [mp ♂ 8 / ♀ 6].

Catabolic Process: Part of metabolism that releases energy. ♂.

Catalepsy: (See Paralysis). A nervous seizure that causes a temporary loss of voluntary motion. Muscles, posture, goes rigid. Link the nervous system/ or muscles [seizure > rigidity]. Ajna. ♊ ☿ / ♂ [♅ > ♄ ♇].
(1) Bob Beamon (29 August 1946, no time). In the 1968 Olympics, the long jumper had a brief cataleptic seizure when it was announced that he had won the gold medal. ☿ [mp ♂/ ♅ ♊ > ☌ ♇].

Cataract: Cloudy area in the lens of the eye that leads to a decrease in vision. 'Clouding' can be represented by Neptune or the Moon. Link eyes/ vision [clouding / loss]. Ajna. ☉ ☽ [♆ ☽ / ♄].
(1) EPA 49-1. P. B. Marston (13 Aug 1850, no time). ☉ [qd ♆ ♓ > ♆ ∠ ♄ ♈ ℞].
(2) EPA 49-2. (20 Jan 1928, no time). ☉ ♑ [⚻ ♆ > ∠ ♄].
(3) EPA 49-3. (20 Oct 1871, no time). ☉ [☍ ♆ ♈ > □ ☽ ♑].

Catarrh - see Post Nasal Drip.

Catatonia: Is a group of symptoms that usually involve a lack of movement and communication. (See Catalepsy).

Celiac Disease - see Coeliac Disease.

Celibacy: Sexually abstinent. ♏ ♂ ♀ > ♄.

Cell Life: The life of God, of Nature, vitalising cells. Hrt. ☉.

Cells of the Body: The cells are the basic building blocks of all living things and are generally ruled by the Sun and Moon. The Sun carries the life-giving 2nd ray and governs the life of cells. The 3rd aspect (the 3rd ray) vitalises physical cells, [1] the energy carried by the Moon via its sign Cancer. Hrt. ☉ ☽.

Cellulite: Excess lumpy, dimpled flesh on thighs, hips, buttocks and stomach. ♃.

Cellulitis: Bacterial infection in the inner layers of the skin. Link the skin [and infection]. Base. ♑ ♄ (♋ ☽) [♅ ♂ ♆].

Central Nervous System (CNS): (See also the Nervous System). The central nervous system is the central communications system in the body, a network of channels that carry electrochemical signals. It is made up of the brain and spinal cord. The brain (under the impression of the soul), controls how we think, learn, move, and how we feel. The spinal cord carries messages back and forth between the brain and the nerves that run throughout the body.

1 Bailey, Alice: Treatise on White Magic, 40.

Astrologically, brain substance is governed by the crown chakra, Aries and Cancer. The CNS by the ajna, Gemini and Mercury, which are the primary rulers of nerves. Venus is a coruler of the nervous system, [1] and Uranus is related. Ajna. ♊ ☿, ♀ (♅).

Cerebellum: The hindbrain or lower brain. Thr. ♊ ☿.

Cerebral/ Cerebrum, Cerebral Cortex: The largest part of the brain has two hemispheres - an outer layer called the cerebral cortex (grey matter) and an inner layer (white matter). The cortex is involved in complex brain functions such as language and information processing. There are four lobes in the cortex: the frontal lobe, parietal lobe, temporal lobe and occipital lobe. Cwn. ♈, ♋ ☽ for brain substance, ♊ ☿ for information processing.

- Cerebral Embolism: A clot inside a brain artery blocks adequate oxygen and blood flow, causing a stroke. Link brain > artery [clot]. Cwn. ♈ ♂, ♋ ☽ > ♃ ♒ [♑ ♄ ♇].
These two examples died from a cerebral embolism.
(1) Jose Perez Jimenez (27 Apr 1887, 04:00, Segure de Leon, Spain). Cwn. ♂ ♉1 > ☍ ♃ ℞ [♃ ⚻ ♇ r8H].
(2) Michel Detroyat (28 Oct 1905, 13:00, Paris, Fr). ♂ ♑12 > ☍ ♆ ♋6 blood-stream [♆ Q ♄ ♒1℞].

- Cerebral Haemorrhage: A rupture in a brain artery. Cause can be an accident, a tumour, stroke or high blood pressure. Link brain / artery [and haemorrhage]. Cwn. ♈ ♂, ♋ ☽ / ♃ ♒ [♂ ♅ ♇].
The following WWII leaders died from this condition.
(1) Franklin Roosevelt (30 Jan 1882, 20:45, Hyde Park, NY). He is reported as having a famous temper, but it was usually reserved for his political opponents. ☿ ♒6 [□ ♇ ♉/♏].
(2) Joseph Stalin (6 Dec 1878, no time). Stalin had a violent temper. But he was able to hold it in check, then release it when it was beneficial for him to do so. ♃ ♒ [⚻ ♅].

- Cerebral Palsy: (See Paralysis). Spastic paralysis of nerves causing jerky movement. This condition is typically caused by damage to the developing brain before or at birth. Afflictions to Sagittarius or Jupiter for impaired movement may also be involved. Link congenital > nerves/ brain [paralysis/ spastic]. Ajna. ♋ ☽ > ♊ ☿ / ♈ ♋ ♂ [♄ ♇/♅].
(1) Astro.com 45734 (9 Feb 1945, 21:06, Evanston, IL). ♄ ♋℞ > ⚻ ☿ ♒ [☿ △ ♅ ♊ r6H].
(2) Astro.com 45741 (4 Nov 1949, 07:30, Fellsway, MA). ☽ > ☍ ☿ [∠ ♄]. ♅ ♋ > ☍ ♀.
(3) Astro.com 45742 (22 Feb 1950, 15:01, Chicago, IL). ☽ > □ ☿ ♒ [☍ ♇1].

- Cerebrospinal Fluid: Clear, colourless body fluid that surrounds the brain and the spinal cord, protecting these organs from sudden impact or injury. This fluid also removes waste products from the brain. ☽ ♆.

Cervical Vertebrae: The neck bones or vertebrae. There are seven (C1 - C7), all in the Taurus ruled region. Thr. ♉ ♀.

- Cervical Osteoarthritis/ Spondylosis: The discs of the cervical vertebrae degenerate, become stiffer. A painful, chronic disease normally caused by aging or disease. Link neck [and stiffen]. Mars for pain may link in. Thr. ♉ ♀ [♑ ♄ ♇].
(1) Ginger Baker (19 Aug 1939, no time). The English drummer for the group Cream, in 2013, reported via social media, that he had chronic back pain from degenerative osteoarthritis. ♄ ♉℞ [□ ♂ ♑℞].

1 Bailey, Alice: Esoteric Healing, 143.

Cervix: Lower end of the womb, at the top of the vagina. Allows both period blood and a baby to pass from the womb through and out of the vagina. Sac. ♋☽.

- Cervical Cancer: Develops over many years as a result of the human papillomavirus. Link the cervix to the cancer formula: Sac. ♋☽ [(♋☽,♆♂ > ♄♇) > ♃☉].
(1) Pam Grier (26 May 1949, 18:30, Winston-Salem, NC). ☽6 [(☌♂, ☽□♄) △♃℞].

Chakras: (See also the chakras listed under their individual names). Where many energy lines cross in the etheric web, the chakras (energy vortexes), form. They receive energies from various sources and pass these to the body. There are hundreds of chakras, mostly minor. Seven chakras are considered major because they are involved with the development of consciousness (crown, ajna, throat, heart, solar plexus, sacral, base). The energies of the seven rays, the signs and planets all flow through one or other of the chakras into the body.

Chemicals, Natural: These are produced by nature without human intervention. EG., water, oxygen and carbon dioxide. In esoteric teachings, chemicals - along with the metals, minerals and radioactive substances, are living subhuman units of the mineral kingdom. [1] This kingdom is governed by the 7th ray, [2] which is carried by Uranus. R7, ♅.

- Chemical Medicines, Drugs: Artificially prepared medicines. ♅♆.

- Chemical Reactions: Are rearrangements of electrons. This is different to a nuclear reaction or fission which involves a change in an atom's nucleus, and which usually produces a different element. That is governed by Pluto. ♅.

- Chemical, Synthetic: These are made by humans. ♆.

Chemotherapy: Cancer treatment that uses powerful chemicals (Uranus), to kill (Pluto) fast-growing cells in the body. The treatment damages the nucleus of cells, which brings this treatment under the 1st ray. ♇♅.

Chest Cavity: It contains the ribs, breastbone, oesophagus, the trachea, windpipe, bronchi, lungs, pleura, the heart and large blood vessels. Hrt. ♋☽.

Chest Congestion - see Breathing Congestion.

Chicken Pox: Highly contagious viral infection, distinguished by an itchy, blister-like rash on the skin. Link skin [virus > rash, blisters]. Thr. Spx. Base. ♑♄ (♋) [♆♂♅ > ♂, ☽♃].
(1) Astro.com 6283 (15 Jul 1927, 14:50, Newark, NJ). ♄♐1℞ [□♆ > □♂].
(2) Astro.com 13943 (27 Dec 1963, 20:45, Phoenixville, PA). ♄6 [□♆ > ♆ qd ☽ r12H].
(3) Jon Rodden (26 Oct 1960, 04:53, Covina, CA). ♄♑ [☍♂, coruler 6H > ♂qd♃♑].

Chilblains: Patches of red, swollen, itchy skin, caused by a combination of cold weather and poor circulation. Link skin [cold > inflammation]. Base. ♑♄ (♋☽) [♄ > ♂☉].
(1) Jim Orchard (14 Feb 1946, 22:36, Blenheim, NZ). ♄♋℞ [☌♂♋℞].

Childbirth: Process of giving birth to a child. Sac. ♋☽ (Asc, 1H).
(1) Queen Victoria (24 May 1819, 04:15, London, Eng). She had 9 children, so was very fertile. ☽☌☉ r5H, ☌ Asc.

Children: Progeny. Young human beings. ♌☉, 5H.

Chills: Feeling of coldness. ♑♄.

1 Bailey, Alice: Treatise of Cosmic Fire, 931,
2 Bailey, Alice: Esoteric Psychology I, 369.

Chin: Front pointed part of the lower jaw. Thr. ♈ ♉.

Chlamydia: A common sexually transmitted bacterial infection that can cause permanent damage to Fallopian tubes. Link sex [bacterial infection]. Sac. ♏♂ ♀ [♅♂♆].

(1) Charlotte Crosby (17 May 1990, no time). The British TV presenter, in her book "Me Me Me," revealed that in the past she had chlamydia. ♀♈ [□ ♅♆].

Chloroform: In the early 1900s, it was used as an anaesthetic to reduce pain during surgery. ♓♆.

Choked - see Strangled for being murdered, and Dysphagia for swallowing difficulties or choking on food.

Cholera: Intestinal bacterial disease that causes severe diarrhoea and dehydration. It is usually spread in water. Link intestines [bacterial infection > diarrhoea/ dehydration]. Spx. ♍☿ [♅♂♆ > ♂/♄].

(1) Zachary Taylor (24 Nov 1784, 10:57, Barboursville, VA). The 12th American President died suddenly from cholera. ☿♏ r8H [⚼ ♅♋6 > ♅☍♄12].

Cholesterol: Waxy, fatty substance in the blood that helps make cell membranes. Bad cholesterol can build up on the walls of blood vessels resulting in high blood pressure and consequent circulation problems. [♃].

Chromosome: A long DNA molecule containing genetic material. Sac. ♒♅.

Chronic Disease: A disease that limits health, lasts one year or more, requiring ongoing treatment. Generally ruled by Saturn, Pluto can substitute - especially if the disease is also terminal. ♑♄ (♇).

Chronic Fatigue Syndrome (CFS): A long-term state of physical or mental exhaustion, fatigue, utter weariness and depression. Medically the cause is unknown. Even if there are contributing problems, the basis is emotional. It is a 4th ray problem caused by constant inner-conflict/ inner-fighting that leads to "constant devitalisation." [1] Consequently, an afflicted Moon (and perhaps Mercury) which carry ray 4, will be central in a CFS pattern. Link emotional/ mental [conflict > exhaustion/ lethargy]. Spx. ☽/☿ [♂♅ > ♄/♆].

(1) Michael Crawford (19 Jan 1942, 06:00, Salisbury, Eng). The British singer/ actor suffered from CFS. ☽♒ [□ ♅6 > □ ♄].

Chronic Obstructive Pulmonary Disease: (COPD. See Bronchitis, Emphysema, Pulmonary Embolisms). Refers to a group of chronic diseases that cause airflow blockage and breathing-related problems. Link the airways [blockages]. Thr. ♊☿ [♄♇].

Chyle: A milky-white digestive juice that aids digestion. Spx. ♋☽.

Cigarettes, Cigars: Thin cylinders of finely cut tobacco rolled in paper for smoking. ♓♆.

- Cigarette Addiction - see Nicotine/ Cigarette Addiction.

Circadian Sleep-Wake Cycle: At morning light, the optic nerve alerts the *suprachiasmatic nucleus* (SCN) in the anterior hypothalamus. The SCN then sends hormones to the cerebral cortex to wake us up. When the optic nerve signals darkness, the SCN turns off the alert and signals the pineal gland to release melatonin. This hormone helps to regulate the circadian rhythm and has a soporific effect upon the system. Link hypothalamus > sleep > wake. Cwn. ♀ > ♆☽ > ☉.

1 Bailey, Alice: Esoteric Healing, 301.

Cirrhosis - see Liver, Cirrhosis.

Claustrophobia: (See Panic Attack). Intense fear of suffocation or being restricted in a confined space. This triggers the flight-flight reaction, and desire to escape. The Asc for reactiveness, may link in. Link emotions [fear > fight-flight]. Spx. ♋ ☽ ♂ [♄ ♇ > ♏ ♂].
(1) Barbara Bain (13 Sep 1931, 20:45, Chicago, IL). ♂ ♎ 6 [□ ♇ ♋]. Asc ♉/♏ [⚻ ♂ 6].
(2) Uma Thurman (29 Apr 1970, 13:51, Boston, MA). ☽ 6 [⚻ ♇]. Asc [□ ♂].

Clavicle: Collarbone. ♊ ☿.

Cleavage: A dissociative type mental disorder - one part of the nature is out of touch with another, feelings of alienation from people and the environment, being torn in two directions. These are negatives traits of ray 5 (carried by Aquarius and Venus). They can result in tissue and energy cleavages in the body - groups of cells repelling other cells. R5, Ajna. [♒ ♅ ♀].

Cleft Palate, Cleft Lip: A congenital problem. Foetal bones in the roof of the mouth do not fuse completely. Jupiter, planet of growth that is responsible for the fusing together of tissue/ bone, etc., may be involved. Saturn rules 'undeveloped.' The top lip is ruled by either Aries or Taurus, the palate by Taurus. Link congenital > lip/ palate [undeveloped/ cleft]. Thr. ♋ ☽ > ♈ ♂/♉ ♀ [♑ ♄/♂].

Cleft lips.
(1) Cheech Marin (13 Jul 1946, 13:00, LA, CA). ♄ ♋ [∠ ♂ r6H, for lip and cleft].
(2) Joaquin Phoenix (28 Oct 1974, no time). ☽ ♈ [disposited by ♂].

Cleft palate.
(1) Astro.com 1052 (22 Mar 1947, 21:05, Chicago, IL). ☽ ♈ > ∠ ♀ [♂ mp ☽/♀].
(2) Astro.com 1470 (8 Oct 1977, 22:20, Mackey Bar, Idaho). ♀ ♍ [mp ☽ ♄/ ☿ ♇].
(3) Astro.com 3679 (14 Apr 1896, 03:25, Bridlington, Eng). ♃ ♋ 6 > △ ♀ ♈ 1 [disp. by ♂].

Clitoris: Main pleasure centre in female sexuality. Sac. ♀ ♂ ♏.

Clot - see Blood Clot.

Club Foot: Congenital defect that affects muscles and bones. The foot is twisted out of shape or position. Link congenital > the foot [twisted/ undeveloped]. Sac. Base. ♋ ☽ > ♓ ♆ ♃ [♅/♄].
(1) Dudley Moore (19 Apr 1935, 18:30, Dagenham, Eng). The British entertainer was born with a club foot and had seven operations as a child. ☽ ♏ 1 > △ ♄ ♓ [☽ ☍ ♅]. ♓ r6H.

Coagulate: In medicine, the clotting of blood. Hrt. ♄.

Coccyx, Coccygeal Vertebrae: Tailbone, the very bottom fused vertebrae. Base. ♐ ♃.

Cochlea: Part of the inner ear involved in hearing. Ajna. ♊ ☿.

Coeliac Disease, Gluten Intolerance: (See Autoimmune Disease). The immune system attacks the small intestine when gluten is eaten. Inner causes are hypersensitivity, feeling malnourished emotionally, etc. Link emotions/ gluten > the intestines [immune reaction]. Spx. ♋ ☽ > ♍ ☿ [♂(☉ ♅)].
(1) Novak Djokovic (22 May 1987, 23:25, Belgrade, Serbia). The tennis great said "going on a gluten-free diet eliminated allergy symptoms." ☿ [mp ♂ ♋ 6 / ☉].
(2) Zooey Deschanel (17 Jan 1980, 06:57, Santa Monica, CA). She said she was "allergic to eggs, dairy, and wheat gluten." Astro.com. ☽ ☿ ♑ 12 [☌ ☉ 1, ☌ Asc].

Cognition: Ability to clearly think, learn, and remember. Ajna. ♊ ☿.

Colds, Common: A viral attack on the airways, producing mucous and phlegm. Link airways [virus > mucous, phlegm]. Thr. ♊ ☿ [♆♂♅ > ♋☽(♆)].
(1) Emily Bronte (30 Jul 1818, 14:49, Thornton, Eng). Caught a cold that would not go away. But it was more than that and she died within three months of being infected. The cold likely evolved into pneumonia. ☿ [△♆♅1 > ∠☽♋8].

Colic: (See Wind). Severe pain in the abdomen caused by wind or a muscle spasm. Saturn may link in for 'obstruction,' air signs or planets for 'wind.' Mars can represent both muscles and pain. Link abdomen/ intestines [and pain]. Spx. ♋☽/ ♍☿ [♂].
(1) Eva Klemperer (12 Jul 1882, 15:30, Konigsberg, Poland). ♅♍ [☌♂♍ r12H].
(2) Jean Driscoll (18 Nov 1966, 09:15, Milwaukee, WI). ♅♍ [☌♂♍].

Collagen: A protein produced by the body, which is essential to connective tissue and skin. Base. ♑♄.

Collarbone: Clavicle. Thr. ♊ ☿.

Colon: Also known as the large bowel and the large intestine. A long, continuous tube running from the end of the small intestine to the anus. The colon/ large intestine absorbs water and salts. It forms and stores faeces, then excretes it via the anus. Specifically ruled by Scorpio, Mars and Pluto. Virgo-Mercury are back-up rulers. Thr. Spx. ♏♂♇ (♍☿).

- Colitis: Inflammatory reaction in the colon. The cause can be due to an auto-immune problem, an infection, or in the case of ischemic colitis, blood flow to the large intestine is temporarily reduced (♄♇♒). Link colon [the cause of the problem > inflammation/ pain]. Spx. ♏♂♇ (♍☿) [the cause > ♂☉].
These examples are from Carter, Encyclopaedia of Psychological Astrology.
(1) EPA p54. (16 Jan 1878, 21:45, Wales). ♂♈8 [□♃♑]. Likely ischemic colitis, with Jupiter in Capricorn representing an artery blockage.
(2) EPA p54. (20 Oct 1901, 13:15, London, Eng). ♂♐ [⚻♆♋6]. A virus.
(3) EPA p54. (24 Feb 1889, 12pm, London, Eng). ♂♈ [□♃♑6]. Most likely ischemic colitis - a blood flow blockage.
(4) EPA p54. (5 Apr 1868, 23:55, Sussex). ☿♓ coruler 6H [☌♂♓]. A virus.

- Colon Cancer - see Bowel Cancer.

- Colostomy: This operation is done to create an opening for the colon through the abdomen. It is needed if stools cannot be passed through the anus, the result of an injury or disease such as bowel cancer. Link the colon > surgical/ bypass. Spx. ♏♂♇ (♍☿) > ♂♅/ ☿.
These two examples had colostomies and continued with active lives afterwards.
(1) Marvin Bush (22 Oct 1956, no time). ♇♍ > qd ♂ / ∠☿.
(2) Otto Graham (6 Dec 1921, 01:50, Waukegan, IL). ♂♎1 > ∠☿♐.

Colour Blindness, Colour Deficiency: Colour is seen, but because some nerve cells in the eyes are missing or do not work correctly, a narrower range of colours are seen. Link sight / nerve cells [deficient]. ☉☽/ ☿♅ [♄].
(1) Paul Newman (26 Jan 1925, 06:30, Cleveland, OH). ☉♒ / ∠♅ [□♄].
(2) Roger Staubach (5 Feb 1942, 04:25, Cincinnati, OH). ☉♒ / ☿♒ [□♄].

Coma, Comatose: Being unconscious, unresponsive, and cannot be woken. Most often the result of a brain injury or stroke, it can also be caused by severe alcohol poisoning or a brain infection. Other planets linking in should explain the cause. Link consciousness [with unconscious]. A planet for the cause will link in. Cwn. ☉, Asc [♆♇ (♄)].

(1) Evel Knievel (17 Oct 1938, 14:40, Butte, MT). A motor cycle stunt performer, in the 1970s. ☉ [□♇6 > △♃1℞]. Knieval was showman and risk-taker (♃1), and potential head injuries were a hazard of the job.

(2) Marie Trintignant French actress (21 Jan 1962, 13:00, Boulonge Billancourt, Fr). In 2003, she was found in a hotel room with a severe head injury. The assailant was never found. She remained in a coma until she died. ☉ [☌ ♄ coruler 8H > ⚻ ♅5]. With the 5H linking in - and Pluto in that house, possibly a violent lover was the assailant.

(3) Mike McKeever (1 Jan 1940, 13:00, Cheyenne, WY). A footballer prone to head knocks and consequent coma. Asc [☌ ♅, ∠♂].

Conception, Impregnation: When sperm impregnates an egg in the Fallopian tube. Sac. ♏♂ > ♋☽.

Concrete Mind - see Mental Body.

Concussion: A traumatic brain injury, which damages brain tissue. Link brain [impact injury]. Cwn. ♈♂, ♋☽ [♈♂♅].

(1) Stephanie Eggink (12 Jul 1988, 10:38, Bellingham, WA). This American mixed martial arts fighter is susceptible to head injuries. ☽♋ [□♂]. ♂ [□♅♄ in the 5H of sport].

Confusion: Cannot think clearly. Ajna. ♊ ☿ [♆].

Congenital Disease/ Disorder/ Defect: A congenital disease or defect is present from birth. Such a disease may be due to a genetic/ karmic mutation being passed down a family line. Birth defects can be environmental or a combination of genetic and environmental. The rulers of birth will be heavily afflicted. Link congenital, birth [disease/ defect]. Sac. ♋☽, Asc [♄♇/♅].

Congestion, Breathing - see Breathing Congestion, Lung Congestion.

Conjunctivitis: Inflammation of the inner eyelid due to an infection. Link the eyes [infection / inflammation]. Ajna. ☉☽ [♂♅♆ / ♂☉].

(1) Karen Allen (5 Oct 1951, 10:11, Carrollton, IL). When the actress was young, she had temporary blindness then later a conjunctivitis condition. ☉ [□♅♋].

Consciousness or Self-awareness: The state of being aware of and responsive to one's surroundings. The source of consciousness is the soul, which (via the antahkarana), uses the mind, the brain and the nervous system [1] to navigate and make sense of the physical world. Depending upon the level of development and the chakras that are awake, consciousness may be emotionally coloured (focused in the solar plexus), intelligent (throat and ajna), or spiritually awake and aware (crown). If for some reason the antahkarana link is disrupted, only animal awareness/ consciousness will be left. The animal brain is the solar-plexus.

The ray energy responsible for consciousness is the 2nd ray, [2] the force which is carried by the Sun, the planet which represents personality consciousness. Mercury (mind) is a substitute ruler. Ajna. R2, ☉ (☿).

1 Bailey, Alice: Education in the New Age, 18,
2 Bailey, Alice: The Externalisation of the Hierarchy, 145.

- Consciousness Thread (Antahkarana): This is the channel of communication between the God spark/ Monad > the soul > and the brain. [1] It is how the soul communicates with its personality aspect (us in our everyday consciousness), and vice versa. It anchors in the region of the pineal gland. [2] Mercury rules the antahkarana. [3] Cwn. Ajna. R2, ♊ ☿ .

Constipation: Difficulty in emptying the bowels, usually associated with hardened faeces. Psychologically, holding onto one's 'shit'. Link the bowel, faeces [and hard]. Spx. ♏ ♂ ♇ (♍ ☿), ♄ [♑ ♄].
(1) Elvis Presley (8 Jan 1935, 04:35, Tupelo, MS). Presley's doctor claims the legendary singer died from chronic constipation. [4] The chart supports that view. ♇ 8 [☋ ♄].

Constitution, Body: The state of health, vitality and wellness in the body. Hrt. R2, ♌ ☉ .

Constrict: Make narrower, especially by applying encircling pressure. Scorpio rules suffocation. ♏ ♇, ♄ .

Contagious Diseases: Two rays are involved with highly communicable diseases and epidemics.
• Ray 4 (Moon, Mercury). Afflicted, this force is conducive to "the rapid taking on of contagious diseases." [5]
• Ray 7 (Uranus). This energy, which is the opposite pole of the power ray (R1), "is largely responsible for infections and contagious diseases." [6]
Of all the signs, Cancer is often implicated in infectious diseases because it carries ray 7, and ray 4 via the Moon. Thr. [☽ ☿ , ♅]. This does not mean this sign is fated to be sick more often than other signs. Personal karma determines that.

Contaminate, Contamination: (See Poison). The presence of an undesirable element that spoils, corrupts, infects, makes unfit or inferior. Neptune can be deviant, insidious. Pluto is a corruptive agent. Esotericist Helena Blavatsky said that "moonlight spoils food and injures health." [7] [♆ ♇ (☽)].

Contractions, Childbirth: The uterus muscles tighten and then relax, to push a baby down the birth canal. Sac. ♄ .

Convulsions: Uncontrollable muscle spasms that can be caused by an illness, drugs or injuries. Link muscles [spasms]. ♂ [♅].
(1) Romeo Beckham (1 Sep 2002, 09:40, London, Eng). Son of celebrity couple Victoria and David, Romeo suffered convulsions at age three. ♂ coruler 6H [♂ ♅].

Copper: Trace mineral that helps the body make red blood cells and keeps nerve cells and the immune system healthy. ♀ .

Cornea: The clear outer layer at the front of the eye, which helps the eye to focus light. Ajna. ☉ .

Corns: Thick, hardened skin on the feet and toes that develops to protect against friction. Base. ♑ ♄ .

---

1 Bailey, Alice: Discipleship in the New Age II, 46.
2 Bailey, Alice: The Rays and the Initiations, 450.
3 Bailey, Alice: Esoteric Astrology, 281.
4 The Daily Telegraph, March 2023.
5 Bailey, Alice: Esoteric Healing, 301.
6 Bailey, Alice: Esoteric Healing, 304.
7 Collect Writings, vol IV, 396-7.

Coronary Thrombosis: Blood clot in a heart blood vessel that restricts blood flow and can cause a heart attack. Link the heart / blood [clot]. Hrt. ♌ ☉/ ♒ ♅ ♆ [♄ ♇].
These men died from a coronary thrombosis, so an 'attack' step (♂ ♅) has been added.
(1) George IV (14 Dec 1895, 03:05, Sandringham, Eng). ♃ ♌ ℞ [□ ♄ > △ ♂ r6H].
(2) James Baxter (29 Jun 1926, 21:30, Dunedin, NZ). ☉ r6H [☌ ♇ > □ ♂ ♈].
(3) Kurt Koffka (18 Mar 1886, 12:45, Berlin, Ger). ☉ [□ ♄ 12 r6H > qd ♂].

Corpses: Dead bodies. R3 rules the body. ☽ ♄ ♇, 8H.

Corruption of Cells: Damage to cells by a corruptive force. Neptune can be deviant, insidious. Pluto is a corruptive agent. Link cell life [and corruption]. Hrt. ☉ [♆ ♇].

Cortisol: A hormone produced by the adrenals in response to danger. It heightens fight-or-flight defensiveness and curbs nonessential functions. Base. ♏ ♂.

Cough: A natural reflex that occurs when the body tries to remove irritants from the airways. Sometimes the cause may be emotional, be nerve related. Link airways [cough]. Thr. ♊ ☿ [♂ ♅].
(1) Andy Kaufman (17 Jan 1949, 18:03, Jamaica, NY). He had a persistent cough because of lung cancer. ☿ [☌ ♂ 6]. ♅ ♊ [⚼ ♂ 6].
(2) Frederic Chopin (1 Mar 1810, 18:00, Zelazowa Pola, Poland). He had severe coughing fits towards the end of his life, indicative of a lung issue. ☿ [□ ♅ r6H].

Covid-19: A new virus that appeared in 2019, killing millions around the world. Congesting the airways, unchecked it can lead to problems such as pneumonia and respiratory failure. Link airways [and viral infection]. Thr. ♊ ☿ [♆ ♂ ♅].
These two stars died from Covid complications. An extra step has been added for death.
(1) Charley Pride (18 Mar 1934, 08:00, Nashville, TN). ☿ ♓ [☍ ♆ ♍ > ⚼ ♃ 6, r8H].
(2) Cloris Leachman (30 Apr 1926, 06:55, Des Moines, IA). ☿ [∠ ♂ > ♂ □ ♄ r8H].

Cowpox: (See Smallpox). A viral skin infection caught from cows and small rodents. It causes pus-like lesions, which ulcerate and scab. Link skin [infection > pus/ scabs]. ♑ ♄ (♋ ☽) [♆ ♂ ♅ > ☽ / ♂].

Cowper's Glands: These are male sex organs, which add fluid to semen during ejaculation. Sac. ♏ ♂ ♇.

Crabs, Pubic: Small parasites that cling to pubic hair and suck blood for nourishment. Sac. [♏ ♂ ♇].

Cramps, Muscle. An uncontrollable and painful muscle spasm. Any muscle can be affected, but the muscles of the calf and foot are particularly prone. Serious stomach cramps can be caused by food poisoning or a stomach infection. Other linking planets may explain the cause of cramps. Link muscles and / or the body part involved [and cramps]. ♂ [♂ ♅].
(1) Astro.com 6496 (24 Sep 1928, 23:30, Winterhausen, Ger). An American infant who died following an operation for stomach cramps within a month of birth. From the astrology, the cause could have been ischemic colitis, which reduces blood flow to the bowel, causing cramps. ☽ ♒ (blood flow in the stomach region) [qd ♇ ♋ 12 (fatal stomach blockage) > ⚹ ♅ ♈ painful cramps].

Cranium: Bone framework enclosing the brain. Cwn. Base. ♈ ♄.

- Craniosynostosis: A congenital deformity. Skull bones close prematurely due to a gene abnormality. Link congenital > skull [gene abnormality]. Cwn. Base. ♋ ☽ > ♈ ♄ [♅].
(1) Dove Arroyave (25 Feb 2020, no time, Los Angeles, CA). Infant daughter of reality star Teddi Mellencamp, who posted on Instagram in 2020, that her baby girl had this condition. ☽ > ⚹♄♑ [♄□♅♉].

Cravings: Extreme desire for something. R6, Spx. Sac. ♉♂.

Cretinism: A congenital problem usually caused by insufficient iodine in the diet during pregnancy. The result is impaired physical and mental development. Link congenital/ pregnancy > thyroid [deficient]. ♋☽ > ♉♀ [♄♇].

Crib Death - see Sudden Infant Death Syndrome (SIDS).

Crippled: A lame person deprived of the use of a limb. Cancer or the Moon may be involved if it is congenital, and Jupiter - Sagittarius for impaired movement. Link limb [crippled]. Sac. Base. ♐♃,♒♅ legs [♄♇].
(1) Gwen Verdon (13 Jan 1925, 09:57, Los Angeles, CA). The Broadway dance and movie star was born with badly twisted legs. Her mother had her put in corrective shoes and started her on dance lessons. By age 4 she was dancing in public. ☽6 congenital > △♃♑ [♃☍♇♋].

In her chart, the ability to heal the congenital condition is shown by a grand trine: ♄,△♇,△♅. Uranus is the 'worker of miracles.'

Crohn's Disease: Chronic inflammation of the bowel. Psychologically, the repression of anger. Link bowel [and inflammation]. Thr. Spx. ♏♂♇ (♍☿) [♂☉].
(1) Linn Lane (1 Jun 1947, 03:47, Bayfield, CO). ♂♉12 [☍☽♏6].
(2) Robin Kaplan (15 May 1968, 08:23, Boston, MA) ☿12 [□♇☌♅♍]. ♂12 [∠♄♈].
(3) Tessa Miller (16 Aug 1988, 07:34, Boise, Idaho). ♇♏ [⚻♂♈8].

Croup: A viral infection that causes swelling in the windpipe and voice box, making it hard to breathe. In serious cases, lack of air causes suffocation. There is a distinctive barking cough. Link airways / throat [and infection]. Thr. ♊☿/ ♉♀ [♂♅♆].
(1) Napoleon Charles Bonaparte (10 Oct 1802, 21:00, Paris, Fr), a nephew of Emperor Bonaparte I. He died aged 4, of croup. ♀6 [⚻♂♋ > ♂□♅ coruler 8H of death].

CROWN CHAKRA (Cwn): (See Chakras and Etheric web).
Consciousness: This chakra is the seat of the soul, and awakens only when we become spiritually alive. Until then, it vitalises basic physical functions. Eventually the transmuted forces of the base centre, flow up and out through this chakra.
Ray and Astrology energies: The primary ray is the 1st of Will and Power. It flows via Pluto, for physical functions, via Vulcan for disciples, and via Uranus for initiates.
Body rulership: This 1000-petal lotus enters through the top of the head and anchors in the pineal gland. The region it vitalises is comparable to that of Aries, including, the brain, sleep and death. (See the Pineal Gland).
Diseases: Those in the head and brain - such as dementia, meningitis, and stroke.

Cruelty: Behaviour which causes physical or mental harm to another. This evil trait is a negative of the 6th ray. It consists of a lack of empathy for others, as well as a driving urge to harm and maim - mentally, emotionally or physically. Spx. R6 [♏♂♆].

(1) Dennis Rader (9 Mar 1945, 14:47, Wichita, KS). He tortured and killed small animals and later did the same to people. An afflicted Moon (☽ ♑6) explains his lack of empathy, an afflicted Venus (♀♈) his narcissism. ☉♓ [mp ♀♈/ ♂8].

Cryogenics: Relating to the production of very low temperatures. ♄.

Crystallises: To harden, give definite or concrete form to. R1 crystallises.[1] ♑ ♄.

Crystals: All atoms are arranged in a regular grid pattern. Crystals are members of the mineral kingdom, ruled by rays 7 and 1. ♄ ♅.

CT scan: Rotating X-ray machines that create cross-sectional images of the body. ♅.

Cushing's Syndrome: The diseased adrenal-cortex produces excess cortisol. This causes a fatty hump between the shoulders, a round face and stretch marks. Link the adrenal-cortex [and excess, fatty]. Base. ♎♀ [♃].
(1) Travis Holder (16 Oct 1946, no time). The American actor reported he had the disease. ♀♐ [♃ is mp ♀/ ♆♎].

Cuts, Cutting: Self-harm. Deliberately causing pain or injury to oneself because of self-hatred, self-disgust. It is a a cry for help. Link the emotions [with cutting]. ♋ ☽ ♂ [♈ ♂].
(1) Angelina Jolie (4 Jun 1975, 09:09, Los Angeles, CA). She admitted to self-mutilation in her teens. Her chart shows deep emotional insecurity, self-dislike, self-disgust and potential for self-harm. Spx. ☽ ♈ [☌ ♂]. ♄ ♋12 [□♂ ☽ ♈].

Cyanide Poisoning: see Poisons - Vegetable.

Cyber Criminals: These are criminals, scammers, bullies, stalkers, who operate via internet and social media. Thr. ♊ ☿ [♆].

Cyst: A noncancerous sac or capsule that is filled with either fluid, blood, tissue, hair, bone, a foreign body, etc. If it is filled with pus, it becomes an abscess. [♋ ☽, ♃].

Cystic Fibrosis: An inherited life-threatening disorder that causes thick, sticky mucous to build up in the lungs, digestive tract, and other areas of the body. Link inherited > the airways/ digestion [mucous/ thick, sticky]. Thr. ♊ ☿/ ♋ ☽ [♋ ☽ > ♃ ♓ ♆].
(1) Annie Tulcin (14 Jun 1953, 17:36, NY, NY). ♅♋ > ☌ ☿ ♋8 [□♆].
(2) Gregory Lemarchal (13 May 1983, 05:08, La Tronche, Fr). ☽4 a family inheritance > ⚹ ☿ ♊1 [☿ mp ♄12 / ♃♋].
(3) James Fletcher Brown (17 Jul 2006, 09:00, Edinburgh, Scot). ☽8 > □ ☿ ♋℞ [☽ ⚹ ♆6].

Cystitis - see Urinary Tract Infection.

Cytokine Storm: Cytokines are warning cells that alert the immune system when the body is attacked by germs. A cytokine storm refers to a severe immune reaction that causes the release of too many cytokines into the blood too quickly. They flood the lungs and can cause serious breathing problems. Hrt. [♓♆].

1 Bailey, Alice; Esoteric Healing, 299.

D

Dead Body: Lifeless body, a corpse, cadaver. ♄♇, 8H.

Deaf: Hearing loss so severe there is very little or no functional hearing. Link the ears [with deafness]. Ajna. Thr. ♊ ☿ [♑ ♄].

(1) Ludwig Van Beethoven (16 Dec 1770, no time). He composed some of his greatest masterpieces while completely deaf. ☿ ♐/♊ [disposited by ♃ ♑; ♃ ⚼ ♄].

Death: The death of the physical body. When breathing stops permanently, when the life-thread from the soul to the heart snaps. Then consciousness gradually moves through the emotional and mental bodies before withdrawing back into the soul. After a period of rest, a new incarnation begins. Link life [and death]. ☉ Asc [♏♇, ♄, 8H].

There are many omens in the chart at the moment of death. For instance, the cause of the death if it is not natural will likely figure. Because death is a blessing for the ill and suffering, often Jupiter makes a beneficial aspect. The following are basics for death.

- The 8H, Scorpio, Pluto, Saturn (the Grim Reaper), and (Mars); are the rulers of death.
- Often at the moment of death, the ruler of the 8H of death will be active by transit, by secondary progression or by solar arc direction.
- Natal planets in the 8H may be active or activated (targeted by transit, progressed planets).
- The ascendant - the representative of the incarnation, may be active or activated.
- The Sun, the primary representative of life, may be activated.

a. In the following examples, all death dates and times are from Astro.com.

b. First, the pattern for the cause of death in the natal chart is given.

c. Then the planet transits, progressions and solar arc directions for the moment of death, are compared to the natal chart - and to each other. Although there may be other things happening in the chart at the moment of death, in these examples, focus remains on the basic indicators of death as listed previously.

(1) Christian Dior (21 Jan 1905, 01:30, Granville, Fr). French fashion designer who died suddenly of heart attack, 24 Oct 1957 at 22:30.
Natal chart: Heart attack ☉ [□♂]. For death ☉ [□♂ > ♂ ⚼ ♇8].
Progressed charts: Asc [☌ t☿, r8H]. Prog Asc [☌ t♄]. n☉ [⚻ t♇]. n♇ is in the 8H

(2) Francois Mitterand (26 Oct 1916, 04:00, Jarnac, Fr). French politician who died of prostate cancer, 8 january 1996 at 08:30.
Natal chart: Cancer and death, ♇♋ [⚹♃8, r6H].
Progressed charts: p Asc [☌n♂ r8H > ☌t♇]. n☉ [□p♂ > p♂⚻n♇].

(3) Jackie Onassis (28 Jul 1929, 14:30, Southampton, NY). Suffering from lymphoma cancer, she died suddenly on 19 May 1994, at 22:15.
Natal chart: Lymphoma and death. ☽ [(□♇♋8) > ∠♃ ♊].
Progressed charts: Asc [☌p♂, ruler of the Asc]. t☿ r8H, [☌♇8]. p☉12 > □n☉ [☍t♃6]. p☿ r8H [☌s.arc ♇, n♇8H]. n☉ [⚻t♄].

(4) Ted Kennedy (22 Feb 1932, 03:58, Dorchester, MA). He died of brain cancer on 25 August 2009 at 22:33.
Natal chart: Brain cancer and death, ♅♈ [(□♇♋) > △♃].
Progressed charts: s.arc Asc [☌t♅ coruler 1H]. p☿ coruler 8H [⚻t♄8, r,Asc]. n☉ [☍t☉8H]. t☿ coruler 8H [Tsq □t♇12 > □t♂6].

(5) Winston Churchill (30 Nov 1874, 01:30, Woodstock, Eng). The great wartime leader died at 08:00, on 24 January 1965.
Natal chart: Death was from complications due to a stroke. ♂1 [☌♃ > ♃☍♆♈8].
Progressed charts: Asc [☌t♂ r8H]. Prog. Asc [□t♄]. ♇8H [□ s.arc ♇]. n☉ [☌ p♂].

Debilitation, Devitalisation: Fatigue, exhaustion in the physical body. Even if there are external factors, it is due to exhaustive inner mental-emotional conflict - a 4th Ray of Conflict problem. This force is carried by the Moon and Mercury. Conflict is also related to ♂. Eventually the energy disturbance can cause organs to malfunction. Link mind / emotions [with exhaustion]. ☿☽ [♄ (♇)].

Decapitate: Cut off the head. Link the head/ neck [and decapitation]. ♈/♉ [♂].
(1) Ann Boleyn (5 May 1507, 11:30, London, Eng), wife of King Henry VIII, was decapitated when she fell out of favour. ♀♈8℞ [☍♃ the king > ♃⚻♂♉/♏ ordering her execution]. Mars disposits Venus.

Decay, Decomposition: The process of rotting or decomposition is associated with the Moon. Here are some quotes.

> The decay of a moon has as great an evil effect upon all that contacts.[1]
>
> Every moon is occultly a "point of corruption."[2]

Saturn is another representative of decay. ☽♄.

Decompression Sickness, the Bends (DCI). It occurs most commonly in scuba or deep-sea divers. If re-surfacing occurs too quickly, nitrogen does not have time to clear from the blood. It forms bubbles, which will damage blood vessels and block blood flow. Link blood [block]. Hrt. ♒♅♆ [♄].

Deep Vein Thrombosis. (See Blood Clot, Pulmonary Embolism). A clot in a vein that blocks blood flow, usually in the legs. Venus rules the veins, but any of the other cardiovascular rulers could substitute. Add in ♂ or ♅ if the clot leads to a heart attack. Link veins [and clot]. Hrt. ♀ [♄♃].
(1) Tab Hunter (11 Jul 1931, 03:00, New York, NY). An American movie heart-throb in the 1950s, he died from complications of deep vein thrombosis. This formula for the blood clot: ♀♋ r6H [qd ♄♑8℞]. This formula for the heart attack that followed ☉ [□♅♈ > ☌♇ for death].

Defecation: Discharge of faeces from the body is a Scorpio/ Pluto function. Traditionally, faeces when viewed as waste, is represented by Saturn. Spx. ♏♇, ♄.

Deformed, Bone Deformities: A distorted body. Serious genetic abnormalities occur when a gene mutates or is damaged at conception. For these, look for major Uranus and Pluto afflictions, because they can produce gross extremes and abnormalities. Jupiter for overgrowth may link in, and Saturn for being deformed generally. Link the body-appearance/ growth [genetic extremes / deformed]. Asc, 1H / ☉♃ [♅♇ / ♄].

1 Bailey, Alice: Treatise of Cosmic Fire, 795.
2 Bailey, Alice: Treatise of Cosmic Fire, 794.

Wikipedia

(1) John Merrick (5 Aug 1862, 13:09, Leicester, Eng). Called the "Elephant Man", he was said to be the "most shockingly disfigured person in history." Parts of his body were grossly enlarged, and his skeleton showed gross (♃), deformities. His birth time is unknown. But the time 13:09, places his Asc and Pluto into positions that match his gross deformities. Asc ♏ □ ☉ [☍ ♇ ♉ 6]. ☽ for the body: Tsq [☍ ♅ / □ ♄].

(2) Astro.com 3015 (31 Mar 1881, 23:34, Chadderton Eng). A British dwarf with deformed knees and feet. His knees bent over each other when he walked. Asc ♐ [☍ ♇6, ⚻ ♄].

Degenerative Disease: The function of the affected organ, gradually but relentlessly changes for the worse over time. This is the 1st ray at work, a process that hardens and ages until death occurs. R1. [♑ ♄ ♇].

Dehydration: This occurs when more fluid is lost than can be taken in. [♄].

Delirium - due to Diabetes. Untreated diabetes causes excess blood sugar (hyperglycaemia), and severe delirium. Link the pancreas [excess sugar > delirium]. Spx. ♋ ☽, ♎ ♀ [♃ ♀ > ♓ ♆].

(1) John Massis (4 Jun 1940, 08:00, Bruges, Belgium), a showman entertainer was found delirious due to untreated diabetes and died. ♀ ♋12 [mp ♃/♆ ♍].

Delirium - due to Mental-Emotional Issues. Generally, delirium refers to being seriously disturbed mentally, with confused thinking and reduced awareness of reality. When the cause is emotional, it means that emotional disturbances are too powerful for the reasoning capacity. Pisces and Neptune are rulers of the emotions and are the prime rulers of delirium. Link the nervous system [and delirium]. Spx. ☉ ♊ ☿ [♓ ♆].

Delirium Tremens (DTs). Confusion, hyperactivity of the autonomic NS (trembling, sweating, nausea, vomiting), due to sudden alcohol withdrawal. Chronic drunks can have DTs even when no alcohol is in the bloodstream. Link nervous system [alcohol/ delirium > hyperactivity]. Spx. ♊ ☿ [♓ ♆ > ♂ ♅].

(1) Dylan Thomas (27 Oct 1914, 23:00, Swansea, Wales). The Welsh poet-writer was an alcoholic, and died from chronic delirium tremens. ☿ [△ ♆12 > ☌ ♂ ♏].

Deltoid Muscles: In the shoulder. Thr. ♂ ♊.

Delusion: (See Grandiose Delusions, Guidance, Mystical Vision, Stigmata). Lacking discrimination, an unshakable belief in something not real. The emotional life is more potent than the intellect. Link the mind [emotionalism/ delusion]. Spx. ♊ ☿ [♋ ☽, ♓ ♆].

Dementia: The term applies to a group of conditions (see Alzheimer's, Huntington's Disease, Lewy Body Dementia, and Vascular Dementia), characterised by impairment of at least two brain functions such as loss of memory and judgement. Disease of brain-cells (neurons), means that the brain can no longer store and access new memories and it atrophies and shrinks. Consequently, the soul/ consciousness, the intelligence, can no longer communicate with the outer world because of the diseased dementia brain. Planets for the intelligence (☿ ♀), or consciousness (☉), may connect in. Link the brain [to aging, atrophy]. Cwn. ♈ ♂, ☽ ♋ [♄ ♇].

(1) Bruce Willis (19 Mar 1955, 18:32, Idar-Oberstein, Ger). The American movie star was diagnosed in 2023. ♂ ♉ 8 [☍ ♄, aging, drying out of the brain]. ☿ ♓ r12H and Asc [☍♇, destruction of cognition].

Dengue Fever: A mosquito borne virus, which attacks the blood causing a fever, rash, muscle and joint pain. In extreme cases there can be a haemorrhage. Mars rules the blood, fever, mosquitos etc., so it will likely be involved in the pattern. Link the blood [virus]. Thr. ♂ ♃ ♒ [♆ ♂ ♅].

(1) Rishi Kapoor (4 Sep 1952, 23:10, Mumbai, India). ♂ r12H [∠♆].

Dental Decay, Infection: Teeth are invaded by bacteria. Link teeth [bacteria > decay]. Thr. ♄ [♅ > ☽ ♄].

Depression: Extended thoughts and feelings of severe despondency and dejection. Link mind/ or emotions [and depression]. Spx. ☿ / ☽ ♂ ♆ [♄].

(1) Bruce Springsteen (23 Sep 1949, 22:50, Freehold, NJ). ☽ [∠♄]. ♂ r6H [☌♇].

(2) Kirsten Dunst (30 Apr 1982, 13:00, Point Pleasant, NJ). The actress revealed in a 2021 interview, that she had suffered with depression in her 20s. Neptune afflicts both the Sun and Moon. ☽ 12 [♄ mp ☽/♆].

Dermis: The thick layer of living tissue below the epidermis which forms the true skin. Contains blood capillaries, nerve endings, sweat glands, hair follicles. Base. ♑ ♄ (♋ ☽).

- **Dermatitis:** (See Eczema). A general term given for inflammation of the skin. Psychologically, emotional irritation and unexpressed anger are causes. Link skin [and inflammation]. ♑ ♄ (♋ ☽) [♂ ☉].

Desire Body: The subtle body which expresses emotions and desires. Spx. Sac. ♂♆.

Destroys: End the existence of, by destroying / killing. ♏♇.

Deviant: Social or sexual behaviours that depart so far from accepted/ moral standards, ; they are considered abhorrent. [♆ (♅)].

Devitalise - see Debilitation.

Diabetes: Blood sugar levels are too high (hyperglycaemia), due to trouble with insulin absorption. Insulin regulates blood sugar levels and enables sugar to enter the body's cells for energy. Some symptoms are: an urge to urinate a lot, thirsty/ hungry, weight loss, blurry vision, exhaustion. Afflictions to Venus and Jupiter that govern sugar, are key.

Type 1 diabetes: There is little or no insulin because the pancreas glands (Islets of Langerhans), are destroyed by the immune system. So, glucose cannot enter cells to give energy. Saturn may link in for tiredness. Link the pancreas [immune attack > excess sugar]. Spx. ♋ ☽, ♎ ♀ [♂ ☉ > ♃ ♀].

(1) Eric Paslay (29 Jan 1983, 01:06, Abilene, TX). ♀ r12H [wide ☌ ♂ > □ ♃].

(2) Marcia Hines (20 Jul 1953, 09:44, Boston, MA). ♀ [∠☉♂♋ > ☌ ♃ coruler 6H].

(3) Mary Tyler Moore (29 Dec 1936, 10:45, Brooklyn, NY). ♀ 12 [∠☉ > ∠♃].

Type 2 diabetes: The ability of body cells to respond to the regulating influence of insulin is impaired. A diet high in fat, calories and cholesterol is thought to be a major cause. Link the pancreas [fatty diet > excess sugar]. Spx. ♋ ☽, ♎ ♀ [♋♃ > ♃ ♀].

(1) Jayj Jacobs (1 Feb 1949, 03:54, Poplar Bluff, MO). ♀ [☌ ♃ r12H].

(2) Spencer Tracy (5 Apr 1900, 01:57, Milwaukee, WI). ☽ [□ ☿ ♓℞ (ruler 6H of diet) > qd ♃ ♐℞]. The Moon is conjunct the 6H cusp, emphasising a problem with diet.

Diaphragm: The major muscle of respiration. ♂ > ☿ .

Diarrhoea: Infection in the bowels. Loose, watery stools. The 'runs.' Spx. Link bowels [infection > diarrhoea]. ♏♂♇ (♍☿) [♅♂♆ > ♏♂♇].
(1) James Polk (2 Nov 1795, 12pm, Pineville, NC). ♂♍8 [wide ⚻♇].

Diet: Kinds of food that a person eats, a special course of food. ♋☽ , ♍☿ , 6H.

Digestion System, Digestion: Its function is to absorb food to provide energy and nutrients. It includes the digestive/ gastrointestinal tract, which is a series of hollow organs and tubes that run from the mouth to the anus. It consists of the mouth, oesophagus, stomach, liver, pancreas, gallbladder, small intestine, large intestine, anus - plus accessory organs like teeth, tongue, salivary glands and digestive juices. The rulers are Taurus and Venus for upper gastrointestinal digestion, Cancer and the Moon for stomach region digestion, Virgo-Mercury for intestinal digestion, and Scorpio for the elimination of waste-food from the end of the gastrointestinal tract. The overall ruler of 'digestion' is Cancer. Thr. Spx. ♋☽ , ♍☿ .

Diphtheria: A serious bacterial infection causing a greyish-white membrane to form over the throat and tonsils, making it hard to swallow and breathe. Link the throat / breathing [bacterial infection > difficulty]. Thr. ♉♀/ ♊☿ [♅♂♆ > ♄♇].
These examples are from Medical Astrology by Daath.
(1) Daath, 82 (4 Nov 1895, 07:30, London Eng). ♀♍ r12H [∠♄12 > ♄☌♂].
(2) Daath, 83-1 (26 April 1894, 06:45, London Eng). ♀ r6H [□♆♊12 > ⚻♄].
(3) Daath, 83-2 (12 Oct 1897, 08:45, Peckham, OK). ♀♍ coruler 6H [□♆♊ > □♇♊].
(4) Daath, 84 (27 Oct 1891, 13:00, Peckham, OK). ♀♏ [disposited by ♂☌♄ r12H].

Dipsomania - see Alcoholism.

Disfigurement: Spoiling the appearance of, defacement. Asc, 1H [♂].

Dislocation: Injury causing the normal position of a body-part to be disturbed. [♅♂].

Dismember: The body/ arms, legs being dismembered. Asc, 1H, ☽ / ☿ ,♃ [♏♂♇].
(1) Katherine Romano (20 Dec 1950, 22:10, Boston MA). The body of the homicide victim, was dismembered. ☽ [□♇12]. 12H for the secret murder and disposal of the body.

Disruption: Unexpected disruption of the functions of systems and organs. [♂♅].

Dissociative Mental Disorder: A disconnection, lack of continuity, between thoughts, memories, surroundings, actions and identity. A lack of reality. This may be due to emotional instability and life-avoidance, or due to a major trauma that is too hard to face. Either way, the root cause is an emotional disturbance, plus isolative tendencies. Link the self, mind, emotions [and isolative/ withdrawal tendencies]. Spx. ☉ Asc/ ☿ ♀, ♋☽ [♄, 8H ♇, 12H ♆].
(1) Anna Lynn McCord (16 Jul 1987, no time), American actress. ☽□☿ [⚻♇♏].
(2) Herschel Walker (3 Mar 1962, no time), American footballer. ☽∠♀ [☌♄].
(3) Jill Janus (2 Sep 1975, 15:00, Cooperstown, NY). ☽♋8 [☌♄]. ☉ [□♆12].
(4) Roseanne Barr (3 Nov 1952, 13:21, Salt Lake City, UT). ☽☍☿ [⚼♄♆8].

Dissolve: Cause to disperse or disappear. ☽ ♆, water signs.

Distention: Swelling and becoming large by pressure from inside. [♃].

Distorted perception - see Glamour.

Distribution: Process of moving substances/ fluids/ impulses through the various tubes in the body. ♊ ☿ ♐.

Diuretics: Medication that helps rid the body of extra water and salt. ♓♆.

Diverticulitis: Bacterial infection in one or more small pouches (diverticula) in the large intestine/ bowel. Link bowel [and infection]. Spx. ♏☌♇ (♍ ☿) [♅☌♆].
(1) Brock Lesnar (12 Jul 1977, no time). ♂ ♉/♏ [qd ♆].
(2) Eddie Van Halen (26 Jan 1955, 01:05, Amsterdam, Netherlands). ☿ [∠♂ r6H, ⚻♅].
(3) Howard Baker (15 Nov 1925, 15:00, Oneida, TN). ☿ r6H [□♅12, ∠♂♏].

Dizzy: (See Imbalance, Vertigo). Sensation of whirling, imbalance. Causes can include an inner ear disturbance, motion sickness, and medication effects. There may be an underlying health condition, such as poor circulation, infection or injury. [♅, afflictions to ♎].

DNA - see Gene, Genetics.

Domestic Violence: Violent behaviour between current or former intimate partners. Link domestic [and violence]. ♋ ☽, 4H [♂ ♅].
(1) Tina Turner (26 Nov 1939, 22:10, Nutbrush, TN). She reportedly suffered domestic violence from her first husband. ☽ [□♂7, r4H].

Dopamine: The 'happy' hormone. It is a primary driver of the brain's reward system and spikes when something pleasurable is experienced. ♀ ♃.

Dorsal region of the back: Back portion of the body. ♌ ☉.

Down's Syndrome: A genetic disorder. An extra chromosome affects the way a child's brain and body develop, leading to developmental and intellectual delays. Link genetic > intellectual [impairment]. Sac. ♒♅ (♋ ☽) > ♊ ☿ [♄♇].
(1) Astro.com 9250 (11 Nov 1942, 01:00, Los Angeles, CA). ♅ ♊ [☌ ♄ ♊ ℞].
(2) Astro.com 14458 (21 Sep 1970, 19:45, Hamburg, Ger). ☽ ♊ > □ ☿ [☽ □♇6].
(3) Astro.com 14464 (11 Nov 1970, 04:05, Hamburg, Ger). ♅ > ∠ ☿ [☍ ♄].
(4) Astro.com 14752 (18 Mar 1979, 03:52, Edmonton, Alberta). ♅℞ > ⚼ ☿℞ [⚻ ♄].

Dreams, Distressing: (See Nightmares). Distressing dreams are expressions of frustrated desire - for love, sex, or for one's ambitions. Link dreams [frustration]. ♓♆, ☽ [♄>♂].

Dream analysis work holds danger and should be avoided. It could bring to the surface things that are undesirable, or penetrate the past and tap into ancient racial evil. On a more mundane level, it could cause sleep disorders. Recommended therapy for distressing dreams is to deal with the underlying frustration by filling the life with constructive and creative projects and to invoke the power of the soul through meditation and positive affirmations.

Drink: Act of ingesting water/ liquid through the mouth. ☽ ♆.

Dropsy - see Oedema.

Drowns: Die through submersion in, and inhalation of, water. Link life/ breathing [and drown]. ☉ Asc/ ♊ ☿ [♓♆ water signs and rulers].

(1) Natalie Wood (20 Jul 1938, 11:16, San Francisco, CA). The Hollywood actress drowned in mysterious (♓♆) circumstances. ☉♋ [□ ☽]. ☉ [☿ mp ☉/♆12]

Drugs: Any chemical that causes a change in physiology or psychology when consumed. Generally ruled by Neptune. ♓♆.

- Drug Addiction: Misuse or abuse of alcohol and drugs, prescribed or illegal. The psychological root is emotional. Link the self/ emotions [drugs]. ☉, Asc / ☽ ♂ [♓♆].
These entertainers all had drug abuse problems.
(1) Elton John (25 Mar 1947, 02:00 Pinner, Eng). ☉ [☍♆℞].
(2) Glen Campbell (22 Apr 1936, 20:14, Delight, AR). ♂♉6 [△♆♍℞].
(3) Natalie Cole (6 Feb 1950, 18:07, Los Angeles, CA). ☽ [☌♆℞].
(4) Pete Townshend (19 May 1945, 15:00, London, Eng). ☽♍/♓12 [mp ♆℞ / ♇].

Dryness: Lack of moisture. [♑♄].

Ducts: Any tube, canal, pipe by which fluid/ air/ or other substance is conveyed. Gemini and Mercury are general rulers. The sign ruling the region a duct is in, is a coruler. ♊☿.

Duodenum: The first part of the small intestine. Absorbs nutrients, water from food. ♍☿.

- Duodenal Ulcer - see Ulcer.

DWARFISM - Disproportionate and Proportionate.

Mostly caused by a random genetic mutation. But they can also be inherited. There are two main types of dwarfism:

- Dwarfism Disproportionate, Achondroplasia. Arms and legs are short in comparison to the head and trunk.
- Dwarfism, Proportionate: The entire body though small, is proportionate.

More research is required with Venus and Libra, which give balance and beauty, to understand why in some cases the bodies are proportionate. In the standards of the day, Lavinia Stratton, a proportionate dwarf, was considered to be beautiful in appearance.

Dwarf significators. The ascendant and 1H for the body and appearance. The growth planets Sun and Jupiter. Venus for the pituitary gland, growth hormones, and right proportion. The main afflictions to look for, are those coming from Uranus and Pluto, because they can give wild/ gross extremes and abnormalities. Saturn, which tends to under-development is often associated with dwarfism. Link the body-appearance/ growth/ pituitary, proportion [genetic extremes/ underdevelopment]. Asc, 1H / ☉♃ / ♀ [♅♇/ ♄].

Disproportionate - Achondroplasia.

(1) Astro.com 4467 (8 Jan 1909, 02:00, Huntington Park, CA). Asc ♏ [♇☍♀]. ☉ [☌♅ 17♑, the Venus decanate].

(2) Peter Dinklage (11 Jun 1969, 01:37, Point Pleasant, NJ). The actor from Game of Thrones. Asc 29♓, the Scorpio decanate [♇⚼♀]. Asc [☍♅♃♇♍ in the Taurus-Venus decanate (22-29 ♍)].

(3)Quanden Bayles (13 Dec 2010, 12:15, Brisbane, Australia). He suffered relentless bullying because of his condition. Asc 28♓, the Scorpio decanate [♀♏8]. Asc [☌♅12].

Proportionate.

(1) Charles Stratton (4 Jan 1838, no time). In the 1920s, he was a huge star in P. T. Barnum's circus. ☉♑/ ∠♀ [☌♅/ □♄].

(2) Herve Villechaize (23 Apr 1943, 23:30, Montauban, France). The 90s TV star was a dwarf. Asc ♐ / ☍ ♀ [♂ ♄ ⛢6].

(3) Lavinia Warren-Stratton (31 Oct 1841, no time). The wife of Charles, and also a huge star in P. T. Barnum's circus. ♀ [qd ⛢].

Dysentery: Bacterial infection in the large intestine (bowel), sometimes accompanied by bloody diarrhoea. Link the large intestine [bacterial infection > diarrhoea]. Spx. ♏♂♇ (♍☿) [⛢♂♇ > ♈♂].

These men died from the disease.

(1) Fernando, Prince of Asturias (4 Dec 1571, 02:30, Madrid, Spain). ♂♍ [□♇ > ☍♇].

(2) Henry V of England (16 Sep 1386, 11:25, Monmouth, Wales). ☿♍ [♄♋8 mp ☿/ ♇♉/♏6].

(3) John Booker (3 Apr 1601, 08:13, Manchester, Eng). ☿♈ [mp ♂♈/ ⛢♉/♏12].

(4) Paul Bert (19 Oct 1833, 16:00, Auxerre, FR). ♂♏ r8H [□♇♑].

Dyslexia: Learning disorder characterised by difficulty reading. Around 10% of the world's population are dyslexic and the numbers are growing. This indicates an evolutionary development prior to a new way of reading/ learning. Link the mind/ learning [difficulty/ evolutionary advancement]. Ajna. ♊☿ [♄/⛢].

(1) Anthony Hopkins (31 Dec 1937, 09:15, Port Talbot, Wales). ☿12 [□♄ > △⛢♉℞]. ⛢ is in the 3H of formal learning and thinking.

(2) Richard Branson (18 Jul 1950, 07:00, Blackheath, Eng). ☿12 [mp ☽/ ⛢♋, ∠♄].

Dyspepsia: Upset stomach. Spx. ♋☽ [♂].

Dysphagia: Coughing or choking when eating or drinking. A planet to represent the obstruction may link in; such as the Moon for food or vomit, or Neptune for a liquid. Link airways [blockage]. Thr. ♊☿ [♄].

(1) Jimi Hendrix (27 Nov 1942, 10:15, Seattle, WA). The Rock guitarist suffocated by inhaling his own vomit. ☿♐ [☍♄♊6℞; ♄∠☽♋ for vomit]. ☽ [♂♇8].

Dysplasia: A broad term for the abnormal development of cells that can cause a wide range of conditions. Link cells [abnormal]. ☉☽ [⛢].

- Dysplasia, Skeletal/ Bone: A category of rare genetic disorders, usually congenital, that cause abnormal development of a baby's bones. Link genetic, congenital > bones [overgrowth]. Sac. ⛢♒, ♋☽ > ♄ [♃].

(1) Rocky Dennis (4 Dec 1961, 10:03, Downey CA). The 1985 drama film Mask, was based on his life. He was born with craniodiaphyseal dysplasia which distorted his face, making it grow twice the normal size. ☽♏ > □♄12 [♂Asc, ♂♃1].

Dystrophy: (See Muscular Dystrophy). A group of genetic diseases that cause progressive weakness and loss of muscle mass. Link genetic [muscles > loss/ weakening]. Sac. ⛢♒ [♂ > ♓♇, ☽].

E

Ears: Organs of hearing and balance. Ajna. Thr. ♊ ☿.

- Ear Ache: Pain in the inner/ outer ear. Link ears [and pain]. Ajna. ♊ ☿ [♂].

- Ear Infection: Link ears [and infection]. Ajna. ♊ ☿ [♅ ♂ ♆].

(1) Lou Ferrigno (9 Nov 1951, 01:30, Brooklyn, NY). Severe ear infections destroyed most of his hearing before he was three. ☿ ♐ coruler 12H [□ ♅ ♋].

- Ear, Middle: Converts air vibrations into fluid vibrations, in the cochlea. Ajna. ♊ ☿.

EARTH ⊕ (planet).

Signs it rules: It is the esoteric ruler of Sagittarius, and hierarchy ruler of Gemini.

Ray: Carries the 3rd ray of Intelligence and Activity, the energy that governs substance, matter, the dense physical bodies of all living things.

Body: The Earth corules the throat chakra and is a ruler of the thyroid gland. All are bathed in the aura of the earth. The quality of the land we live on affects health - toxic regions have an adverse the effect, fresh and green areas have a positive effect.

Disease: Afflictions indicate difficulty absorbing planetary prana and physical body devitalisation.

Psychology: Once we are on the Spiritual Path, the Earth begins to affect consciousness. It is a counterbalance to the excesses of the ego, which are represented by the Sun. The qualities of the sign it is in (the sign opposite the sun sign), help balance the nature.

Eat: The process of ingesting food. ♋ ☽.

- Eating Disorders - see Anorexia and Bulimia.

- Eating Habits: The foods habitually selected to eat, the manner of eating and eating habits. Spx. ☽ ♋, ♍ ☿, 6H.

Ebola Virus: A virus that impairs blood clotting, resulting in massive haemorrhaging. Link blood [virus > haemorrhage]. ♂ ♃ ♒ (♅) [♆ ♂ ♅ > ♂ ♅ ♇].

The following physicians died from the disease after catching it from their patients. Birth times are unknown.

(1) Dr. Ameyo Adadevoh (27 Oct 1956). ♂ ♓ [□ ♆ > qd ♇].

(2) Dr. Godfrey George (9 Jul 1960). ♂ ♉ [☍ ♆ ♏ > ♆ disposited by ♇].

(3) Dr. Olivet Buck (2 Oct 1953). ♅ [mp ♃/♇ ♌].

Ectopic Pregnancy: A pregnancy in which a fertilised egg embeds outside the uterus. The foetus has to be aborted before it grows too large, so Scorpio and its planets may link in. Link foetus [and abnormality]. Sac. ♋ ☽, 5H [♅].

(1) Sophie Rhys-Jones (20 Jan 1965, 12:46, Oxford, Eng). Her 5H of children is very afflicted with the malefics Mars, Pluto and Uranus located there with the Moon. But thanks to modern medicine and good aspects to Mercury (which rules the 5H in her chart); she has two healthy children. ☽ 5 [☌ ♅ ♇ 5].

Eczema: Skin is dry, itchy, inflamed. Link skin [dry > inflamed]. ♑♄ (♋☽) [♄ > ♂☉].
(1) Kenneth Lee Adelman (9 Jun 1946, 10:51, Chicago, IL). He had sarcastic political views. Such bitterness affects health - he developed chronic eczema. Base. ♄♋ [mp ♂♌12 / ☉].

Egg Ovum: The female reproductive cell. Sac. ♋☽.

Ego: A person's sense of self-esteem, self-importance. ♌☉.

- **Egoism:** The sense of "I-ness." Excessive concern for oneself. ♌☉ (♅).

- **Egomania:** (See Megalomania). Extreme egocentricity. Link self [extreme]. ♌☉ [♅♇].

Ejaculation: Ejecting semen from the body following sexual stimulation. Sac. ♂.

Elbow: Joint between the forearm and the upper arm. Thr. ♊☿.

Electric Shock, Electrocution: A sudden discharge of electricity through the body. [♒♅].

Shock treatment for a mental disorder.

Link the body/ or the 6H of health [and electrocuted]. ☽♄♂, Asc, 1H, 6H [♒♅].
(1) Alda Merini (21 Mar 1931, 05:00, Milan, Italy). ☽ r6H [☌♅].
(2) Daniele Evenou (21 Feb 1943, 21:00, Tunis, Tunisia). ♀6 [⚹♅♊]. ♆ r6H [△♅♊].
(3) Vivian Leigh (5 Nov 1913, 17:16, Darjeeling, India). ♇♋ coruler 6H [⚻♅♒].

Electrocuted.

Link the life / body [and electrocuted]. ☉, Asc, 1H [♒♅].
(1) Claude Francois (1 Feb 1939, 06:05, Ismailia, Egypt). He was accidentally electrocuted when he tried to change a light bulb after stepping out of a bath. ☉♒1 [□♅♉/♏].

Electrical Nerve Signalling: Energy by which the nervous system (Gemini, Mercury, Venus, Uranus), sends signals throughout the body. Ajna. ♒♅ (♊☿).

Electrolytes: Essential minerals like sodium, calcium and etc. ♄♅.

Elimination - see Excretion.

Emaciation: State of being abnormally thin or weak. [♑♄].

Embolism: (See Cerebral Embolism and Pulmonary Embolism). A blocked artery - usually by a blood clot. Link artery [and blockage]. Hrt. ♃♒ [♑♄♇].

Embryo: Foetus. Unborn offspring in the process of development. Sac. ♋☽.

Emergency: A serious, unexpected situation requiring immediate action. [♂♅].

Emetic: A substance causing vomiting. ♂.

Emollient: Moisturising treatments. ♋☽.

EMOTION, EMOTIONAL: Emotion is a strong feeling deriving from one's perceptions of life, circumstances and relationships. The emotional body from which these feelings arise, is also known as the astral and desire body. Troubled emotions are the cause of most mental disorders and individual, physical diseases.

The astral plane is the water plane, so all water signs can represent the emotions. Emotional habits and negative core-beliefs are governed by Cancer and the Moon. Passionate, desirous, heroic and angry emotions are governed by Mars. Refined emotions by Neptune. In the following sections, ♋☽♂ will be given as the rulers of the emotions. But Neptune or planets in Scorpio or Pisces could substitute. Spx. ♋☽♂ (♆, ♏♓).

- Emotional Repression: Using the will to repress the emotions. Spx. ♋ ☽ ♂ [♑ ♄ ♇].

- Emotional Shock: Unexpected event/ trauma so upsetting it makes it hard to function normally. Link emotions [and shock]. Spx. ♋ ☽ ♂ [♅].

(1) Stephen Sondheim (22 Mar 1930, 21:00, New York NY). He said he suffered a tremendous emotional shock when his parent's separated. ☽ ♑ [□ ♅ r4H].

Emphysema: A disease that belongs in the Chronic Obstructive Pulmonary Disease group. It is caused by inhaling toxins that damage airways. Smoking (Pisces, Neptune) is a major cause. Link airways [smoking/ toxins > obstructive]. Thr. ♊ ☿ [♆/ malefics > ♄ ♇]. These four died from the disease.

(1) Allan Sherman (30 Nov 1924, 13:30, Chicago, IL). ☿ ♐ coruler 6H [□ ♂12 > qd ♇].

(2) Dick York (4 Sep 1928, 01:00, Fort Wayne, IN). ♂ ♊12 [☍ ♄6].

(3) Eleanor Bach (11 Jan 1922, 00:17, Kulpmont, PA). ☿ ♑ r12H [qd ♆ r6H).

(4) Gene Tierney (20 Nov 1920, 17:15, Brooklyn, NY). ☿ ♏6℞ [□ ♆].

Enamel: Tooth enamel, the hard mineralised surface of teeth. Base. ♑ ♄.

Encephalitis: Infectious viral disease, which inflames brain tissue causing swelling. Link the brain [virus > inflammation/ swelling]. Cwn. ♈ ♂, ♋ ☽ [♆ ♂ ♅ > ♂ ☉/ ♃].

(1) Liza Minnelli (12 Mar 1946, 07:58, Los Angeles). The singing, acting star had viral encephalitis of the brain. ☿ ♈12 [☍ ♆6 > qd ♃6℞].

Endocardium: Innermost membrane (♋ ☽, ♑ ♄) of the heart. Hrt. ♋ ☽, ♑ ♄ > ♌ ☉.

- Endocarditis: Bacteria in the bloodstream inflames the endocardium, damaging heart valves. Link the heart [bacteria > inflammation]. Hrt. ♌ ☉ [♂ ♅ ♆ > ♂ ☉].

(1) Arnold Schwarzenegger (30 Jul 1947, 04:10, Graz, Austria). ☉ ♌ [∠ ♅ ♂12].

(2) Barbara Walters (25 Sep 1929, 06:50, Boston, MA). ☉12 [☍ ♅ ♈].

(3) Robin Williams (21 Jul 1951, 13:34, Chicago, IL). ☉ [mp ♅ ♂/ ♇ ♌].

Endocrine System, Ductless Glands: An intelligent messaging system comprised of 7 major ductless glands. Each gland is a physical anchor for the forces of the 7 major chakras. These are the pairings: Crown-pineal, Ajna-pituitary, Throat-thyroid, Heart-thymus, Solar-plexus - pancreas, Sacral-gonads, Base-adrenals.

These glands act like a network of pharmacies. They collaborate to dispense hormones/ chemicals directly into the blood to balance and regulate health. Some consider the master gland to be the pituitary, while (esoterically), the thyroid is "the keystone of the endocrine system," [1] holding the structure together. The system is generally governed by R3 and overall, by Mercury and Venus. But each gland is also conditioned by its chakra, ray, and the sign and planet that rules the location it is in. Ajna. Thr. R3, ☿ ♀ (♄),

Endometrium: The layer of tissue that lines the uterus. Sac. ♋ ☽.

- Endometriosis: Tissue that normally lines the uterus grows abnormally outside of it. Link the uterus [and abnormal/ insidious growth]. Sac. ♋ ☽ [♅ ♆ / ♏ ♇].

(1) Cyndi Lauper (22 Jun 1953, 23:00, Astoria, NY). ☽ ♏ [△ ♅ ♋6].

(2) Dolly Parton (19 Jan 1946, 20:25, Sevierville, TN). ☽12 [mp ♂ ♄ ♋℞ /♆].

(3) Pamela Anderson (1 Jul 1967, 04:08, Ladysmith, Canada). ☉ ♋ [⚼ ♆ ♏6].

Enema: Injections of fluids to cleanse and empty the bowel. ♓ ♆ > ♏.

1 Bailey, Alice: The Soul and its Mechanism, 46.

Energy, Energises: Vitalising energy comes from the Sun, is transmitted to earth and all life on it, by golden angels:

> The Transmitters of Prana.. devas who vitalise and produce energy, nourish and preserve all forms.. originate in the sun. [1]

> Energy is a life fluid circulating throughout the entire body of the Logos, and vivifying the tiniest atom in that whole. [2]

Mars represents kundalini fire, which warms the physical body and "vitalises via the blood stream." [3] ☉ ♂.

- Energy Low: Devitalising of energy. ☉ ♂ [♄].

Enlargement: An increase in size, anatomic swelling or prominence. [R2, ♃].

Enlightenment: The evolutionary goal for all souls - a consciousness filled with spiritual love, light and wisdom. Jesus' transfiguration in the Bible represents this. ☉ > ☿ ♀ ♃.

Enteric Nervous System: Governs the function of the gastrointestinal tract. Thr. Spx. ♍ ☿ .

- Enteric Fever - see Typhoid Fever.

- Enteritis (Gastro): An infection picked up by eating contaminated food, causing inflammation in the small intestine. Link the intestines [infection > inflammation]. Spx. ♍ ☿ (♏ ♂ ♆) [♂ ♅ ♆ > ♂ ☉].

(1) Jacques Cousteau (11 Jun 1910, 13:06, St. Andre de Cubzac, Fr). At ten, he was diagnosed with chronic enteritis. ♂ ♋ [♂ ♆ ♋ r6H > ☍ ♅ for inflammation].

Enzymes: A substance that causes a chemical reaction. ♅ .

Epidemics/ Plagues: A disease that spreads rapidly. Rays 4 and 7 and their planets, are at the root of rapidly moving, widespread diseases. In ancient times these were called plagues.

> Occultly, the 4th Ray of Conflict, lies behind epidemics. They are a consequence of the many conflicts that humanity is constantly embroiled in and that leads to "constant devitalisation, debility and a rapid taking on of infections and of contagious diseases." [4]

The 4th ray is carried by Mercury, which is responsible for air-borne epidemics; and the Moon, which is responsible for epidemics spread by contaminated food, water and unhygienic living conditions. Another ray involved in epidemics is the 7th, a force carried by Uranus, the prime ruler of bacterial infections.

> (R7) energy is largely responsible for infections and contagious diseases. [5]

Jupiter-Sagittarius and the 9H may link in for global epidemics, and Scorpio and Pluto for the mass-death effect. [☽ ☿ ♅].

Epidermis: The surface tissue of the skin, overlying the dermis. Base. ♑ ♄ (♋ ☽).

Epididymis: (See Testiculitis). Testicle tubes that store sperm. Sac. ♏ ♂ .

Epilepsy: A central nervous system disorder. Brain activity becomes abnormal causing seizures. The nervous system is governed by the ajna chakra, which is coruled by Gemini, Mercury and Venus. Link nerves [and seizures]. Ajna. ♊ ☿ (♀ ♒ ♅) [♒ ♅].

1   Bailey, Alice: Treatise of Cosmic Fire, 924.
2   Bailey, Alice: Treat se on White Magic, 364.
3   Bailey, Alice: Esoteric Astrology, 211.
4   Bailey, Alice: Esoteric Healing, 301.
5   Bailey, Alice: Esoteric Healing, 304.

(1) Florence Joyner (21 Dec 1959, 00:11, Los Angeles, CA). ♀♏ [□♅].
(2) John Roberts (27 Jan 1955, no time), Chief Justice. ☿♒ [⚻♅].
(3) Prince, the rock star (7 Jun 1958, 18:17, Minneapolis, MN). ♀♉6 [□♅].
(4) Vincent Van Gogh (30 Mar 1853, 11:00, Zundert, Holland). ☿ [☌♇☌♅♉].

Epithelial Membranes: They are coated with mucous secretions and line the digestive, respiratory, urinary and reproductive tracts. ♋☽.

Epstein Barr Virus (Mononucleosis/ Glandular Fever): (See Chronic Fatigue Syndrome). This virus is thought to be a cause of chronic fatigue. Thr. Spx. [♆♂♅].

Equilibrium: A state of mental, emotional, physical balance. ♎♀.

Eruption: A spot, rash, or other mark appearing suddenly on the skin. [♂].

Escapism: Diversion from unpleasant/ boring aspects of daily life, through fantasy, alcohol, drugs. Spx. [♓♆].

Esophagus - see Oesophagus.

Ether: A liquid that is used as an anaesthetic. ♓♆.

Ethers: The finer levels of matter of the physical plane, which normally cannot be seen by the naked eye. The etheric web - the transporter of energy into the physical body, is formed from matter at this level. ♒♅.

- Etheric Web or Body: This is the fiery energy web upon which the dense physical body is constructed. According to occult teaching, the physical body is formed of two parts, the dense physical body, and the etheric body. The dense physical body is formed of matter of the lowest three subplanes of the physical plane. The etheric body is formed of the four highest or etheric subplanes of the physical plane. (There are 7 subplanes in a plane, and 7 planes in the solar system).

The etheric body anchors in the sacral centre, [1] where it vitalises the dense physical body. The 7th ray (Uranus) and Aquarius rule the ethers and the etheric web. [2]

> Uranus is sometimes called the planet of the violet force and its graduates wield the power of cosmic etheric prana. [3] The 7th ray is the violet ray, and it uses the ethers as its medium. [4]

Other associations are Gemini which conditions the web, [5] and the Moon (veiling Vulcan), which governs etheric circulation. [6] Sac. ♊♅ (☽).

Euthanasia: The practice of intentionally ending life to eliminate pain and suffering. Here is an esoteric view on this subject from the Master Djwhal Khul.

> Frequently, lives are preserved in form - both in old age and in infancy - that could be well permitted liberation. They serve no useful purpose and cause much pain and suffering to forms which nature (left to herself) would extinguish. Through our overemphasis on the value of form life, fear of death, uncertainty as to the fact of immortality, and also through our deep attachment to form, we arrest the natural processes and hold the life, which is struggling to be free,

1 Bailey, Alice: Esoteric Healing, 45.
2 Bailey, Alice: Treatise on White Magic, 373; Esoteric Astrology, 303.
3 Bailey, Alice: Treatise of Cosmic Fire, 1178.
4 Bailey, Alice: Treatise of Cosmic Fire, 326.
5 Bailey, Alice: Esoteric Astrology, 357.
6 Bailey, Alice: Esoteric Healing, 143.

confined to bodies quite unfitted to the purposes of the soul. [Note that suicide is not being advocated]. This preservation is, in the majority of cases, enforced by the subject's group and not by the subject himself—frequently an unconscious invalid, an old person whose response apparatus of contact and response is imperfect, or a baby who is not normal. These cases constitute definite instances of an offsetting of the Law of Karma. [1]

Because the death is for compassionate reasons, Neptune and Jupiter will link into the pattern. Link life [death > compassion]. ☉, Asc [♏♇♂, 8H > ♃ ♆].

(1) Hugo Claus (5 Apr 1929, 21:00, Brugge, Belgium). Due to Alzheimer's, he requested euthanasia in 2008. Asc ♏ [△♇8 > ☍ ♃].

(2) Vincent Humbert (3 Feb 1981, 10:32, Evreux, Fr). At age 19, an accident left him a quadriplegic, blind and mute. He begged to be able to die. Asc [☍♇ r8H > △♆].

Evolutionary Advancement: (See Dyslexia, Synesthesia). Improved development in the body to ensure a better chance of survival. Spiritually, the development of higher soul powers. ♒♅.

Excretion, Elimination, Excrement: Elimination of body waste is the end process of digestion and is a Scorpio function. Excrement/ faeces are co-ruled by Saturn. Spx. ♏♇♄.

Exhaustion: (See Chronic Fatigue). Extreme physical, emotional and mental tiredness. [♄].

Exocrine Glands: These glands make and secrete sweat, tears, saliva, oil, milk and digestive juices. Such glands are generally ruled by Cancer and the Moon, plus the sign that rules the part of the body, which the gland is located in. ♋☽.

Exoteric and Esoteric: Exoteric refers to information intended for, and likely to be understood by, the general public. Exoteric planets are the traditional planet rulers. They rule the personality life. In this book, esoteric refers to the soul. Esoteric planets carry the transforming energies of the soul. Uranus generally rules 'the esoteric.' But each sign has its own esoteric ruler. Exoteric ♄ / and esoteric ♅.

Extra Body Parts: A congenital, Jupiter, and ray 2 (the growth force in the universe), problem. Something goes awry and over-building occurs with cells. Ray 2 [♃].

Extropia: A type of eye misalignment, where one eye deviates outward. Can be constant or intermittent, always one eye or both Link eye [deviate]. Ajna. ☉☽ [♅].

(1) John Paul Sartre (21 Jun 1905, 18:45, Paris, FR). His right eye deviated. ☉ [☍♅].

(2) Marty Feldman (8 July 1934, no time). He had prominent, misaligned eyes. ☽ [□♅♈].

Extroverted: Outgoing and socially confident. ♐♃, fire and air signs.

Eyes: Organs that allow us to see. The eyes are in the Aries part of the body, but vision, sight and the right eye, are ruled by the Sun.

The physical eye came into being in response to the light of the sun. [2]

The Moon is said to rule the left eye, but can represent problems in both eyes. Uranus and Mercury share rulership for the retina and optic eye nerves. Ajna. ♈☉☽ (☿♅).

- Eye Lens: The lens' work with the cornea to focus light correctly on the retina. Ajna. ♈☉.

- Eye Lids: They protect and lubricate the eyes. ♈♋☽.

---

1 Bailey, Alice: Esoteric Healing, 350-351.
2 Bailey, Alice: Treatise on White Magic, 213.

F

Face: The front part of a person's head from the forehead to the chin. The ajna chakra - ruled primarily by Venus, rules the face. 'Showing one's soul to the world.' Ajna. ♈ ♀.

Faeces: Waste matter remaining after food has been digested. Thr. Spx. ♏♇♄.

Fainting: Brief unconsciousness caused by a sudden drop in blood pressure, which reduces blood flow and oxygen to the brain. Link consciousness > blood flow [unconscious]. Cwn. Hrt. ☉, Asc (☿) > ♒♅♆ [♄♆ (♇)].
(1) Alanis Morissette (1 Jun 1974, 09:51, Ottawa, Canada). The Canadian singer was mugged in 1993. As a direct consequence of this, she had long periods of crying and fainting spells. ☉♊ [☍♆; ☉ disposited by ☿ > ☿☌♄].
(2) Carl Jung (26 Jul 1875, 19:24, Kesswil, Switz.). At age 12, the famous psychologist developed fainting spells. ☉♌ [□♆]. ☿6 [♆ mp ☿/♄1].

Fallopian Tubes: Two long, slender tubes connecting the ovaries to the uterus. Sac. ♋☽♏.

Famine: Widespread scarcity of food that results in starvation. Can be caused by insect swarms (Mercury), climate (Saturn for cold, Mars, Sun, fire signs for heat), and war (Mars). Link food, nourishment [to the cause of the famine > starvation]. ♋☽ [cause > ♑♄].
(1) Eclipse chart (10 Jan 2020, 22:21, Nairobi) for February 2020, East Africa famine due to a locust plague. There were major crop losses and communities starved. ☽♋ [☍☿ for locust plague > ☍♄♇♑].

Fanatical: Obsessively concerned with something. Spx. R6 [♂].

Fantasise: Daydreaming about something desired. Spx. R6, ♓♆.

Fasting: Abstention from eating and sometimes drinking. Spx. ♄.

Fat, Fatness - see Obesity.

Fatigue: (See Chronic Fatigue). Extreme tiredness. Other planets will be involved if there is a specific cause. For example, ♉♀ if caused by thyroid trouble, or ♏♂ for adrenal overload. Link energy/ vitality [with fatigue]. Thr. Hrt. Spx. ♂☉ [♑♄].

Fear: (See Phobias, Panic Attacks). Be afraid of someone/ something dangerous, painful, or harmful. Spx. [♑♄].

Feebleness: Lacking physical strength or vigour. Link energy or vitality [with feebleness]. Hrt. Spx. ♂☉ [♄♆].

Feet: End parts of the legs on which a person stands or walks. Base. ♓♆.

Females: Adult women. ♋☽.

- **Female Problems**: These are problems with the reproduction organs. Afflictions from planets representing the problem. Sac. ♋☽ [malefics].

- **Female Reproduction Organs, Cycles.** Ovaries, uterus. Sac. ♋♏☽.

Femoral Artery: Main blood vessel supplying blood to the lower body. Starts in the upper thigh. Hrt. ♃ ♐ ♒.

Femur: Thigh bone. Longest, strongest bone in the body. Base. ♐ ♃.

Fertile: (See Barren, Childbirth). The ability to conceive children or young. Generally governed by Cancer and the Moon. Afflictions from Saturn-Pluto undermine fertility. Sac. ♋ ☽.

Fever: A temporary rise in body temperature; the result of an immune response. Hrt. [♂ ☉, fire signs].

Fibrillation: Muscular twitching. ♂ [♅].

Fibrin: Protein made by the liver involved in forming blood clots in the body. ♄.

Fibroids: They are non-cancerous growths found in the muscle wall of the uterus. Link the uterus / muscles > [fibroids]. Sac. ♋ ☽ > ♂ [♃].

Fibrosis: (See Pulmonary Fibrosis, Pulmonary Silicosis). The thickening and scarring of connective tissue, usually as a result of injury. Silicosis is caused by inhaling silica dust. Link connective tissue [thickening/ scarring]. ♑ ♄ [♃/♑ ♄ (♇)].

Fibula: Long bone in lower leg, the lateral side of the tibia. Base. ♒ ♅.

Fight or Flight: Adrenal medulla function, an automatic and defensive body reaction to something perceived as dangerous or frightening. Base. ♏ ♂ ♇.

Filtering: (See Kidneys, Nephrons). The filtering apparatus in the kidneys - *nephrons*, clean the blood and remove waste. ♓ ♆ (♋ ☽).

Fingernails: Hard covering at the end of a finger. Thr. Base. ♊ > ♄.

Fingers: Any of the five terminating members of the hand. Thr. ♊ ☿.

Fistula: Abnormal tubal connection between two organs or vessels that do not usually connect. Link the organ involved [and abnormality]. Organ [⚻ ♅].
(1) Count Gondomar (1 Nov 1567, no time). The Spanish Ambassador to James I of England spent a summer at Greenwich "as the air there was better for his anal fistula" - an infected tunnel between the skin and the anus. ♂ [⚻ ♅]; ♇ [□ ♅].

Fits - see Seizures.

Flabbiness: Being soft and fat, loose flesh. [☽ ♃].

Flatulence: Intestinal gas due to food fermentation, passed from the anus. Spx [♋ ☽].

Flesh: The soft muscular tissue of the body. Base. ♋ ☽.

Fluid in the Body: Liquids in the body, which contain ions and cells essential to body function. They have various tasks. Common fluids are, blood, lymph, saliva, semen, vaginal fluids, mucous and urine. Water is the main fluid - 55-60% of body fluid. White fluids are generally ruled by Cancer and the Moon, Pisces and Neptune. Blood - red fluid, is ruled by Mars. ♋ ☽, ♓ ♆.

- Fluid Waterways: Either blood (♂ ♒), or lymphatic (♓ ♆), circulation in the body.

Fluoride: Mineral that helps keep bones and teeth hard and strong. ♄.

Foetus. Unborn offspring in the process of development. Sac. ♋ ☽.

Food: Nutritious substance eaten/ drunk, to maintain life and growth. Generally governed by Cancer and the Moon, which are the rulers of digestion. Additionally, nutrition, diet and eating habits are governed by Virgo and the 6H. Spx. ♋ ☽ (♍ ☿, 6H).

- Food Allergies: (See Allergic, Peanut Allergy). Allergic to certain foods. Emotional hyper-sensitivity underlies allergies, placing the Moon and Cancer central to this problem since they rule the emotions, and also food and milk. Link digestion [emotions/ food > immune reaction]. ♋ ☽, ☿ ♍ [♋ ☽ > ♂ (☉ ♅)].

(1) Astro.com 11564 (9 May 1950, 22:49, Los Angeles, CA). Milk allergy. ☽ ♓, qd ♂ ♍ [☽ disposits ♅ ♋].

(2) Astro.com 12801 (8 Feb 1955, 12pm, Ukiah, CA). ♃ ℞, ♅ ♋ [□ ♂ ♈ coruler 6H]].

- Food Poisoning: The result of eating contaminated, spoiled, or toxic food. There are four common types: (i) Chemical poisoning (♅). (ii) Microbial - bacteria, viruses, mould, fungi, toxins (♂ ♅ ♆). (iii) Physical contamination - hair, pest bodies etc. (iv) Allergy reactions - gluten, peanuts etc (♂ ♅). Link food [and poisoning]. Spx. ♋ ☽, ☿ ♍ [♂ ♅ ♆].

(1) Patric Walker (25 Sep 1931, 12:18, Hackensack, NJ), died from salmonella (bacterial) poisoning. ☽ ♓ r8H [⚹ ♂ ♏ > △ ♆ ♋8]. ♆ ♍ [∠ ♆ ♋8].

Foot: End part of the leg on which we stand or move. Base. ♓ ♆.

Forehead: The part of the face above the eyes. Ajna. ♈ ♂.

Foul Smells: Strong unpleasant odour. Spx. [♂ ♄].

Fractures: A break or a crack in a bone. Link bones [fracture]. ♑ ♄ [♂ (♅)].

(1) Fausto Coppi (15 Sep 1919, 21:30, Castellanza, Italy). The Italian bicycle racer had numerous bone fractures during his career. ♄ [☍ ♅].

Free Radicals: Unstable atoms that can damage cells, causing illness and aging. [♅ ♆].

Friedreich's Ataxia - see Ataxia.

Frigidity: Failure to respond sexually. Link sexuality [and frigid]. Spx. Sac. ♏ ♂ ♀ [♑ ♄].

Fructose: A form of sugar. ♀ ♃.

Fruitful: Female abundant fertility. Positive aspects from Jupiter help. Sac. ♋ ☽,

Fungus: A spore-producing organism feeding on organic matter. ♋ ☽, ♓ ♆.

- Fungal Infection: A skin disease caused by a fungal infection. Common types are *Tinea* (also known as athlete's foot when feet are affected, or jock itch in the groin), and *Candida* or *Thrush* for candida infections in the mouth or vagina. See those entries. Link skin or the body part affected [and fungus]. ♑ ♄ (♋) [♋ ☽, ♓ ♆].

G

Gallbladder: Storage pouch for bile, which breaks down the food we eat. Spx. ♋ ☽ , ♄ .

Gallstones: Hardened deposits of digestive fluid that form in the gallbladder. Spx [♑ ♄].

Gambling Addiction: The urge to gamble due to uncontrollable emotion/ desire. The 5H rules gambling. Link emotion/ desire [and gambling]. Spx. Sac. ♋ ☽ ♂ [♐ ♃, 5H].
(1) Darry-Cowl (27 Aug 1925, 18:00, Vittel, Fr). ♂ [□ ☽ ♐].
(2) Eddie Fisher (10 Aug 1928, 07:42, Philadelphia, PA). ☽ ♊/♐ [☍ ♄ ♐℞. r5H.
(3) Gladys Knight (28 May 1944, 19:52, Atlanta, GA). ☽ ♌ [☌ ♃. ♃ □ ☿ 5].

Ganglion: Relay stations between neurons. Ajna. ♊ ☿ .

Gangrene (Skin Necrosis): Dead tissue caused by an interrupted supply of blood. The cause can be an injury, an infection, or an environmental condition such as intense cold. Link tissue, skin / blood [dead]. ♋ ☽ / ♑ ♄ / ♂ ♃ ♒ (♆) [♏ ♇ ♄, 8H].
These three men died from gangrene or a gangrene related disease.
(1) Edouard Manet, 23 Jan 1832, 19:00, Paris, Fr). ♄ > ⚻ ♅ ♒6 [♅ ⚹, ♇ ♈8].
(2) Jean Lully (29 Nov 1632, 16:30, Florence, Italy). ☽ ♋ [∠ ♇ ♉12 > ♇ ☌ ♃ ℞].
(3) Lawrence Oates (17 Mar 1880, 06:20, Putney, Eng), Antarctic explorer. ☽ [♇ mp ☽/♆].

Gas - see Flatulence.

Gastric Juice: A digestive juice secreted by the stomach glands. Spx. ♋ ☽ .

Gastric Ulcer - see Ulcer.

Gastrointestinal Tract - see the Digestion System.

- **Gastroenteritis** - see Enteritis.

- **Gastrointestinal Motility:** The movement of food from the mouth through the throat, oesophagus, stomach, small and large intestines and out of the body. Spx. ♋ ☽ / ♊ ☿ ♐.

GEMINI. ♊.

Rulers: The exoteric ruler is Mercury, the esoteric ruler is Venus, the hierarchy ruler is the Earth.

Rays: Gemini carries R2 of Wisdom. It also carries R4 via Mercury and R5 via Venus. Being the third sign, it is also a carrier of R3. [1] Gemini's energy is versatile, airy, light and can be unstable.

Body: Gemini corules the ajna and throat chakras, the pituitary and thymus glands, reactivating the immunity power of the latter in spiritually advanced adults. [2] It governs the fluid reactions of the entire nervous organism. Gemini is also related to the older parts of the brain – the brainstem (pons, medulla oblongata) and cerebellum, which control Gemini-

1 Bailey, Alice: Esoteric Astrology, 357.
2 Bailey, Alice: Esoteric Astrology, 367.

type functions such as breathing and balance. It rules the ears, eye nerves, the bronchial tract, oxygenation of the blood, all tubes in the body, the shoulders, arms, hands, fingers and the 'grasping' and 'balancing' movements of the body.

Disease: When planets are afflicted in Gemini, or when Gemini rules the 6H, it indicates trouble with nerves or airways, and/ or with mobility, which is governed by its opposite sign Sagittarius. As an afflictor - being an air sign, Gemini promotes the rapid spread of air-borne pathogens and pollutants that can evolve into epidemics such as influenza.

Psychology: Gemini carries the relationship ray (R2), and is the great sign of intelligence and communication, ruling mental development and intelligent self-expression. Its higher keynote is, 'I see my other self, and in the waning of that self, I grow and glow.' This refers to an intelligent awareness of being dual-natured, repudiation of the lower self and identification with the true self, the soul.

Gender Dysphoria: Distress caused by feeling that one's gender identity does not match the sex which was registered at birth. Link self / gender [distress, confusion]. ☉, Asc / ♀ ♂ [♓♆].

Gene, Genetics: (See also Permanent Atoms). Genes are segments of DNA (Deoxyribonucleic Acid), the hereditary, karmic, material transferred from parents to offspring. But not all genes/ karma are necessarily passed on. Diseases can be inherited genetically, but a gene mutation that causes a disease can occur during gestation due to an environmental or karmic reason.

Our genes determine what we look like and give us our basic characteristics. This inherited information is stored in energy units called 'permanent atoms', which are located on the 1st etheric subplane of the Physical Plane. They are governed by R7, a force carried by Uranus. Here are supportive quotes.

> In these atoms the past memory of the personal self is stored; these are in the nature of 'memory cells' and are the repositories of past experience, of gained quality, and of the particular note which the body of which it is the nucleus has achieved. They are material in nature, are connected only with the form aspect, and are imbued with as much of the quality of consciousness as the soul has succeeded in developing in the three worlds. [1]

The physical permanent atom, is governed by Aquarius, [2], and the seventh ray. [3] Inherited genes are also represented by Cancer, which carries R7 and therefore by its ruler the Moon. Sac. ♒♅ (♋☽).

- Genetic Disease: A disease caused by changes or mutations to DNA. Can be inherited or a 'spontaneous mutation' which happens when genetic material is damaged as it passes from parent to child. So, a child can have a genetic disorder that the parent does not have.

The latter could fit into the congenital disease category, which refers to a disease being present from birth. Sac. [♒♅ (♋☽)].

Genitals: The sexual/ reproductive organs on the outside of the body. Sac. ♏♂♇, (♀).

- Genital Warts: A small bump on the genitals. A common sexually transmitted infection caused by the human papilloma virus. Link the genitals [and warts]. Sac. ♏♂ ♀ [♄].

1 Bailey, Alice: Esoteric Astrology, 303.
2 Bailey, Alice: Esoteric Astrology, 303.
3 Bailey, Alice: Treatise on White Magic, 373.

Geriatric: Relating to old people, especially those receiving special care. ♑ ♄.

Germs: An infectious agent that can cause disease. Similar terms are antigens and pathogens. The 7th ray carried by Uranus is particularly related to germs, their breeding and proliferation. This force flows through Cancer, which is the danger sign for the breeding of germs since it rules breeding and damp, dark places where germs flourish. Mars is traditionally viewed as an infectious agent, Neptune rules viral infections. Pluto rules toxic agents and could be included. [R7, ♂ ♅ ♆ (♇)].

Gestation: The process of developing inside the womb between conception and birth. Sac. ♋ ☽.

Gigantism - see Acromegaly.

Gingivitis: also known as Periodontitis and Pyorrhoea. Gum disease occurs when bacteria in plaque infects the gums, causing them to become red, puffy and to bleed easily. Link gums/ teeth [bacterial infection]. Thr. ♉ ♀/ ♑ ♄ [♅ ♂ ♆].
(1) George Washington (22 Feb 1732, 10:00, Colonial Beach, VA). He had inflamed gums, lost all his teeth and wore wooden dentures. ♀ r6H, ☌ ♄ ♈12 [♂ disposits ♄].

Glamour: The distortion of perception due to one's emotional prejudices and biases. This is the root cause of most modern psychological problems. Being unhappy with reality, the desire life projects what it hopes or expects to see, onto the self, others, or onto life generally. This distortion is primarily a lower R6, Neptune problem. Spx [R6, ♆ ♓ (☽ ♂)].

Glands, Glandular Systems - see Endocrine System and Exocrine Glands.

Glandular Atrophy: Loss or serious impairment of a gland through injury or disease. Link the ruler of the body part in which the gland is located; and atrophy. [♄ ♇].

Glandular Fever - see Epstein-Barr Virus.

Glaucoma: The optic nerve is damaged/ diseased, causing blindness. Link vision / the optic nerve [and blindness]. Ajna. ☉ ☽/ ♊ ☿ ♅ [♄ ♇].
(1) Jose Feliciano (10 Sep 1945, 10:00, Lares, Puerto Rico), was blind from birth as a result of congenital glaucoma. ☽ ♏1, ☌ Asc [□ ♄ ♋].
(2) Ray Charles (23 Sep 1930, no time), did not lose his sight until he was 7 years, caused by juvenile glaucoma ☉ [□ ♄ ♑1].

Glioblastoma, Brain Cancer: (See also Brain Cancer). Is a fast-growing and aggressive brain cancer/ malignant tumour, which invades nearby brain tissue. Link the brain [and the cancer formula]. Cwn. ♈ ♂, ♋ ☽ [(♋ ☽ > ♄ ♇) > ♃ ☉].
The disease killed these two men.
(1) Chris Duncan (5 May 1981, 20:30, Tucson, AZ). ♂ ♉ [(qd ♇) > ☌ ☉6, coruler 8H].
(2) Sam Bottoms (17 Oct 1955, 20:40, Santa Barbara, CA). ☽ ♏6 [(☌ ♄) > □ ♃].

Glottis: Part of the larynx consisting of the vocal cords. Thr. ♉ ☿.

Glucose: A form of sugar most used by the body. ♀ ♃.

Gluten: A protein found in wheat, barley, and rye. Gluten acts like a binder, holding food together and adding a 'stretchy' quality. ♋ ☽.

- Gluten Allergy - see Coeliac Disease.

Gluteus Muscles: Any of the large, fleshy muscles of the buttocks. ♐ ♃ > ♂.

Gluttony: Habitual greed or excess in eating. Thr. Spx [♉♐♃].

Glycogen: A substance deposited in bodily tissues as a store of carbohydrates. ♀.

Goitre: Due to an iodine deficiency, the thyroid swells to try and capture all the iodine it can. Link thyroid/ iodine [deficiency > swell]. Thr. ♉♀ [♄ > ♃].
(1) Carl Lewis (1 Jul 1961, 07:49, Birmingham, AL). ♀♉ [△♄♑℞6 > ♄☌♃℞].
(2) George Bush Snr (12 Jun 1924, 10:30, Milton, MA). ♀♋℞ [☌♇♋ > ♇⚻♃℞].
(3) Rod Stewart (10 Jan 1945, 21:45, Highgate, UK). ♀6 [☉♑ mp ☽♐/♀].

Gonads: Sex-glands. The physical body anchorage for the forces of the sacral chakra. The testes in men secrete the hormone testosterone. The ovaries in women secrete oestrogen and progesterone. Sac. ♏♂ men, ♋☽♀ women.

Gonorrhoea: (See Sexually Transmitted Disease). Link sex [bacterial infection]. Sac. ♏♂♀ [♂♅♆,♇].
(1) Tallulah Bankhead (31 Jan 1902, 21:00, Huntsville, AL). In 1933, the actress nearly died following a hysterectomy due to uterus damage from gonorrhoea. ♂♒5 [△♆, r6H].

Gorging Food: Overindulging on food, gluttony. Thr [♉♐♃].

Gout - see Arthritis.

Grandiose Delusions: (See Delusion, Megalomania). These are unfounded on inaccurate beliefs that one is super-important, has special powers, has a special mission in life that is more important than anyone else's. Link self [delusion, emotionalism > grandiose] Spx. ☉, Asc [♋☽, ♓♆ > ♌♇♅].
(1) Adolf Hitler (20 Apr 1889, 18:30, Braunau, Austria). Some psychiatrists believe Hitler had this disorder. He does have a pattern. ☉☍Asc (looking at, and admiring himself). Asc [☌♅ that he is brilliantly unique]. Actually, he was. ☉ [♀♂ mp ☉/♇ very admiring of himself, of his power].

Grave's Disease: An autoimmune disease that damages the thyroid. Underlying the condition are pent up virulent emotions and difficulty in speaking one's truth. Link thyroid [autoimmune attack]. Afflicted emotions may link in. Thr. ♉♀ [♂☉].
(1) Barbara Bush (8 Jun 1925, 19:00, Rye, NY). Former US President George Bush Snr., and his wife Barbara Bush were both diagnosed with Graves' disease. It suggests his position as US President made them reticent to say what they really thought, and from expressing their anger. ♀ r6H [□♅. ♅□☉].
(2) George Bush Snr (12 Jun 1924, 10:30, Milton, MA). ☿♉ [□♂6].

Gravel: Also known as 'sand', multiple small stones passed in the urine. Base [♄].

Grieve, Grief: Intense sorrow, especially caused by someone's death. Spx. ♆.

Groin - Abductor Muscles: These muscles allow for leg/ hip movement. They are located at the juncture of the lower abdomen and the inner part of the thigh. ♂.

Group Problems: (See Grandiose Delusion). Those who still have aggressive and prideful egos, who want the influence and power of the teacher or leader of their group, and make trouble to get it. They influence others, expanding their discontent and jealousy. If this is not curbed, they can destroy the group and psychically harm the teacher. Link group [egoism > delusion]. ♒♅ 11H [☉♂♅ > ♆♓].

Growth: Developing, ripening and maturing - physically or psychologically, are functions of ray 2 which rules every unit of life. [1] The Sun and Jupiter carry the 2nd ray. Hrt. ☉ ♃.

- Growth Stunted - see Dwarfism.

- Growths: Over-growth of tissue, both malignant and nonmalignant. Link tissue [growths]. ♋ ☽ [♃].

Guidance (Unwise): (See Delusion, Mystical Vision, Stigmata). This occurs when a mystic (one who is drawn to the spiritual life), believes he hears voices or urges (from God, the Christ, Baba, etc), commanding him to do something. But usually only a person's own internal dialogue is heard. But there is a danger. Those who open themselves to blind, unreasoning guidance may become negative, impressionable automatons, helpless victims of circumstance, self-hypnotised tools used by others. Link the self/ mind [and delusion]. ☉ Ascendant, ☿ [♆♓].

Guillain-Barre Syndrome: (See Autoimmune Disease). The immune system attacks the peripheral nerves and it can lead to paralysis. Link nerves [immune attack > paralysis]. Ajna. Hrt. ♊ ☿ (♀≈♅) [♂☉ > ♄♇].
(1) Anita Cortesi (1 Oct 1955, 17:45, Zurich Switz.). The Swiss astrologer was paralysed by this disease. ♅ [♂♍6 mp ♄/♅♌].

Guilt, Guilty: Feeling responsible or regretful for a perceived offence, which is real or imaginary. Spx [♆].

Gullet - see Oesophagus.

Gums: Tissue of the upper and lower jaws that surrounds the base of the teeth. Thr. ♉ ♀.

- Gum boils: An abscess on the gums, caused usually by bacteria. Link gums [infection > pus]. Thr. ♉ ♀ [♂♅♆ > ♋ ☽].

Gunshot: Penetrating injury caused by a bullet shot from a gun. Link the life, the body [and gun/ assassination]. ☉, Asc, 1H [♂/ ♏♂♇].
These three died from being shot.
(1) John Kennedy, President (29 May 1917, 15:00, Brookline, MA). Kennedy was assassinated, shot in the head and killed. Asc [⚷♂8].
(2) Sabine Bohain (7 Feb 1965, 17:15, Ollioules, Fr), was shot and killed by her husband. Asc ♌ [∠♂, ☍☉7].
(3) Vincent Van Gogh (30 Mar 1853, 11:00, Zundert, Holland). Suffering from depression, he shot himself in the chest. ☽6, ruler of Asc and the chest [□♂].

Gut - see Digestion System.

Gynaecological: Area of medicine concerned with disorders and functions of female reproduction. Sac. ♋ ☽.

---

1   Bailey, Alice: Esoteric Psychology I, 334.

H

Habits: Routines of behaviour that are repeated regularly. ☽.

Haematuria: Blood in the urine. Common causes are a urinary tract infection, excessive exercise, sexual intercourse, an injury or a kidney stone. Link blood > urine [and the cause]. Base. ♂ ♃ ♒ > ♎ ♀ [cause].

Haemoglobin: A red protein responsible for transporting oxygen in the blood. Hrt. ♂.

Haemolysis: Destruction of red blood cells before the body can make replacements. It is caused by parasites, viruses or bacteria. The most well-known cause of this disease is malaria. Link blood > red cells [and destruction]. Hrt. ♂ ♃ ♒ > ☉ ♂ [♄ ♇].

Haemophilia: Blood does not clot because of a gene mutation. Look for afflictions to Saturn, the clotting factor - especially from insidious Neptune, and corruptive Pluto. Uranus-Aquarius may link in for genes. Link blood/ cells [clotting factor > corrupted]. Hrt ♂ ♃ ♒/ ☉ [♄ > ♅ ♆ ♇].

(1) Alfonso, Prince of Asturias (10 May 1907, 12:30, Madrid, Spain). ☉ [mp ♄/♆].

(2) Alexei, Czar (12 Aug 1904, 13:15, Petrodvorec, Russia). ☉ ♌ [☍ ♄ ♒ ℞ > ♅ ☍ ♇].

(3) Eric Dostie (28 Mar 1989, 18:56, Northampton, MA). ☉6 [□ ♄ > ♄ ☌ ♆ ♑].

(4) Queen Victoria (24 May 1819, 04:15, London, UK). Although she did not inherit this defective gene, she passed it onto several of her children. It seems karmic since this happened around the time that royal houses were losing their power. ☉, ruler of the 5H of children, passing on cells with [⚹ ♄ ♓ > ♄ □ ♆ corrupted clot-factor].

Haemorrhage: Acute loss of blood from a ruptured blood vessel. Link blood vessel [and haemorrhage]. Hrt. ♃ ♒ [♂ (♅ ♇)].

These three examples died from a brain haemorrhage. Mars can represent both the brain and the haemorrhage.

(1) Karl Pius, Archduke of Austria (4 Dec 1909, 23:00, Vienna, Austria). ♃ [☍ ♂ ♈ 8].

(2) Nico (16 Oct 1938, 17:30, Cologne, Ger). ♃ ♒ ℞ [⚻ ♂ 6, r8H].

(3) Punch Sulzberger (5 Feb 1926, 03:00, New York, NY). ☉ ♒ [∠ ♂ 1 > ☍ ♆ ♌ 8].

Haemorrhoids: Swollen, lumpy veins in the rectum and anus that cause discomfort and bleed. Link veins/ rectum [lumpy > bleed]. Thr. Spx. ♀/ ♏ ♂ ♇ [♃/♄ > ♂].

(1) Astro.com 8395 (13 Jun 1939, 10:18, Beacon Hill, MA). ♀ △ ♂ ♒ 6 [♂ □ ♄ ♈].

Hair: Any of the fine threadlike strands growing from the skin. Base. ♑ ♄, ♈ ♂.

Halitosis: Bad breath caused by odour-producing bacteria that grow in the mouth. Thr. [♄].

Hallucinations: Perceiving something not present. Spx [♓ ♆].

Hallucinatory drugs: Those that can produce altered states of consciousness. [♓ ♆].

Hamstrings: Tendons at the back of the thighs that attach the thigh muscle to the bone. Base. ♐ ♃.

Handicap: Limitation that acts as an impediment to. [♄].

Hands and Arms: Upper limbs including the wrist, palm, fingers and thumb. Thr. ♊ ☿.

Hardens: Making tissue more firm/ compact/ dense. [♑ ♄].

Harelip - see Cleft Palate, Cleft Lip.

Hashimoto's disease: (See Autoimmune Disease). The immune system attacks the thyroid causing inflammation and symptoms such as tiredness, weight gain and muscle weakness. Link thyroid [immune attack > inflammation/ impairment]. Thr. ♉ ♀ [♂ ☉ > ♂ ☉/ ♄].
(1) Gigi Hadid (23 Apr 1995, 06:26, Los Angeles, CA). ♀ ♈ 12 [⚻ ♂ ♌].
(2) Michelle Visage (20 Sep 1968, 12:08, Perth Amboy, NJ). ♀ r6H [☉ ♇ mp ♀/♂].

Hay Fever: (See Allergies). An allergic response to irritants in the air causing itchy, watery eyes and sneezing. The inner cause is emotional hypersensitivity. Link airways [emotions/ irritants > immune reaction]. Thr. Spx. ♊ ☿ [♋ ☽ /♂ > ♂ (☉ ♅)].
(1) Astro.com 3118 (13 Mar 1884, 03:34, New Orleans, USA). ☿ ♓ [♆ mp ☿/♂].
(2) Astro.com 7160 (4 Dec 1932, 05:54, Chicago, IL). ☿ 1℞ [□ ♂ ♍].

HBP - see Blood Pressure High.

Head: Upper part of the human body, on the neck. Cwn. ♈ ♂, 1H.

- **Headaches**: Continuous pain in the head. Cwn. [♈ ♂].

- **Head Centre** - see Crown Chakra.

- **Head Injuries:** Various types of injuries to the head. [♈ ♂].

Health, Heal, Healing: Heal/ healing is the process of making or becoming sound or healthy again. All easy aspects (trine, sextile) from planets to the rulers of the 6th or 12th houses (the health houses), or to planets within these houses, are beneficial for healing and health. So are easy aspects to a planet that represents a troubled organ - especially if these aspecting planets are Jupiter and Venus, the greater and lesser benefics. A strong Sun by sign, house and aspect (especially easy aspects from Jupiter or Mars), greatly boosts vitality, which is the master healing/ health agent. Another factor that benefits healing is a strong and positive will (♌ ☉ ♇). A determination to heal acts as a powerful health tonic, just as giving in to an illness has the opposite effect. Virgo is the healing sign and Mercury the healing planet. ☉ ♀ ♃, ♍ ☿, 6H.

- **Healers:** Those whose profession is to heal or alleviate sickness symptoms. ♍ ☿, 6H.

- **Healing, Alternative, Natural**: Healing practices that rely on ancient cultural knowledge or noninvasive treatments such as herbal, homeopathic, acupuncture. ♍ ☿ > ♅, 6H.

- **Healing, Esoteric:** The healer draws in healing energies from the soul and via the ajna and hand chakras, directs these to the troubled chakra/ organ of the person who is being healed. It also involves the use the creative imagination/ the power of thought, to move and direct energy currents. ♍ ☿ > ♅, 6H.

- **Healing, Faith**: This is healing achieved by religious belief and prayer, rather than by medical treatment. ♓ ♆, 6H, 9H.

- **Healing, Orthodox Church:** The sacrament of the unction of the sick, is the Church's specific prayer for healing. ♓ ♆, 6H, 9H.

- **Health Pattern, Disease Pattern:** In a natal chart, a group of interconnected planets that represent a disease and the organs it affects.

- **Health Tonic:** A substance that stimulates well-being, which invigorates, restores, or refreshes. Jupiter restores health and the Sun and Mars have a tonic effect upon the body. ☉♂♃.

- **Health Triangle:** This is a pattern in the natal chart that represents a serious disease or problem. It is formed from a minimum of three planets in aspect. Planet 1 represents the organ that is diseased. Planet 2 represents the psychological or genetic/ karmic cause of the disease. Planet 3 (and others) represent the disease and its results - the impairments, damage and limitations caused by the disease. Organ [Cause > Disease/ Effect].

(1) James Cheek (4 Dec 1932, 14:30, Roanoke Rapids, NC). He was born with congenital cataracts. Organ affected: the eyes. [Cause: karmic conditions from the past, represented by the Moon > Disease effect: cataracts]. ☉ [□ ☽ > □♆♍].

Hearing: The faculty of perceiving sounds via the ears. The senses are part of the peripheral nervous system. Ajna. ♊ ☿.

- **Hearing deficient/ loss:** Difficulty hearing because of trouble in the ear. Link ears/ hearing [loss]. Ajna. ♊ ☿ [♑ ♄ ♇].

HEART, the: (See Cardiovascular). The primary organ of the circulatory system that pumps blood through the body. The heart is represented by the Sun (and Leo). Mars can substitute because it rules the heart muscle. So can Jupiter which rules the heart chakra in spiritually advanced people. Just as the Sun is the vitalising organ in the solar system that gives life to all in its influence, so is the heart the vitalising, life-giving organ in the human body. Hrt. ☉ (♌).

- **Heart Arrhythmia, Heart Atrial Fibrillation:** Irregular, often rapid heart rate, causing poor blood flow. Link heart [and arrhythmia]. Hrt. ☉♌ [♅].

(1) Barry Bonds (24 Jul 1964, 17:13, Riverside, CA). ☉♌ [☍ ☽ ♒, ☽ ⚻ ♅].

(2) Ed Koch (12 Dec 1924, 03:00, Bronx, NY). ☉ [□ ♅].

(3) Jim Duggan (14 Jan 1954, 03:38, Glen Falls, NY). ☉ [☍ ♅].

(4) Nicolas Portal (23 Apr 1979, 13:15, Auch, Fr). ☉ [qd ♅].

- **Heart Attack (Myocardial Infarction):** (See Coronary Thrombosis). Sudden blockage of blood to the heart. Rapid intervention is required to avoid death, actual or to a part of the heart. Link the heart / blood flow [blockage > attack]. Hrt. ☉♌ / ♒♅♆ [♄♇/♃ > ♂♅]. These four died of a heart attack. Jupiter represents an artery blockage.

(1) Gerard Philipe (4 Dec 1922, 14:00, Cannes, Fr). ☉8 [⚻♇ > □♅♓].

(2) Jean Carmet (25 Apr 1920, 12:00, Tours, Fr). ☉ [□♃♌1 > ☍♂].

(3) Maurizio Merli (8 Feb 1940, 13:00, Rome, Italy). ☉♒ [∠♃ > □♅12].

(4) Michel Berger (28 Nov 1947, 17:15, Neuilly sur Seine, Fr). ☉6 [☌♃ > □♂♌].

- **Heart Burn** - see Acid Reflux.

- **Heart, Congenital Problem:** A heart problem existing from birth. Link heart [congenital > defect]. Hrt. ♌☉ [♋ ☽ > ♄♇].

(1) Shaun White (3 Sep 1986, 04:37, Easter Cross, CA). The champion snow-boarder was born with a congenital heart defect. ☉1 [wide ☌ ☽ > □ ♄ r6H]

- **Heart Disease:** Heart conditions that include diseased vessels, structural problems and blood clots. Link the heart [and disease]. Hrt. ♌☉ [♄♇].

- **Heart Failure**: The heart does not pump blood as well as it should. Link the heart [and failing/ weak]. Hrt. ♌☉ [♓♆].
(1) Elizabeth Taylor (27 Feb 1932, 02:30, London, Eng). ☉♓ [☍♆♍].

- **Heart Murmur:** It is caused by rapid, choppy, turbulent blood flow through the heart. Link the heart [and choppy, turbulent]. Hrt. ♌☉ [♅♆].
(1) Dean Corll (24 Dec 1939, 20:45, Fort Wayne, IN). ☉ coruler 12H [⚼ ♅ ♉].
(2) Sophia Stallone (27 Aug 1996, 00:29, Sth Miami, FL). Sylvester Stallone's daughter. ☉ [⚻♅♒].

- **Heart Muscle:** The muscle tissue that forms the heart. Hrt. ♌☉♂.

- **Heart Palpitations:** Feelings the heart is racing/ fluttering but not usually a sign of heart disease. It is most likely connected with an emotional upset - so, the emotional planets or signs may link in. Link heart [racing/ fluttering]. Hrt. ♌☉ [♂/♅].
(1) Wilbur Wright (16 Apr 1867, no time). After some teeth were knocked out in an ice-hockey accident, he developed heart palpitations. ☉ [□♂♋].

- **Heart Valves**: The valves on the lower chambers of the heart that prevent the backward flow of blood. ♒♅.

HEART CHAKRA (Hrt): (See Chakras and Etheric Web).
Consciousness: It is the organ of spiritual love, and begins to open once conscious soul contact has been made. It comes alive in the higher sense when we begin to transmute lower desire into inclusive love, and become group/ soul conscious. Eventually the transmuted forces of the solar plexus centre, flow up and out through this chakra.
Ray and Astrology energies: The heart chakra is the channel for Ray 2 of Love and Wisdom, flowing via the Sun and Jupiter. Leo is associated.
Body rulership: This 12-petal lotus enters the spine between the shoulder blades, around T5, anchoring in the thymus gland. Life force enters this centre via the sutratma, vitalising the heart, the cardiovascular system, the entire organism - including the vagus nerve.
Diseases: Those of the cardiovascular system - the heart, blood, devitalisation. Problems with cell life, with the autonomic nervous system, the vagus nerve, with the immune system and autoimmune diseases.

Heat: Warmth, a high degree of hotness. ♂☉, fire signs.

- **Heatstroke:** The body overheats, due usually to prolonged exposure to a high temperature. [♂☉ fire signs].
(1) Matthew Power (22 Oct 1974, 03:55, Middlebury, VT). An American journalist who suffered from heatstroke while bush-walking and died. ☉ [☌♅♂ r8H].

Hepatic Portal System: Venous system that returns blood from the digestive tract and spleen to the liver. Hrt. ♀ (♒♅).

Hepatitis: Liver infection and inflammation often caused by a virus, but can be also caused by drugs. Most common types are A, B and C. Link liver [virus > inflammation]. Spx. ♃ [♆♂♅ > ♂☉].
These examples all had hepatitis C.

(1) Buddy Turman (12 Apr 1933, 21:30, Noonday, TX). American professional boxer. ♃♍℞ [☌♆♍ > ☌♂♍ r12H].
(2) Greg Allman (8 Dec 1947, 15:39, Nashville, TN). ♃ [□♂ rules 12H]. He believed he got hepatitis C from a dirty tattoo needle.
(3) Naomi Judd (11 Jan 1946, 18:45, Ashland, KY). ♃ [□♂♋12]. The singer committed suicide in 2023

Hereditary Diseases: Genetic abnormalities passed from parent to child. Sac [♒♅, ♋☽].

Hernia: A tear in the abdomen wall that allows the contents inside to protrude outward. Link abdomen [and tear]. Spx. ♋☽, ♍☿ [♂].
(1) Jim Hodgson (8 Sep 1947, 01:55, Hawkwell, Eng). ☿♍ r12 [□♅12].

Herpes: (See Sexually Transmitted Disease). A virus spread through sexual contact, causing contagious sores on the genitals. Link genitals [virus > sores]. Sac. ♏♂ [♆♂♅ > ♂].
(1) Don Heche (20 Mar 1937, 13:15, Bluffton, IN). His actress daughter Ann, said her father had herpes, and passed it to her when he raped her as a child. ♅♉/♏ r8H [☌♀ > ♀⚻♂5]. He had hidden, unhealthy desires (♇☌☽♋12).

- Herpes, Oral: A virus that is spread orally and which causes contagious cold sores around the mouth. Link mouth [virus > sores]. Thr. ♉♀ [♆♂♅ > ♂].

Hiccough: Involuntary sounds made by spasms of the diaphragm. Representatives of the vocal cords may link in. Link diaphragm [spasms]. Thr. ♂ (♋☽) [♅].
(1) Charles Osborne (2 Apr 1894, no time, Anthon, Iowa). Reports say that after an accident, Osborne hiccupped for 68 years straight. ♂♒ [disposited by ♅℞].

High Blood Pressure - see Blood Pressure High.

High Temperature: A temporary increase in average body temperature. Hrt [♂☉].

Highly Strung: Nervy and easily upset. Link nerves [intensity]. Spx. ♊☿ (♀♒♅) [♂♅].

Hippocampus: (See Triune Brain). An integral part of the limbic system (the desire or emotional brain), related to regulating learning, memory. Short term memories are stored in the hippocampus. Thr. ♉♀ (☽).

Hips: Area below the waist and above the legs at either side of the body. Base. ♐♃.

- Hip Dislocation: The head of the thighbone is forced out of its socket. Base. ♐♃ [♂].

- Hip Problems: Link the hips [and planets representing the cause]. Base. ♐♃ [malefics].
(1) Jeanne Calment (21 Feb 1875, 07:00, Arles, Fr). She lived until 122 years of age. Calment broke her hip in 1990. ♃℞ [☍♆], suggests weakening, osteoporosis.

Histamine: A neurotransmitter necessary to maintain wakefulness and alertness. Ajna. ♊☿♅.

HIV, Human Immunodeficiency Virus: (See Acquired Immunodeficiency Virus - AIDS). This virus attacks and destroys the immune system.

Hives: Itchy, raised red areas on the skin caused by a stress reaction. Link skin (♋☽) [red, itchy]. ♑♄ [♂].
(1) George Stephanopoulos (10 Feb 1961, 10:17, Fall River, MA). The American political commentator said his work was so stressful he broke out in hives. ♄♑ [⚻♅♌ substituting for Mars].

Hoarding: A psychological disorder where, people hoard possessions. The root cause is fear of being vulnerable, being exposed to harm, a fear of life. Possessions are ruled by the 4H. Since Cancer and the Moon are the natural rulers of that house and of the emotions, study them closely. Scorpio and Pluto which govern 'compulsive' urges may be involved. Link emotions / the home [fear/ compulsive > hoarding]. Spx. ♋ ☽, 4H [♄/♆ >♃ (♅ ♋)].
(1) Delta Burke (30 Jul 1956, 11:24, Orlando, FL). ☽ ♉ [△♃ ♍ r6H > ♃ ♂ ♇]. ♄ r4H [□♇ > ♇ ♂ ♃ ♍].
(2) Kevin McCrary (13 Aug 1948, 09:04, New York, NY). ☽ [△♇ > ♂ ♃ ℞ r4H].

Hoarse Throat: Strained voice. Thr. ♉ ♀ [♄].

Hodgkin and Non-Hodgkin Lymphoma: (See Lymphoma). Bone marrow produces abnormal white blood cells (lymphocytes), resulting in cancer in the lymphatic system. The difference between the two diseases is the type of cell affected.

Homeostasis: A state of balance among all the body systems needed for the body to survive and function correctly. ♎ ♀.

Homosexuality: Sexually attracted to people of one's own sex. Sac. ♂ ♀ > ♅.

Hormones: The body's chemical messengers, dispensed by the body's pharmacy, the endocrine glandular system. ☿ for messenger, ♅ for chemical/ hormones. ☿ ♅.

- Hormonal Imbalance: This is due to an imbalance in hormones. ☿ [♅].

Horse Riding Accident: Statistics suggest that horse riding is more dangerous than motorcycle riding and automobile racing. Link horses [and accident]. ♃ ♐ [♂ ♅].
(1) Christopher Reeve (25 Sep 1952, 03:12, Manhattan, NY). A horse-riding accident: ♃ ℞ [♐ ♂ ♐]. The actor broke his back: Asc [♂ ♇ ♌].

Hospitals: An institution providing medical/ surgical/ nursing treatment. ♓ ♆, 12H.

Houses: Brief overviews.

1H: (See also - Ascendant). The physical body, the appearance. In the body - the head and brain (via Aries).

2H: Personal possessions, money, business matters. Values, material and spiritual, gains and losses. In the body - the throat (via Taurus).

3H: The local environment, neighbours, siblings, extended family, communications, the lower mind. In the body - the nervous system (via Gemini).

4H: Family, mother, home, emotions, unhealed psychological patterns, life endings. In the body - stomach (via Cancer).

5H: Children, one's personal creativity, love, hobbies, pleasure. In the body - the heart (via Leo).

6H: The health house, acute illnesses, the struggles and crises we go through in order to survive and to get on with others. Service, work, co-workers, skills. In the body - nutrition, eating habits, digestion (via Virgo).

7H: Marriage, others, attitude to formal relationships, the law and justice. In the body - the kidneys (via Libra).

8H: Death, resources of the partnership, other people's money, emotional crises, divorce, transformation. Physical death. In the body - sex, excretion (via Scorpio).

9H: Collective mind, society's beliefs, morals, philosophy, higher learning, the high court, judges, legal matters. In the body - mobility (via Sagittarius).

10H: Authority, corporate structures, father, the government, status, recognition. In the body - the body structure (via Capricorn).

11H: Group and friend relationships, social reform, politics, revolution, hopes and wishes. In the body - circulation (via Aquarius).

12H: Health - asylums, hospitals, chronic diseases. Self-undoing, negative core-beliefs, confinement, hidden enemies. In the body - unconsciousness, sleep (via Pisces).

Humerus: Bone of the upper arm. Thr. ♊ ☿.

Huntington's Disease: Hereditary dementia. (See Dementia). Symptoms may differ from other forms of dementia. EG. People with Huntington's may have a good memory of recent events, but forget how to do things. Planets for the intelligence (☿ ♀), or consciousness (☉), may connect in. Link the brain [to aging, atrophy]. Cwn. ♈♂, ☽♋ [♄♇].
(1) Sophie Daumier (24 Nov 1934, 05:30, Boulonge sur Mer, Fr). ♅♈6 [□♇♋].
(2) Woody Guthrie (14 Jul 1912, no time). ♂☌6H cusp [□♄♊].

Hydrocephalus: Fluid accumulation in the brain, enlarging the head and sometimes causing brain damage. Link brain [fluid > excess, enlarging]. Cwn. ♈♂,♋☽ [♓♆,♋☽ > ♃].
(1) Otto Hitler (17 Jun 1892, 08:00, Braunau am Inn, Austria). The younger brother of Adolf, died at 7 days old, of hydrocephalus. ♃♈ brain, excess [□♀♋12; ♀∠♆ r8H].

Hydrophobia: (See Rabies). A morbid dread of water, extreme fearfulness of swallowing liquids, painful spasms of the throat. There are two causes. Traumatic experiences involving water, and symptoms of a rabies infection. Link the self/ emotions [fear > water]. ☉ Asc, ♋☽♂ [♄ > ☽♆ water signs].
(1) Michael Jordan (17 Feb 1963, 13:40, Brooklyn, NY). After witnessing the death of a childhood friend, Michael Jordan was terrified of the ocean. ♂ [Tsq: ☍♄ > □♆♏].

Hydrotherapy: A branch of alternative medicine, hydrotherapy is the use of water for therapy, rehabilitation, exercise, relaxation. It is very beneficial for emotional healing and purification. ♓♆.

Hygiene: Life-style practices performed to preserve health. ♍☿, 6H.

Hyoid bone: U-shaped bone situated at the root of the tongue. Thr. ♉♀.

Hyperactivity: This is due to overstimulated emotions. Spx. ☽♂♆ water [♂♅].

Hypercritical: Meticulously or excessively critical. Thr. ♍☿ [♄]

Hyperglycaemia: (See Diabetes). High blood sugar. A condition affecting people who have diabetes. Glucose tends to build up in the bloodstream.

Hyperpituitarism: Overproduction of pituitary hormones. This can lead to conditions like Gigantism and Acromegaly. Link pituitary [overproduction]. Ajna. ♀☿ [♐♃].

Hypersensitive: Extreme sensitivity to substances or conditions. Spx [♓♆].

Hypertension - see Blood Pressure High.

Hyperthyroidism: Immune system attack causing the overproduction of thyroid hormones. Link thyroid [immune attack > overproduction]. Thr. ♉♀ [♂☉ > ♃].

Hypertrophy: An increase and growth of muscle cells. ♃ > ♂.

Hyperuricaemia: Too much uric acid in the blood, usually due to diet. Link blood [uric acid > excess]. Hrt. ♂ ♃ ♒ [♏ ♂ ♇ > ♃].

Hypnotherapy: Use of hypnosis as a therapeutic technique. ♆.

Hypochondria: Obsessed with the idea of having a serious but undiagnosed medical condition. Link the self / the 6H, 12H [and obsessed]. Spx. ☉, Asc, 6H ♍ ☿, 12H [♏ ♇].
(1) Jason Mantzoukas (18 Dec 1972, 16:40, Nahant, MA). The American actor was born with an egg allergy and experiences anaphylaxis if ingested. He has cited this allergy as the cause of his hypochondriac tendencies. ☉6 [□ ♇].

Hypogeusia. (See Ageusia). Reduced ability to taste - sweet, sour, bitter, or salty things. There are various causes. Link nerves, taste [reduced]. ♊ ☿ [♄].

Hypoglycaemia: Low blood sugar due to too much insulin. Cause can be due to diet or a side effect of diabetes medication. Link blood sugar [deficient]. Spx. ♎ ♀ ♃ [♄ ♇].
(1) Marcia Hines (20 Jul 1953, 09:44, Boston, MA). She had diabetes and hypoglycaemia. ♀ [♇ ♌ 12 mp ♀/♄ ♎]. Sugar (♀), deficient in the blood stream (♇ ♌/♒), due to wrong dosage of medicine (♄ ♎).

Hypopituitarism: Deficiency of one or more of the pituitary hormones. Link pituitary [deficient]. Ajna. ♀ ☿ [♑ ♄ ♇].

Hyposmia: (See Anosmia). Reduced ability to smell. There are various causes. Link nerves, smell [reduced]. ♊ ☿ [♄].

Hypotension: Low blood pressure (fainting, dizziness), because the brain does not receive enough blood. Link blood [pressure deficient]. Cwn. Hrt. ♂ ♃ ♒ [♄].
(1) Simon Cowell (7 Oct 1959, no time), reported he had low blood pressure. ♃ [□ ♇; ♂ mp ♃/♇].

Hypothalamus: A gland located above the pituitary. It is the master switchboard for the endocrine system, regulating its activity. Its main function is homeostasis, keeping the body-state stable by monitoring and regulating. Ajna. ☿ ♀ ♎.

Hypothyroidism: (See Iodine Deficiency). Insufficient thyroid hormone can cause mental health issues, shock and coma. Link thyroid [insufficient]. Thr. ♉ ♀ [♄ ♇].
(1) Hillary Clinton (26 Oct 1947, 18:45, Chicago, IL). In 2015, she was treated for hypothyroidism. ♀ ♏ 6 [□ ♄ ♇].

Hysterectomy: A surgical operation to remove all or part of the uterus. Link uterus [surgery > removal]. Sac. ♋ ☽ [♂ > ♄ ♇].
(1) Frieda Hughes (1 Apr 1960, 05:45, London, Eng). ☽ [□ ♇6 > ♇ ☍ ♂12].
(2) Roseanne Barr (3 Nov 1952, 13:21, Salt Lake City, UT). ♅ ♋6 [Tsq: ☍ ♂ ♑12 > □ ♄].
(3) Tallulah Bankhead (31 Jan 1902, 21:00, Huntsville, AL). ☽ ♏ [□ ♂ > ⚻ ♇].

Hysteria: Exaggerated, uncontrollable emotion or excitement. Spx. [R6, ♂ ♆].

I

IBS - see Irritable Bowel Syndrome.

Ileum: The final portion of the small intestine that connects to the large intestine. Spx. ♍ ☿.

- Ileitis: Inflammation of the ileum. Spx. ♍ ☿ [♂ ☉].

Ilium: Upper portion of the hip bone and pelvis. Base. ♐ ♃.

Illness: A disease or period of sickness affecting the body or mind. [♄].

Illusion: A false idea or belief. The misinterpretation of ideas. ♊ ☿ [♓ ♆].

Imbalance: Lacking right-relation, a balance disorder. [♎ ♅ (♀)].

Immune System: Governed by the vitalising power of the Sun, the heart chakra and heart..

> When vitality is great and the life force has free and unimpeded circulation, germs cannot find a lodging and there will not be the risk of infection. [1]

Mars energy, which contributes to healthy blood cells and whose function is to protect against external attack is a substitute ruler for the system.

Water signs and their rulers service and assist the immune system. White immunity blood cells originate in bone marrow (Cancer, Moon). They migrate to guard peripheral tissue, circulating in the blood and the lymphatic system (Neptune). Cancer imparts the protective nature of the system and Scorpio the killing function. Hrt. ☉ ♌ (♂).

- Immune Attack - see Autoimmune Disease.

-Immune Deficient: An impaired immune system. The decreased ability of the body to fight infections and other diseases. Link immune system [deficient]. ☉ ♌ (♂). [♄ ♇].

(1) David Vetter (21 Sep 1971, 07:00, Houston, TX). "The Bubble-Boy," born with severe immunodeficiency, he lived in a plastic bubble for 12 years until he died. ☉1 r12H [☌ ♇].

- Immunosuppression: Suppression of the immune system and its ability to fight infections/ disease. Link immune system [suppression]. Hrt. ☉ ♌, ♂ [♑ ♄ ♇].

Impetigo: A skin bacterial infection that causes red sores. The inner cause is bubbling and unexpressed anger. Link skin [bacterial infection > sores]. Base. ♑ ♄ (♋ ☽) [♂ ♅ ♆ > ♂].

(1) Alexandra Cane (9 June 1991, no time). Had a battle with impetigo. ♄ ♒℞ [☍ ♂ ♌].

(2) Amy Winehouse (14 Sep 1983, 22:25, Enfield, UK). ♄6 [mp ♂/☽].

Impotent, Impotency: When a man cannot get or keep an erection firm enough for sexual intercourse. The cause can be the result of illness or psychological. Potency problems can occur at any age if there is stress and doubt about an ability to cope, or about one's manhood. Pisces and Neptune tend to dilute the sexual drive. Link the self/ sex [and impotent]. Sac. ☉ Asc / ♏ ♂ [♄ (♓ ♆)].

(1) Arthur Bremer (21 Aug 1950, 14:40, Milwaukee, WI). Asc / ∠♂♏ [□♄].

(2) John Wayne Gacy (17 Mar 1942, 00:29, Chicago, IL). Asc / ☍♂ [☍♄].

1 Bailey, Alice: Esoteric Healing, 321,

Impregnate: Make a woman pregnant. Sac. ♏♂ (☽).

Impulse Control Disorder: Failure to resist a temptation, an urge, or an impulse. Mars represents our impulses, so it will be dominant in the chart. In contrast, the Sun - the self, or the mind - Mercury; may be weaker. Link impulses [powerful]. ♂ [♅♇].
(1) Mike Tyson (30 June 1966, no time). A psychiatric report said "Mike Tyson has impulse control problems." The birthtime is not known, but Mars is likely in hard aspect to the ascendent. ♂ [□♅, □♄].

Incarnate - see Reincarnate.

Incest: Sexual relations in the family, between people closely related - such as between siblings. Link family [abnormal/ unhealthy > sex]. Sac. ♋☽, 4H [♅/♆ > ♏♂♇].
(1) Astro.com 8168 (8 May 1938, 23:52, Los Angeles, CA). Incest victim, abused by her father from age 7. She has Mars in the 4H, a common placement with sexual abuse in the home. In her chart, it rules the 10H of the father. ☽8 [☌♆♍8 > ♆□♂4]. Asc [☍♇♋].

Incontinence: Inability to control the flow of urine from the bladder (urine incontinence), and/ or stools from the bowel (faecal incontinence); due to weak pelvic floor, sphincter muscles. Neptune and the Moon rule liquid flows, and can weaken. Link bowel, bladder [weak]. Base. ♏♂ (♍☿) [♆♓, ☽].
These incontinence examples all had spina bifida.
(1) Astro.com 14659 (6 Jul 1976, 21:00, West Richland, WA). ☿6 [⚼☽♏].
(2) Astro.com 14672 (9 Nov 1976, 19:15, New York, NY). ♂♏ [⚻☽12].
(3) Astro.com 14891 (27 Jun 1983, 06:20, Cheyenne, WY). ♂12 [⚻☽♑, ☍♆6].

Incubation Period: Time it takes for an infection to develop. [♋☽].

Incurable Disease: A terminal disease causing death. [♏♇,8H].

Indigenous Diseases: These are syphilis, cancer and tuberculosis; diseases native to humanity as a whole because of their prolific nature through the ages. Syphilis is related to the physical body and sacral chakra. Cancer is related to the emotional body and solar plexus. Tuberculosis is related to the mental body and the throat. (See the individual diseases).

Indigestion: Stomach pain, discomfort, due to difficulty digesting food. Spx. ♋☽♍ [♂].

Infant, Infancy: A very young child or baby. ♋☽. Older children are ruled by ♌☉, 5H.

- Infant Mortality - see Sudden Infant Death Syndrome.

- Infantile Paralysis - see Polio, Paralysis.

Infection: An infection occurs when germs invade the body, increase in number and cause a body reaction. Two rays are involved. Ray 4 (☽), is behind "a rapid taking on of infections." [1] Ray 7 (♅) is "largely responsible for infections and contagious diseases." [2]

There are four types of infections generally ruled by the following: viral (Neptune) bacterial (Uranus), fungal (Moon, Neptune), and parasitic (Pluto). Additionally, Mars is a general representative for infection. An infection could be represented by any of these planets and their signs, but to simplify just three will be presented for infection: [♂♅♆].

Infertility - see Barren.

---

1 Bailey, Alice: Esoteric Healing, 301.
2 Bailey, Alice: Esoteric Healing, 304.

Inflammation: This is an immune response, which sends out inflammatory cells to attack pathogens or heal damaged tissue. In the following sections, inflammation will be presented as ♂ ☉. But Uranus, or planets in the fire signs could substitute. Hrt [♂ ☉ (♅) fire].

Influenza: An influenza virus attacks the airways, causing fever, a runny or stuffy nose. R4 is behind the spread of influenza epidemics. [1] The collective fear and worry in humanity is the root cause of influenza. [2] Inner conflict wears down immunity, it debilitates, opening our systems up to the spread of disease. Consequently, the Moon and Mercury that carry R4, are often implicated with influenza. Link the airways [virus > mucous/ emotions]. Thr.
♊ ☿ [♆♂♅ > ♋ ☽ (♓♆)].
These aristocratic ladies died from influenza.
(1) Louise Margaret (25 Jul 1860, 05:30, Potsdam, Ger). ☿ [♐♂♑/♋,℞6].
(2) Marie-Adelaide Therese (14 Jun 1894, 21:00, Berg, Luxembourg). ☉ ♊6 [□♂♓].
(3) Viktoria Margarete (17 Apr 1890, 15:30, Potsdam, Ger). ☿8 [mp ☽/♆♊].

Ingestion: Taking into the body by mouth. Thr. ♉ ♀.

Inherited Disease: (See Congenital Disease and Genetic Disease). A disease caused by a genetic mutation that is passed down the family line. [♒♅, ♋ ☽].

Injury: An instance of being injured. ♂ (♅).

Insanity, Madness: The mind is unable to function through the brain and nervous system because of a serious brain defect, brain injury, brain disease (such as dementia), or the consciousness thread from the soul is not anchored in the brain. Only the animal awareness of the physical body is present. Link intelligence > the brain [serious break-down]. Cwn. Ajna. Spx. ♊ ☿ / ♈♂,♋ ☽ [R1, ♄♆].

Insanity - Psychological: (See Delusion). A serious mental illness caused by a too powerful and unstable emotional body. It is a natural and temporary stage on the journey to enlightenment. The emotional body (the connection to the astral plane), is currently more powerful and dominant than the awakening mind.

> The astral plane.. is the realm of delusion, of fog, of mist and of glamour. [3]

When common-sense and discrimination are not present, images built in the imagination can seem real. For example, religious mystics can get lost in visualisations such as talking to an image of Jesus or God; believing them to be real occurrences. Future growth opportunities via reincarnation will correct this. The 12H, which is related to Pisces and Neptune, may be involved. Link the mind/ emotions [delusion]. Spx. ♊ ☿/ ♋ ☽ [♓♆, 12H].

Insects: The insect kingdom is generally ruled by Mercury, especially flying insects. The troubling proliferation of insects that is injurious to human life is related to widespread negative thinking. Here is a quote:

> The vast assembly of insects which now haunt our planet and cause increasing concern to the scientist, agriculturist, and all those dealing with the welfare of the human animal, are the direct result of thought precipitation. [4]

This is especially true of flying swarms of insects such as locusts, moths and grasshoppers that destroy crops. ♊ ☿ .

---

1   Bailey, Alice: Esoteric Healing, 301.
2   Bailey, Alice: Esoteric Healing, 70.
3   Bailey, Alice: The Rays and the Initiations, 64.
4   Bailey, Alice: Treatise on White Magic, 542.

However, biting, stinging, parasitic, blood-sucking, poisonous insects are ruled by Scorpio, Mars and Pluto. ♏♂♇.

Insidious Tissue Changes: The gradual and secret causing of harm/ disease in tissue, not usually discovered until well advanced. Link soft tissue [insidious changes]. ♋ ☽ [♆].

Insomnia: (See Caffeine Induced Sleeplessness). Inability to sleep. There are many causes such as stress, illness, pain, medication and neurological problems. An irregular sleep schedule such as staying active through the night and sleeping mainly in the day can upset the circadian sleep cycle, causing insomnia. A too busy mind and life style is another cause. So is a deeply disturbed emotional life: anxiety, depression, panic attacks, and a hypervigilant 'fight-flight' reaction that wakes up its owner during the night at the least disturbance. This latter can be shown by malefics linking into the rulers of sleep, or being located on an angle in the chart (especially the Ascendant or IC).

Sleep is ruled by Neptune (ruler of the astral plane to which consciousness goes when we sleep), and the Moon (ruler of 'night time'). Link sleep [to hyper-alert]. Spx. ☽ ♆, 12H [♂ ♅].

(1) Audie Murphy (20 Jun 1924, 19:00, Kingston, TX). The decorated American soldier of WWII, may have had PTSD. He suffered from chronic insomnia. ♆ ☍ ☽ [☽ ☌ ♂].

(2) Franz Kafka (3 Jul 1883, 07:00, Prague, Czech). This Austrian novelist was mentally hyperactive, a chronic worrier, which contributed to his problem. ☽ [□ ♅]. ♆ [☌ ♂].

Instinct: This is an innate, fixed pattern of behaviour in animals (including in the human animal body), in response to certain stimuli. The animal brain and instinctual reactions, are largely located in the solar plexus chakra, [1] co-ruled by Mars and Cancer-Moon. The fight-flight system is an integral part of instinct. Spx. R3, ☽ ♂.

Insulin: A hormone produced in the pancreas that regulates glucose in the blood. ♎ ♀.

Integumentary system: Skin and its appendages that act as a physical barrier protection for the body. Base. ♑ ♄.

Intelligence: This is an evolving faculty: the capacity for abstraction, logic, understanding, self-awareness and learning from experience (across lives). The throat [2] and ajna chakras develop intelligence. "The presiding Intelligence, the Self, is seated on the throne between the eyebrows." [3] Ajna. Thr. ♊ ☿ ♀.

Intercostal Muscles: The muscles that fill the space between the ribs. ♂.

Intestines, Large: Also known as the large bowel and the colon. A long, continuous tube running from the end of the small intestine to the anus. The large intestine absorbs water and salts. It forms and stores faeces, then excretes it via the anus. Specifically ruled by Scorpio, Mars and Pluto. Because Virgo rules the small intestine - and Mercury the moving of substances through the body; they corule the bowels. Thr. Spx. ♏♂♇ (♍ ☿).

Intestines, Small: Also known as the small bowel. A long, continuous tube that runs from the stomach to the beginning of the large intestine. It digests food and absorbs nutrients. Virgo and Mercury rule the small intestines, and Mercury governs the process of moving the digested mass (chyme) through the tube. Thr. Spx. ♍ ☿.

1 Bailey, Alice: Esoteric Psychology II, 434.
2 Bailey, Alice: The Externalisation of the Hierarchy, 92.
3 Bailey, Alice: Treatise on White Magic, 206.

- Intestinal Pain/ Cramps: Pain from inside the abdomen dues to intestinal cramps. Spx. ♋ ☽ / ♍ ☿ [♂].

Intoxicant: An intoxicating substance. [♓ ♆].

Intoxicated: Drunk or under the influence of drugs. [♓ ♆].

Introverted: Shy, quiet, inwards-looking person. ♄ .

Intuition or Pure Reason (Buddhi): Intuition is defined as: "Literally the synthetic and immediate grasp of the truth as it essentially exists.. perfect insight." [1]

The intuition is an expression of Ray 2 of Love and Wisdom. [2] It is governed by the head chakra, [3] and by Mercury, which is called "the star of intuition." [4] ☿ .

Invalid: Someone who is sick. [♄].

Iodine: Trace mineral that makes thyroid hormones. ♉ ♀ .

- Iodine Deficiency - see Cretinism, Goitre, Hypothyroidism.

Ions - see Atoms.

Iris: The coloured tissue at the front of the eye. The iris changes how dilated the pupil is. ♈ ☉ .

Iron: An essential mineral for blood production - for the manufacture of haemoglobin. It is essential for transferring oxygen in the blood from the lungs to the tissues. ♂ .

Irregular: Not regular. [♅].

Irritable Bowel Syndrome (IBS): Pain, diarrhoea, wind and constipation in the large intestine. Medically, the cause is not known. Alternatively, it is considered a manifestation of emotional unhappiness, pain, irritation and of not being able to rid oneself of those feelings. Crudely put, 'holding onto one's shit.' Link large intestines [diarrhoea, pain, irritation]. ♏ ♂ ♇ (♍ ☿) [♂ ♅].

(1) Cybil Shepherd (18 Feb 1950, 19:52, Memphis, TN). In 2004, she revealed that she had secretly suffered from IBS for more than 20 years. ♄ ♍ 12,℞ [mp ♂ ♆/♇].

(2) Tyra Banks (4 Dec 1973, 19:13, Inglewood, CA). In 2006, the USA model revealed she had IBS. ☿ ♏ r12H [♐ ♂ ♈].

Irritation: Inflammation or other discomfort in a body part caused by reaction to an irritant. Spx. Thr [♂ ☉].

Ischium: Bone of the pelvis that forms the lower and back part of the hip bone. Base. ♐ ♃ .

Islets of Langerhans: Endocrine glands in the pancreas, which secrete *insulin* and *glucagon* into the blood to control blood sugar levels. Spx. ♎ ♀ (♋ ☽).

Itch: Irritating sensation in the upper surface of the skin. [♂].

---

1   Bailey, Alice: Esoteric Psychology I, 134.
2   Bailey, Alice: Esoteric Psychology I, 134.
3   Bailey, Alice: The Externalisation of the Hierarchy, 92.
4   Bailey, Alice: Treatise of Cosmic Fire, 370.

J

Jaundice: Bilirubin in the blood causes yellow discolouration of the skin. It is usually a symptom of liver disease. Chronic jaundice is often caused by alcohol abuse (♆♂). Link liver [alcohol abuse]. Spx. ♃ (♋☽) [♆♂].

(1) Eduard Eyth (2 Jul 1809, 06:30, Heilbronn, Ger). A German poet who "died of jaundice". ♃♈ [☍♂, ⚼♆].

(2) Friedrich, Archduke of Austria (14 May 1821, 03:30, Vienna, Austria), died from jaundice. ♃♈12 [☌♄, ♄☌♂♈ - ♂△♆]. ♃ rules the 8H.

(3) Henri Matisse (31 Dec 1869, 20:00, Le Cateau, Fr). A damaged liver and jaundice left him bedridden for long periods of time. Matisse (☉), was an alcoholic [□♆], which led to chronic liver damage ☉ [□♆ > △♃℞,☌♇♉].

Jaws, Mandibles: Bony framework of the mouth, containing the teeth. Some astrologers place the upper jaw under Aries, the lower jaw under Taurus. Thr. ♈♉.

Jejunum: In the small intestine - absorbs sugars, amino acids, and fatty acids. Spx. ♍☿.

Joints: Part of the body where two or more bones meet to allow movement. Base. ♑♄.

- Joint Inflammation, Pain: Inflammation in joints, causing pain. Base. ♑♄ [♂☉].

Jugular Veins: Major blood vessels in the neck that stretch from the head to the upper chest. Hrt. ♉♀

JUPITER. ♃.

Signs it rules: Jupiter is the exoteric ruler of Sagittarius and Pisces, the esoteric ruler of Aquarius, and it is the hierarchy ruler of Virgo.

Houses it rules: The 9H and 12H.

Rays: Jupiter's personal force is the 2nd ray of Love and Wisdom, the energy of the soul or consciousness. It also carries rays 4, 5 and 6 via its signs Sagittarius and Pisces. Jupiter's force expands, builds, preserves life and restores health.

Body: Governs the heart chakra in spiritually advanced people. Rules the arteries, arterial blood, the liver, the sciatic nerve, the hips, thighs, strength, movement and locomotion. It is the prime representative for growth and for the fusing of bones and tissue together.

Disease: When afflicted, Jupiter can represent trouble in the liver, or with locomotion via Sagittarius. As an afflictor, its building and growth function (ray 2) can go awry, leading to overeating, obesity, extra body parts and unhealthy growths - tumours, cancer, etc. It can also loosen muscles that need to be firm.

Psychology: Carries the expansive 2nd ray, which develops consciousness, expanding it so that it becomes inclusive, wise and group oriented. When misused we see amorality, exaggeration, gluttony, greed, materialism, excessive pleasure seeking and wastefulness.

K

Karmic Diseases: Karma is the law of cause and effect, and Saturn is the Lord of Karma. Everything is causal. The natal chart is karmic. It contains seeds planted in a previous life that require balancing and healing in the present. This is why babies can have debilitating diseases - the causal roots lie in a past life. Some karmic seeds are retributive, others bring rewards. All is determined by our past actions. [♄].

Keloid: A raised scar after an injury has healed. Base. ♄ ♃ .

Keratitis: Inflammation of the cornea. Eye redness, pain and blurred or decreased vision are symptoms. Link cornea [infection]. Ajna. ♈ ☉ ☽ [♂ ♅].

Keystone of the Endocrine System: This is the thyroid gland, [1] it locks the system together. Taurus and Venus govern the thyroid, and Saturn is the ruler of the throat chakra that anchors in the thyroid. (See the Endocrine System). Thr. ♉ ♀ ♄ .

Kidneys: The waste-disposal system of the body, filtering toxins from the blood and producing urine. Base. ♎ ♀ .

- Kidney Disease - see Nephritis.

- Kidney Failure - see Uraemia.

- Kidney Filtering - see Nephrons.

- Kidney Stones: Hard objects, made up of millions of tiny crystals. Can cause acute pain when passed. Link kidneys [stone/ mineral]. Base. ♎ ♀ [♄ ♅].
(1) Jeraldine Saunders (3 Sep 1923, 12:15, Los Angeles, CA). ♀ ♍ [♂ ♅. ♅ ⚹ ♄ ♎].
(2) Lyndon B Johnson (27 Aug 1908, 05:40 Stonewall, TX). ♀ ♋ [♂ ♅ ♑].

Kill: To deprive of life. [♏ ♂ ♇].

Knees, Knee Joints: Joint where the bones of the lower and upper legs meet. Base. ♑ ♄ .

- Knee problems: They are various. Link knees [and cause]. ♑ ♄ [malefics].
(1) Betty Dion (28 Sep 1919, 17:36, Columbia City, IN). Born with a knee dislocation (♅). She had 15 surgeries to deal with a deteriorating joint. ♄6 [♂ ♅12].
(2) Pearl Bailey (29 Mar 1918, 07:20, Newport News, VA). In 1990, an arthritic knee was replaced with a metal and plastic joint. ♄ arthritic knee [♂ ♇ false joint].

Knife Injury, Knifed: Injured by a knife thrust. Link self, body [knife]. ☉, Asc, 1H [♂].
(1) Johny Stompanato (19 Oct 1925, 17:00, Woodstock, IL). Lover of actress Lana Turner, stabbed to death by her teenage daughter. Asc ♈ [♂ ♎6, □ ♇4]. Killed at home (4H).

Kundalini: The fire of matter, of the physical body, located in the base chakra. [2] Kundalini (latent) is represented by Mars, kundalini in intelligent expression by Mercury. Base. [3] ♂ ☿ .

---

1 Bailey, Alice: The Soul and its Mechanism, 46.
2 Bailey, Alice: The Soul and its Mechanism, 106.
3 Bailey, Alice: Treatise of Cosmic Fire, 181.

L

Labia: Inner/ outer folds of the vulva, either side of the vagina. Sac. ♏ ♀ .

Labyrinthitis: An infection that inflames inner ear nerves. Link ears, nerves [infection / inflammation]. Ajna. ♊ ☿ (♀ ≈ ♅) [♂ ♅ ♆, ♂ ☉].
(1) Rachel Goswell (16 May 1971, 04:00, Fareham, Eng). English singer-songwriter from the 1980s. She became partially deaf because of labyrinthitis (a viral infection) which occurred in 2006. ☿ ♈ 1 [□ ♂ ≈].

Laceration: A deep cut or tear in skin or flesh. [♂].

Lachrymal Apparatus: Makes tears. ♋ ☽ .

Lactation: Producing/ releasing milk from the mammary glands in the breasts. Spx. ♋ ☽ .

Lacteal: This is a lymphatic capillary located in the intestines, which absorbs dietary fats. Spx. ♍ ☿ .

Lame: Unable to walk easily, the result of an injury or illness affecting the hip, leg or foot. Link hip, leg, foot/ mobility [the cause > lame]. ♐ ♃ ,≈ ♓/ ♐ ♃ [cause > ♄].
(1) Mark Akenside (20 Nov 1721, 20:00, Newcastle upon Tyne, Eng). He was left lame from a wound he received as a child, from his butcher father's cleaver. ♂ muscle [qd ♅ lower leg injury > ⚹ ♄].
(2) Sir Walter Scott (15 Aug 1771, no time). The Scottish novelist, poet and historian, survived a childhood bout of polio in 1773, ☿ [♂ ♆], which left him lame: ♃ ♑ ℞ [⚹ ♄].

Large Intestine - see Intestines, Large.

Larynx, Voice Box: Area of the throat containing the vocal cords, used for breathing, swallowing and talking. Thr. ♉ ♀ (♊ ☿).

- Laryngeal Cancer: Forms in the tissues of the larynx. Link the larynx [and the cancer formula]. Thr. ♉ ♀, ♊ ☿ [(♋ ☽ > ♄ ♆) > ♃ ☉].
(1) Astro.com 4145 (6 Apr 1904, 01:32, Gueret, Fr). ♀ [Tsq: (□ ☽ ♐ 12 > □ ♇)].
(2) Dexter Gordon (27 Feb 1923, 11:00, Los Angeles, CA). ♀ ♑ [(☍ ☽ > □ ♄) > ⚹ ♃ 6].
(3) Katherine Boehrer (25 Sep 1923, 08:27, Waco, TX). ♀ 12 [(☍ ☽ > □ ♇ ♋) ♂ ☉].

- Laryngitis: Inflammation of the larynx from overuse, irritation or infection. Untreated it can lead to severe breathing problems and even death. Link larynx [inflamed/ hoarse]. Thr. ♉ ♀ (♊ ☿)[♂ ☉/ ♄].
(1) George Washington (22 Feb 1732, 10:00, Pope's Creek, VA). The great American statesman died of a larynx-related illness. ♀ r6H [△ ♂ ♏, ♂ ♄ ♈ 12].

Lassitude: Tiredness, weakness, lack of interest in daily activities. Thr. Spx [♄].

Lead: Chemical element/ heavy metal, found in the environment that can be dangerous for health. [♄].

- Lead Poisoning: Acute poisoning due to absorbing lead. It attacks the brain and central nervous system, causing coma, convulsions, even death. Lead-based paints were a problem in the 90s. Link brain or/ and nervous system [and lead]. ♈♂, ♋☽/ ♊☿ [♑♄].
(1) Heinrich Heine (13 Dec 1797, 15:20, Dusseldorf, Ger). In 1997, an analysis of the poet's hair revealed that he had suffered from chronic lead poisoning. ♃♈ [□♄♋ r8H].

Learning: Acquiring knowledge/ skills through study, experience, learning. Thr. ♊☿.

- Learning Difficulties: Problems with reading, writing and/or maths. Thr. ♊☿ [♄].

Legionnaires' Disease: A serious form of pneumonia (lung infection). The infection inflames air sacs in the lungs, which can fill with fluid and pus. It is caused by a bacterium commonly found in potting mix, and can be spread through air-conditioned buildings. Link lungs [bacterial infection > fluid/ pus]. Thr. ♊☿ [♂♅♆ > ♋☽♆].
(1) Bonnie Paulley (11 Mar 1930, 04:30, Bonneville, WY). ☿♓ [☌♂♒ > ☍♆♍℞].
(2) Ross Burden (16 Dec 1968, no time). He was being treated for leukaemia, but died from Legionnaires' disease caught from the hospital's infected water supply. ☿ [□♅ > ∠☽♏; > □♇ for his death].

Legs: Limbs used for supporting the body and walking. The legs for mobility, are generally ruled by Sagittarius and Jupiter. Base. ♐♃.

LEO. ♌.

Rulers: The exoteric ruler is the Sun, the esoteric ruler is the Sun unveiling Neptune, the hierarchy ruler is the Sun unveiling Uranus. As spiritual development occurs, the Sun unveils the higher forces of Neptune and Uranus, which can then flow through consciousness.

Rays: Carries R1 of Will and Power, R5 of Concrete Mind; and R2 via the Sun. Its energy is fiery, intensely hot, concentrated, and carries power.

Body: Leo governs the heart chakra and the life stream (sutratma, which anchors in the heart). Leo and the Sun represent the heart, the life and vitalisation of the body via the cardiovascular system, and the vitality and effectiveness of the immune system. They also govern the spinal column and vertebrae.

Disease: When planets are afflicted in Leo, or when Leo rules the 6H, it indicates trouble with the heart and cardiovascular system, which it rules with its opposite sign Aquarius. Because the heart organ is central to physical plane life, its diseases are dangerously life threatening. Being hard-hearted can cause hardening of the heart; being weak-hearted can cause heart failure. As an afflictor, Leo burns and inflames.

Psychology: Leo's evolutionary task is to produce a fully self-conscious, intelligent and integrated personality. A person who is fully aware of his/ her individual and independent self and destiny. Then later, enable the purified personality to identify consciously with the soul. Hence Leo's higher keynote: 'I am That, and That am I.' ♌☉

Leprosy: An infection caused by a slow-growing bacteria that affects mainly the nerves and skin. Link the skin / nerves [and bacterial infection]. Ajna. Base. ♑♄ (♋☽) / ♊☿ (♀♒♅) [♅♂♆].
These cases are from Max Heindel's, Astro-Diagnosis.
(1) P301-4. (11 Sep 1885, 01:00, Calcutta, India). ♄♋12 [□♅].
(2) P305-7. (19 Mar 1896, 19:50, Calcutta, India). ♄ [☌♅♏].
(3) Father Damien (3 Jan 1840, 12:30, Ninde, Belgium) ☿☌♄ [□♅♓12].

Lesion: Abnormal tissue that can be benign or cancerous. Link tissue and [abnormal/ or insidious]. ♋ ☽ [♅, ♆].

Lethargy: (See Narcolepsy). A lack of energy and enthusiasm. ☉ ♂, Asc [♄ ♆ ♓].
(1) Astro.com 12077 (29 Jan 1952, 15:30, Santa Monica, CA). Born into a narcoleptic family, he was narcoleptic and lethargic. ☉ [∠ ☽ ♓]. Asc [□ ♄ ♆].

Leucoma/ Leukoma: A scarring and clouding of the cornea due to trauma, inflammation or an ulcer. The cornea loses its transparency, its ability to transmit light. If the trouble is large and central, it can cause blindness. Link vision [scarring/ loss of sight]. Ajna. ☉ ☽ [♄ ♇].
(1) Jean-Paul Sartre (21 Jun 1905, 18:45, Paris, Fr). He had a leucoma in his right eye, which reportedly he developed due to influenza, at age four. ☉ [☌ ♇ r12H].

Leukaemia: Cancer in the blood and bone marrow, caused by the rapid production of abnormal white blood cells.

> Many children get the disease. Whenever children are involved with life-threatening diseases, it is important to remember that esoteric astrology is founded on the fundamental laws of reincarnation and karma - viewing karma in its energy-balancing function and not as an agent of retribution. In each new incarnation we bring through patterns from the past to be healed. Cancer involves the suppression of emotion and this pattern will be found in the charts of children who develop the disease - see the chart for Robin Bush.

Link blood/ bone marrow [cancer formula]. Hrt. ♂ ♃ ♒/ ♋ ☽ [(♋ ☽ > ♄ ♇) > ♃ ☉].
(1) Janette Moore (3 Jul 1963, 13:05, Melbourne, Australia). Australian scientist diagnosed with acute leukaemia. Moore subsequently had a successful bone marrow transplant to improve chance of remission. ♄ ♒ [(□ ☽ ♏) > ⚹ ♃ 6].
(2) Joan Blondell (30 Aug 1906, 19:55, Manhattan, NY). The American actress died of leukaemia. ☽ ♑ [(∠ ♄ ♓ 12) > ♄ ☍ ☉ 6].
(3) Jose Carreras (5 Dec 1946, 04:00, Barcelona, Spain). Spanish operatic tenor. In 1987, at the height of his career, he was diagnosed with acute leukaemia. Given a '1 in 10' chance of survival, he fought for recovery and then resumed his career. ♂ for blood and emotions [(⚼ ♄ ♌) ♄ □ ♃].
(4) Robin Bush (20 Dec 1949, 07:25, Los Angeles, CA). Robin was the daughter of a famous family - George and Barbara Bush. She died at age 3 from leukaemia. ☽ ♑ / ☍ ♅ ♋ 6 [(∠ ♇ 8) > ♅ ☍ ☉ 12].

Lewy Body Dementia: A form of dementia (see Dementia). Lewy body targets problem-solving and reasoning function. Planets for the intelligence (☿ ♀), for consciousness (☉), and hallucination (♅ ♆), may connect in. Link the brain [to aging, atrophy]. Cwn. ♈ ♂, ☽ ♋ [♄ ♇].
(1) Adlai Stevenson III, 10 Oct 1930, 17:13, Chicago, IL). American politician who died from complications of Lewy body dementia, in 2021 at age 90. ♅ ♈ 12 [□ ♄, □ ♇ ♋].
(2) Robin Williams (21 Jul 1951, 13:34, Chicago, IL). The multitalented actor developed this form of dementia. In 2014, he killed himself - allegedly to avoid its ravages. ♃ ♈ 6 [qd ♄, □ ♅ ♋].

Libido: In psychology, libido refers to sexual desire, or the emotion and mental energy related to sex. Another term for it is "sex drive.". Sac. ♏ ♂ ♀.

LIBRA. ♎.

Rulers: The exoteric ruler is Venus, the esoteric ruler is Uranus, the hierarchy ruler is Saturn.

Rays: Carries R3 of Intelligence; R5 via Venus, and R7 via Uranus. Energy is mental, airy and fast-moving.

Body: Libra governs the belt area of the body, close to where the solar plexus enters. It supports the work of the solar plexus, sacral and base chakras, and is related to the ajna (via Venus), from where homeostasis (the balancing function of the body) is managed. Balancing and regulating the body's processes comes under its jurisdiction. Such as glucose balancing via the pancreas gland and Islets of Langerhans; and balancing water/ blood/ acid levels via the adrenals, kidneys, the urinary tract and bladder. Libra is related also to relationships and sex.

Disease: When planets are afflicted in Libra, or when Libra rules the 6H, it indicates trouble with the kidneys. Libra can also represent head problems, which are governed by its opposite sign Aries. As an afflictor, Libra diseases are adaptive, infectious, acute and may strike suddenly - like cystitis. It indicates imbalance - problems like vertigo.

Psychology: The evolutionary goal in Libra is to find psychological and spiritual balance. Its higher keynote is, 'I choose the way which lies between the two great lines of force.'

LIFE, Life Principle, Life Stream: The stream of dynamic life (1st aspect), is seated in the heart and controls the mechanism through the medium of the blood stream. [1]

> This life principle controls the mechanism through the blood stream, for 'the blood is the life,' and uses the heart as its central organ. [2]

A smaller stream of the universal energy - prana, distinctive from the individualised life force, is taken into the body via the breath and spleen, where it rises into the heart to join the life-stream. The latter energises and holds in coherency the physical body. Prana vitalises the atoms and cells of which that body is composed. [3]

> The ascendant is a representative of life, of a new incarnation and can represent 'the self'. Hrt. ♌ ☉, Asc.

- Life Breath: The breathing/ oxygenation process that carries life/ vitality/ prana from the Sun into the lungs. Thr. Hrt. ☉ > ☿ .

- Life Thread and Life Stream: The Life Thread is the medium or vessel that carries the stream of life into the body. Synonyms for the thread are Sutratma, Silver Cord and Thread Soul. [4], [5]. This thread and the stream of life it carries, originates from our highest spiritual aspect - the spiritual spark or Monad. The thread anchors in the heart, and from there the life-force animates every part of the physical body. Hrt. ☉.

> The life thread comes directly from the monad or the ONE. This thread is anchored in the heart during incarnation. There is the seat of life. [6]

> From the heart, the life-stream uses the blood stream and arteries to animate every part of the organism. [7]

1   Bailey, Alice: Education in the New Age, 18.
2   Bailey, Alice: Education in the New Age, 18.
3   Bailey, Alice: Esoteric Healing, 428-429.
4   Bailey, Alice: Education in the New Age, 32.
5   Bailey, Alice: Treatise on White Magic, 495.
6   Bailey, Alice: Education in the New Age, 146.
7   Bailey, Alice: From Intellect to Intuition, 54.

Ligaments: Tough, flexible fibrous tissue connecting two bones or cartilages or holding together a joint. Base. ♑ ♄.

Light: Electromagnetic radiation that can be detected by the human eye. Ray 2 is the "light-carrier." [1] ☉.

Lightning Strike - see Electric Shock.

Limbic System - see Triune Brain.

Limits: Puts restrictions on. [♄].

Limping: (See Lame). Favouring one leg. Link mobility/ legs [limping]. Base. ♐ ♃ [♄].

Lipids: Fatty acids or their derivatives such as natural oils, waxes steroids. ♃.

Lipoedema: Mainly affects women. Painful swelling in the legs, thighs, buttocks, arms because of the abnormal accumulation of fat under the skin. [♐ ♃/ ♓ ♆ for swelling].
(1) Kirstie Alley (12 Jan 1951, no time). Her legs were disproportionate in appearance when compared to the rest of her body. ♃ ♓ swelling thighs, buttocks [⚳ ♆].

Lips: Two fleshy parts forming the upper/ lower edges of the mouth opening. Ruled generally by Taurus, some astrologers allocate the top lip to Aries. Thr. ♈/☍ ♀.

Lisp: A speech defect. Thr. ♊ ☿ [♅ ♄].

Listless: Lacking energy or enthusiasm. Thr. Spx. [♄].

Liver: Large organ in the upper abdomen that cleanses the blood and aids digestion by secreting bile. The liver is generally ruled by Jupiter. Cancer and the Moon are the overall rulers of digestion so could substitute for Jupiter. Spx. ♃ (♋ ☽).

- Liver Cancer: The disease attacking the liver. Link the liver [to the cancer formula]. Spx. ♐ ♃ [(♋ ☽ > ♄ ♇) > ♃ ☉].
These three men died from liver cancer. Jupiter can double up for both the liver and cell overbuilding.
(1) Allen Ginsberg (3 Jun 1926, 02:00, Newark, NJ). He was an American poet and writer. ♃12 [(Tsq. ☍ ♆6 > □ ♄ ♏8)].
(2) Lou Reed (2 Mar 1942, 10:00, Brooklyn, NY). American musician, songwriter, and poet. ♃ ♊ r12, r8H [♇ mp ♃/♆♍6].
(3) Richard Cromwell (8 Jan 1910, 07:00, Los Angeles, CA). American actor who worked with Bette Davis and Henry Ford. ♃ r12H [(G.cross □ ♆ ♋ > ☍ ♄) □ ☉].

- Liver Cirrhosis: Scar tissue replaces healthy liver tissue, impairing blood flow. Alcohol abuse is the most common cause. Link liver > blood flow [and scarring]. Spx. ♐ ♃ [♑ ♄].
(1) Florence Aadland (20 Sep 1914, 23:50, Salt Lake City, UT). She was an alcoholic (♂ □ ♆ ♋), and died from the disease. ♃8℞ > ☌ ♅ ♒ [⚻ Asc, Asc ☌ ♇ ♄ 12].
(2) Larry Hagman (21 Sep 1931, 16:20, Fort Worth, TX). A drinker for many years, in 1992 he was diagnosed with cirrhosis of the liver. He had a successful liver transplant. ♃ > ☍ Asc ♒ [♃ ⚻ ♄ ♑12].

Lockjaw - see Tetanus.

Locomotion - see Movement.

---

1 Bailey, Alice: Esoteric Psychology II, 359.

Locomotor System/ the Musculoskeletal System: Consists of the skeleton, skeletal muscles, ligaments, tendons, joints, cartilage and connective tissue. They work together to allow the body to move. Base. ♐♃ (movement), ♑♄ (the body structure), ♂ (muscles).

- Locomotor Ataxia: Inability to precisely control one's body movements. Usually results from damage to the cerebellum that controls muscle coordination. Link nerves > mobility [the cause / difficulty]. Ajna. ♊☿ (♀♒♅) > ♐♃ [the cause/ difficulty].
(1) Edouard Manet (23 Jan 1832, 19:00, Paris, Fr). During the second part of the French artist's life, he contracted syphilis (♇♈8). This caused brain damage and the onset of locomotor ataxia. ☿ > ∠♃♒6 [☿□♇♈8 syphilis destruction of brain cells].

Looseness, Loosens: Loss of tone in muscles. Jupiter stretches, frees, loosens. Venus is related to a prolapse, the Moon and Neptune weaken. [☽♆(♀)].

Loss of Consciousness: Become unconscious. Link consciousness/ awareness [and lack of]. Cwn. Ajna. ☉☿ [♄♇].

Lou Gehrig's Disease - see ALS.

Low Blood Pressure - see Blood Pressure Low/ Hypotension.

LSD: A psychedelic drug. [♆].

Lumbago: Pain in the lower back, a region generally ruled by Libra. Link the lower back [and pain]. Base. ♎♀ [♂].

Lumbar vertebrae: Consists of five bones in the lower back - L1 to L5, in the Libra region. They are the largest vertebrae in the spine. Base. ♎♀.

Lunacy - see Insanity, Madness.

Lungs: Respiration organs that supply the body with oxygen and remove carbon dioxide. The lungs are the agents of spirit, because they bring into the physical body via the breath, 'the life aspect.' The bronchi are vitalised by the throat chakra, the lungs themselves by the heart chakra. [1] ♊☿, (☉) for the heart chakra rulership.

- Lung Cancer: Link the lungs [cancer formula]. Thr. Hrt. ♊☿ [(♋☽ >♄♇) > ♃☉].
These three died from lung cancer.
(1) Alain Corneau (7 Aug 1943, 02:15, Orleans, Fr). A French film director. ♅♊12 [☉♃♇ mp ♅/☽].
(2) Andy Kaufman (17 Jan 1949, 18:03, Jamaica, NY). ☿ [(☌♂6 > ☍♇) > ♇⚻♃6].
(3) Anthony Burgess (25 Feb 1917, 12pm, Manchester, Eng). British novelist who wrote Clockwork Orange. ☿ coruler 12H [(♃ mp ☿/♇♋12)].

- Lung Congestion: Mucous build up in the passages of the lungs. Link lungs [mucous]. Thr. Hrt. ♊☿ [♋☽].

- Lung Infection - see Pneumonia.

Lupus: A rogue immune system attacks anywhere in the body with a consequent loss of body function. Symptoms can include fatigue, joint pain, rash and fever that periodically flares up. In the section for Autoimmune Disease, we read:

> Underneath autoimmune disease is self-hatred, anger directed at oneself. Influenced by this negativity, the immune system attacks the body.

1 Bailey, Alice: Esoteric Healing, 602.

Examine Mars for rage, anger and an immune attack. Link the body part affected [immune attack > and impairment]. Hrt. Spx. Body part [♂☉ > ♄♇].

(1) Selena Gomez (22 Jul 1992, 07:19, Grand Prairie, TX. American actress who had a public and tumultuous relationship with pop-star Justin Bieber. In a 2007 Instagram post she wrote, "I needed a kidney transplant due to my lupus." Kidneys [immune attack > impairment]. ♀☌Asc [♂♉ > ☍♄ r6H].

Lyme Disease: A form of arthritis caused by bacteria transmitted by a tick-bite. Saturn rules both joints and arthritis so it can double up for both. Link joints [ticks > arthritis]. Base. ♑♄ [♏♂♇ > ♄].

(1) Avril Lavigne, 27 Sep 1984, 07:55, Belleville, Ontario). ♄♏ [in a ♏ stellium with ♇].

(2) Debbie Gibson (31 Aug 1970, 02:57, Brooklyn, NY). ♄ coruler 6H [□♂].

(3) Henri Fantin-Latour (14 Jan 1836, 15:00, Grenoble, Fr). Died from Lyme disease. ♄♏ r8H [☉♑8 mp ♄/♇].

Lymphatic System (Lymph and Lymph Nodes): The lymphatic is part of the immune system, containing a network of vessels through which lymph fluid flows. This fluid contains immune lymphocyte cells to fight pathogens, and chyle to assist digestion. Within the network are lymph nodes (small clumps of tissue) that are mainly in the neck, armpit, and groin area. They clean lymph as it moves through them, filtering out viruses, bacteria and fungi that can cause illness. Thr. ♓♆ (♋☽).

- Lymphoma: Cancer that starts in the lymphocytes, the white blood cells in the lymphatic system. There are two main types of lymphoma: Hodgkin lymphoma and non-Hodgkin lymphoma; but the astrology is the same in both, and in all types of lymphoma.

The key to finding all patterns related to the disease cancer is to look for emotional repression first and build the pattern around that. This is simplified with this disease since the rulers of the lymphatic system also rule the emotions. This is a clue that the trigger for this disease is feeling deeply deprived of emotional nurturing, and a sense of being unable to do anything about it. Link the lymphatic system [and the cancer formula]. Thr. Spx. ♓♆, ♋☽(♋☽ >♄♇) > ♃☉].

(1)Non-Hodgkin's. Frances McEvoy (11 May 1929, 04:05, Phoenix, AZ). American professional astrologer. ♆♌ r12H [(∠♇♋) > □♃1].

(2) Non-Hodgkin's. Jackie Onassis (28 Jul 1929, 14:30, Southampton, NY). The chart of the American First Lady also shows repression of anger, which had a very unhealthy effect on her life and her body. It killed her. ☽♈ [(□♇♋8) > ∠♃♊].

(3) Hodgkin's. Delta Goodrem (9 Nov 1984, 00:36, Sydney, Australia). The chart of the Australian songstress shows repression of anger. ♆ [(⚼☽ > ☍♄) ☽△♃♑6].

(4) Hodgkin's. Richard Harris (1 Oct 1930, 11:20, Limerick, Ire). The English actor had deep and unresolved emotional issues, which led directly to the manifestation of lymphoma and his death. ☽♑ [(☍♇♂♋8) > ♇☌♃♋].

(5) Lymphoma. Ray Katt (9 May 1927, 07:00, New Braunfels, TX). The American professional baseball player had the same aspect as Harris (♂♇♋), indicating he also suffered from intense rage and anger. Additionally, his Sun is in the 12H, indicating a very private person who does not like to show his feelings. ☽♆ [(□♄6) > ⚻♃♓].

M

Macular: Part of the retina at the back of the eye. It is made up of densely packed light-sensitive cells that allow for clear central vision. Ajna. ☉ (☿ ♅).

- Macular, Dry Degeneration: The cause may be a combination of family genes and environmental. Blurred vision develops as the eye ages. Link vision [and dryness]. Ajna. ☉ ☽ [♄].

(1) Bunny Mellon (9 Aug 1910, 02:00, Manhattan, NY). ☉♌ [♇12, mp ☉/♄].

(2) Dabney Coleman (3 Jan 1932, 09:40, Austin, TX). ☉♑ [disposited by ♄].

- Macular, Wet Degeneration: Blurred vision or a blind spot in central vision usually caused by blood vessels that leak fluid or blood into the macula. Link vision [and wetness/ blood]. Ajna. ☉ ☽ [♋♆/ ♂♃♒].

(1) Collen McCullough (1 Jun 1937, 19:30, Wellington, Australia). She was diagnosed with haemorrhagic macular degeneration in 2004. ☉☌6H cusp [□♆♍/ qd ♂℞].

(2) Judi Dench (9 Dec 1934, no time). ☉ [□♆].

Magnesium: Supports muscle and nerve function, and energy production. ♒♌.

Malaise: Indefinite feeling of debility or lack of health. Thr. Spx [♄].

Malaria: (See Poison - Animal Kingdom). A disease caused by a parasite, which is normally spread by infected mosquitoes. These parasites grow inside red blood cells and destroy them. Link blood [parasites / destroy]. Hrt. ♂♃♒ [♏♂♇].

(1) Lord Byron (22 Jan 1788, 14:00, London, Eng). He died of a feverish sickness that doctors concluded was "a virulent form of malaria and remorseless bleeding." ♀♒ r12H [☌♇ r6H].

Malformation: An abnormally formed part of the body. [♅].

Malnutrition: Lack of proper nutrition due to a lack of food, or eating poor quality foods. Link food/ nutrition [with lack of, poor]. Spx. ♋☽ / ♍☿ 6H [♄ (♇)].

(1) Jean Marais (11 Dec 1913, 12:30, Cherbourg, Fr). In 1998, he was hospitalized with malnutrition, dying a few months later. ☽ [♄ mp ☽/♇♋ r8H].

(2) Mario Capecchi (6 Oct 1937, 09:30, Verona, Italy). Italian-born Nobel Prize winner suffered severe malnutrition as a child. ☽♏12 [□♇♋]; ☿♍ [☍♄4].

(3) Salvador Dali (11 May 1904, 08:45, Figueras, Spain). In 1984, he thought he could not swallow and suffered from severe malnutrition. ☽ coruler 12 [∠♄]; ☿ r12H [□♄].

Mammary Glands: The breasts. Glandular organs located on the chest. In females, their primary function is to secrete milk for infants. Spx. ♋☽.

Mandible - see Jaws.

Manganese: Trace mineral that helps the body form connective tissue, bones. ♑♄.

Manic Depression - see Bipolar.

Manipulation, Manipulative Therapy: Involves a practitioner using his/ her hands to manipulate a body to encourage natural healing. ☿.

Manipulative: Exerting a controlling influence over a person or situation for selfish gain. Manipulation is a negative activity of ray 3, carried by Saturn. Alternatively, Mercury, the ruler of the 3rd sign Gemini, is the great trickster. R3. Thr. [♄ ☿].

MARS. ♂.

Signs it rules: Mars is the exoteric ruler of Aries and Scorpio, the esoteric ruler of Scorpio, and the hierarchy ruler of Sagittarius.

Houses it rules: the 1H and the 8H.

Ray: Mars' personal force is the 6th ray of Idealism and Devotion. This is the force of the emotional/ astral plane, which when there is little discrimination, deludes and glamourises. Mars also carries R1 of Will and Power (via Aries); and R4 of War and Conflict (via Scorpio).

Body: Via Aries, Mars governs the brain, face and skull. On its own Mars governs: the solar plexus (emotional) and sacral (sex) chakras, the sympathetic nervous system, the fight-flight instinct, the adrenals and adrenaline.

> Mars function is the protection of the body from external attack and its basic survival when threatened. [1]

Mars represents kundalini fire (the fire of matter) that warms the physical body from the base chakra. It rules and controls the muscled, blood filled, sexual, animal, physical form; the blood, haemoglobin, energy, vitalisation, purification, sex, reproduction and excretion.

> Mars vitalises, purifies and stimulates all aspects and organisms in the body, via the blood stream. [2]

Disease: When afflicted: Mars can represent problems with muscles, the adrenals, with a lack of energy, with the blood, with the sex and elimination organs. As the afflictor, it represents hot diseases - fever, inflammation, autoimmune attacks, ulcerated conditions, skin eruptions and the poisoning of the blood (through toxic emotions). It represents surgery.

Psychology: The negative effect of the 6th Ray via Mars, is aggression, anger, hate, fanaticism, self-deception, cruelty, violence, rampant and uncontrolled desire. In contrast, some higher qualities are heroism, courage, spiritual idealism and aspiration.

Masochism: Deriving sexual gratification from one's own pain/ humiliation. [♏♂♇].

Massacre: Indiscriminate/ brutal slaughter of many people. [♏♂♇].

Mastitis: Inflammation, pain, swelling and redness of breast tissue that may be an infection. It commonly affects breast-feeding women. Link breasts [infection > inflammation]. Spx. ♋☽ [♂♅♆ > ♂☉].

These breast-feeding women had mastitis. Because birth times are unknown, the Moon's positions are approximate. Positions given here are for 12 noon.

(1) Chelsea Houska DeBoer (29 Aug 1991, no time). ☽♈ [⚻♂6].

(2) Meghan King Edmonds (26 Sep 1984, no time). ☽ [∠♅♐].

(3) Nicole 'Snooki' Polizzi (23 Nov 1987, no time). ☽♑ [☌♅♐].

Mastoid Bone: Part of the temporal bone of the skull. Full of air cells, it protects delicate structures of the ear and the temporal bone during trauma. Cwn. Base. ♉♀.

1 Jansky, Robert: Modern Medical Astrology, 6.

2 Bailey, Alice: Esoteric Astrology, 211.

- **Mastoiditis:** A serious bacterial infection in the mastoid bone, which fills with pus. Link the mastoid [infection/ pus]. Cwn. Base. ♉ ♀ [♂ ♅ ♆/ ♋ ☽].
(1) Princess Margaret of Sweden (15 Jan 1882, 15:10, Bagshot, Eng). Died from a mastoid infection. ♀ [qd ♂ 12℞ / ∠ ☽]. ♀ disposits 4 planets in Taurus, including ♄ r8H.
(2) Male, Astro-Diagnosis, Heindel, p187. (8 May 1865, 13:45, no location), had an operation for mastoiditis. 4 planets in Taurus, including Venus. ♀ ♉ ℞ [⚹ ♂ ♋6/ ♂ □ ☽].

Masturbation: Stimulating one's genitals to achieve an orgasm. Sac. ♏ ♂.

Maternal: Relating to a caring mother. Spx. ♋ ☽.

Maternity: Period during pregnancy and shortly after childbirth. Sac. Spx. ♋ ☽.

Measles: A viral infection that infects the airways, then spreads through the body. It causes a fever and a red, blotchy rash. Vaccines have largely eliminated its effects in the West. Untreated, it is dangerous for children and can kill. Because it can affect different parts of the body, planets representing the organs vary. Link airways/ life/ the body [and infection]. ♊ ☿ / ☉ Asc/ ☽ ,1H [♂ ♆ ♅].
These examples (from Carter's, Encyclopaedia of Psychological Astrology), died.
(1) Page 124-1 (20 Aug 1876, 18:39, London, Eng). ☉ ♌ [☌ ♂ ♅ > died ♅ □ ♇].
(2) Page 124-2 (28 Sep 1919, 07:00, Bristol, Eng). ☉ ♎ [∠ ♂ ♌ r8H died].
(3) Page 124-3 (14 Feb 1883, 13:30, Carlisle, Eng). ☉ ♒ [disposited by ♅ r8H died].
(4) Page 124-4 (19 Dec 1869, 07:35, Sunderland, Eng). ☉1 coruler 8H [☌ ♄ died > ♄ ⚻ ♅].

Medical Profession: Is the practice, diagnosis, treatment and prevention of diseases. The 6H governs all things to do with medicine, health and healing. ♍ ☿, 6H.

- **Medical Science:** The scientific foundation that the practice of medicine is built on. ♄ for conservative medicine, ♅ for modern, scientific medicine. ♍ ☿, 6H > ♄ ♅.

- **Medical Treatment, Alternative:** Noninvasive, alternative style modalities such as naturopathy, homeopathy, acupuncture. ♍ ☿, 6H > ♅.

- **Medical Treatment, Mainstream:** Application of medicine by professionals credited by government; to diagnose, treat, injury and disease. ♍ ☿, 6H > ♄.

- **Medicine:** A drug/ preparation for the treatment or prevention of disease. ♍ ♄ ♆, 6H.

Medulla Oblongata: It is a part of the brainstem, connecting the brain to the spinal cord. That makes it an important transit hub between the brain and nervous system. It also regulates important automatic functions. Cwn. Thr. ♊ ☿.

Megalomania: Obsession with the exercise of power. This is a trait of the 1st ray of Will and Power, which is carried by Pluto, Aries, Leo and Capricorn directly, and by Saturn via Capricorn. Venus or Uranus may link in for narcissism. Link the self [extreme lower will]. R1. Base. ☉, Asc [♌, ♇ (♄ ♅)].
(1) Jim Jones (13 May 1931, 22:00, Lynn, IN). He was the leader of the People's Temple Church in America, and ordered the mass murder of his followers in Guyana, when authorities began investigating his criminal activity. His psychological and astrological profiles fit the megalomania type. Asc ♑ [♄1 ☍ ♇; ♇ □ ♀ ♈].

Melancholy: A feeling of pensive sadness. Link emotions [melancholy]. Spx. ♋ ☽ ♆ [♄].

Melanoma - see Skin Cancer.

Melatonin: A pineal gland hormone secreted in association with the sleep-wake circadian cycle. ♎ (♆♇).

Membranes: Body membranes are thin sheets of tissue. There two main membrane categories. (i) Epithelial membranes (mucous, serous, synovial), that secrete mucous or fluid to protect the body. (ii) Connective tissue (ligaments, tendons, cartilage, and parts of bone) that bind the various parts of the body together, protecting and supporting.

Generally, connective or calcified tissue (bone, tooth enamel) are ruled by Capricorn; softer moist tissue by Cancer. Since these signs are polar-opposites, they can substitute for each other. Base. ♑ ♄ (♋ ☽).

Memory: A mental ability to encode, store, and retrieve information - a Gemini, Mercury function. Studies in 2016-2017 reveal that short term memories are formed in the hippocampus and other related structures in the temporal lobe. Long-term memories are stored in the brain's cortex. Damage or disease to these regions of the brain (as happens with dementia) impairs memory. Thr. ♊ ☿.

Men: Adult or mature male human beings. ☉, 10H.

Meniere's Disease: An abnormal build-up of fluid in the inner ear causing vertigo. Link ears [fluid > imbalance]. Ajna. Thr. ♊ ☿ [♋ ☽ ,♓ ♆ > ♎ ♅].
(1) Adrienne Monnier (26 Apr 1892, 02:00, Paris, Fr). ☿ ℞ [☌ ☽ ♈/♎ r6H].
(2) Dana White (28 Jul 1969, 15:02, Manchester, CT). ☿ [♅♎ mp ☿/♆].
(3) Les Paul (9 Jun 1915, 02:00, Waukesha, WI). ☿ ♋ r6H [☽ □ ♅ ♒].

Meninges: Connective membranes that cover the brain and spinal cord, and that secrete fluid to aid in their protection. Cwn. Base. ♋ ☽.

- **Meningitis**: Infection that causes inflammation in the meninges. Mars rules the brain, infection and inflammation so may double up in its representation. Link meninges [infection > inflammation]. Cwn. ♈ ♂, ♋ ☽ [♆ ♂ ♅/ ♂ ☉].
(1) Alexander Eben (11 Dec 1953, 02:42, Charlotte, NC). ☽ [△♂coruler 6H > ♂ ☌ ♆].
(2) Jerry Lewis (16 Mar 1926, 12:15, Newark, NJ). ☽ coruler 12H [□ ♂].
(3) Oscar Wilde (16 Oct 1854, 03:00, Dublin, Ire). ☽ [□ ♅ ♉ r6H].

Menopause: Ending of menstruation. Link menstruation [cease]. Sac. ♏♂ (♋ ☽) [♄ ♇].

Menstruation, Menstrual Cycle: Regular discharge of blood/ tissue from the inner lining of the uterus. Sac. ♏♂ (♋ ☽).

- **Menorrhagia**: Abnormally heavy, painful menstrual bleeding. Link uterus / menstruation [pain / heavy (bleeding)]. Sac. ♋ ☽ / ♏♂ (♋ ☽) [♂/ ♇ ♄].
(1) Chloe Dalton (11 Jul 1933, no time). The Australian Olympiad shared on social media, she had this painful disorder. ☽ ♈ [⚻♂, ⚼♇].

Mental Body/ Concrete Mind/ Lower Mind: The mind is the machine that builds thought-forms/ mind-pictures, when we think. It holds within itself "all knowledge and memory." [1] Lower mind expresses through the throat chakra, higher mind through the ajna and heart chakras. [2] Thr. ♊ ☿.

- **Mental Asylum, Psychiatric Hospital:** Custodial, mental health care. ♓♆, 12H.

1 Bailey, Alice: The Rays and the Initiations, 460,
2 Bailey, Alice: Esoteric Healing, 45.

- Mental Illness, Mental Instability: A wide range of conditions that affect mood, thinking and behaviour. Until the mind has been developed and stabilised, all thoughts are filtered through an emotional nature tinged with fear, insecurity, defensiveness, personal biases and prejudices. If there also happens to be a lack of common sense and for example - great stress, social isolation, or mental or physical abuse, in hyper-emotional people this could lead to mental imbalance and problems. Link the self/ mind/ emotions [with a planet that indicates the type of illness or instability]. The 12th house may be prominent. Thr. Spx. ☉/ ♊ ☿/ ♋ ☽ ♂ [malefic].

- Mental Retardation Severe, Imbecility: There are two primary causes. (i) Brain tissue/ structural problems such as dementia or hydrocephalus. (ii) The consciousness thread from soul to the brain, has become disconnected, leaving only an animal consciousness present. Thr. ♊ ☿ [♑ ♄].

> Those gaps in the relation of the physical body to the subtle bodies which show as imbecilities and psychological troubles. [1]

- Mental Rigidity: Rigid, partisan thinking. Thr. ♊ ☿ [♑ ♄].

MERCURY ☿ .

Signs it rules: Mercury is the exoteric ruler of Gemini and Virgo, the esoteric ruler of Aries, and it is the hierarchy ruler of Scorpio.

Houses it rules: the 3H and 6H.

Rays: Mercury's personal force is the 4th ray of Harmony through Conflict. It also carries R2 of Wisdom and R6 of Idealism via its signs Gemini and Virgo.

Body: Mercury governs the following. The ajna and throat chakras, is a backup ruler for the pituitary gland and is related to the thymus. All nerves; sound, speech, hearing; the shoulders, arms, hands and fingers. Respiration, the airways, oxygenation of the blood, the bronchial tree, upper lungs and the intestines. All tubes in the body through which information or matter is transported. It is also a back-up ruler for movement/ mobility.

Disease: Mercury afflicted, indicates potential trouble primarily with the nervous system and communication. As the afflictor, it can indicate wrong connections in the body, misdirected or wrong messaging, and the rapid spread of germs through the air to cause an epidemic.

Psychology: Mercury is always related to cognition, intelligence and communication. Negative traits are duality, flightiness, instability, worry, agitation, agonising and inner suffering. But Mercury is the ruler of the mind at all levels - lower mind, higher mind and of the intuition. Here are two powerful quotes:

> Mercury, the Messenger of the Gods is the agent of the third aspect (active intelligence), and of the second aspect (love-wisdom).. the expression of the concrete and the abstract mind of God. Mercury is the synthesis of manas-buddhi, mind-wisdom which expresses itself through the human soul. [2]

> Mercury, the star of the intuition. [3]

Metabolism: The process where nutrients mix with oxygen to make energy. The thyroid gland is the controller of the metabolism of energy, [4] which is why trouble in that gland seems to quickly upset energy levels. Thr. ♉ ♀ > ♂ .

1   Bailey, Alice: Esoteric Healing, 302.
2   Bailey, Alice: Esoteric Astrology, 281.
3   Bailey, Alice: Treatise of Cosmic Fire, 370.
4   Bailey, Alice: The Soul and its Mechanism, 46.

Metacarpal Bones: Tubular bones from the wrist to the first knuckle in the fingers/ thumb. Thr. ♊ ☿.

Metastases: The development of secondary malignant growths at a distance from the primary site of cancer. Significators can be Jupiter and the Sun. Neptune and Pisces, which can expand or seep through defined boundaries, are sometimes involved. [♓♃ ♆].

Metatarsal Bones: The bones of the forefoot. Base. ♓♆.

Microbes, Micro-organisms: Microscopic cellular organisms. Trillions of microbes live in and on the body, helping to digest food and protect against infection. There are also microbes (bacteria, viruses), injurious to health. ♇.

Middle Ear Balance Problems: (See Meniere's Disease, Vertigo). An infection of the middle ear that upsets balance. ♊ ☿ [♂ ♅ ♆].

Migraine: Severe headache in cranial nerves, throbbing pain, often accompanied by nausea and sensitivity to light and sound. The cause is unknown. Esoterically, trouble between the ajna and pituitary glands can cause migraine, along with eye and nerve troubles. Of the ray forces, the 5th ray via the ajna, carried mainly by Venus and Aquarius, is involved.

> Emerging as a result of this fifth ray force is migraine, caused by a lack of relationship between the energy around the pineal gland and the pituitary body. [1]

Based on this quote, hypothetically, the psychological cause of migraine is chronic mental detachment and isolation, which has a negative effect on brain function. Link nerves [cleavage > pain]. Ajna. ♊ ☿ [♀ ♒ ♅ > ♂].

These ladies suffered from migraine.

(1) Charlotte Bronte (21 Apr 1816, 14:41, Thornton, Eng). ☿ ♈ [♄ ♒6 is mp ☿/♆]. ♆ increases nerve sensitivity.

(2) Lisa Kudrow (30 jul 1963, 04:37, Encino, CA). ☿ [☍ ♄ ♒; ☿ mp ♂/ Asc].

(3) Loretta Lynn (14 Apr 1932, 16:00, Van Lear, KY). ☿ ♈ ℞ [☌ ♅ ♈ > ☌ ♂ ♈].

Milk: Breast milk used to nourish infants. Spx. ♋ ☽.

Mind - see Mental Body.

Minerals: Crystalline structures. The mineral kingdom is governed by the 7th ray, [2] which is carried by Uranus. The 1st ray is also related to this kingdom. [3] ♄ ♅.

- Mineral Poisoning: (See Poisons, Toxins - Mineral Kingdom). Being poisoned by a mineral substance. [♄ ♅].

Miracle Healing: This is healing which seems to defy the laws of nature. ♍ ♅.

Miscarriage: Expulsion of a foetus from the womb before it can survive independently. Often there are afflictions to the 5H of children, or to Cancer and the Moon, which represent childbearing. Saturn may link in for denial of children. 'Expulsion' can be represented by Mars, Uranus or Pluto. Link foetus [expulsion]. Sac. ♋ ☽ ,5H [♂ ♅ ♇].

(1) Sophia Loren (20 Sep 1934, 14:10, Rome, Italy). The actor miscarried several times before finally bearing two children. ☽ [☍ ♂]. ♇ ♋ [□ ♅ ♉/♏]. ♀ r5H [∠♇].

Misdiagnosis: Wrong diagnosis for a health condition. [♆].

---

1 Bailey, Alice: Esoteric Healing, 302.
2 Bailey, Alice: Esoteric Psychology I, 369.
3 Bailey, Alice: Esoteric Psychology I, 44. Bailey, Alice: Esoteric Astrology, 386.

Modern Medicine: Latest medical science, discoveries, technologies. ♍♂ > ♅.

Molecules - see Atoms.

Moles: Noncancerous growths on the skin. Link skin [growth]. Base. ♑♄ (♋☽) [♃].

Monad: The spiritual Spark, the God aspect in our nature which anchors in the pineal gland. The life thread comes directly from the monad and anchors in the heart. [1] Cwn. ☉♅.

Mononucleosis - see Epstein Barr Virus.

Moods, Mood Swings: Emotions that go up and down. Energy oscillations are innate to the 4th ray, carried by the Moon and Mercury. The Moon rules moods; and an unstable emotional body lies behind the swings. Spx. ♋☽ [♅].
(1) Kelly Osbourne (27 Oct 1984, 20:00 London, Eng). ☽6 [♂♅].

MOON. ☽.
Signs it rules: The Moon is the exoteric ruler of Cancer, the esoteric ruler of Virgo (veiling Vulcan), and the hierarchy ruler of Aquarius (veiling Uranus). The Moon rules the form. On the spiritual path as we refine the nature - the veiling effect of substance/ of the Moon, is removed, and the higher energies of Vulcan and Uranus shine through consciousness.
House it rules: the 4H.
Rays: The Moon's personal force is the 4th ray of Harmony through Conflict. It also carries R3 of Intelligence and R7 of Ceremony-Order-Magic via Cancer.
Body: The Moon is related to the solar plexus chakra and digestion via Cancer. The Moon is the "Mother of the form" [2] and is a general ruler of the physical body - and of flesh, tissue, body fluids, body cycles (including the cycling of energy through the etheric web), secretions, mucous, the lymphatic system and peristalsis, women, female cycles, reproduction, female reproduction organs (ovaries and uterus), and motherhood.
Disease: When afflicted, in the body, the Moon indicates trouble mainly with digestive organs, reproduction - and in the charts of women, trouble with female cycles. As the afflictor, it represents excess damp and water, toxic thick liquids such as pus, excess mucous or phlegm that causes coughing and interferes with airways.
Psychology: The Moon in the chart represents where emotional conflict will play out, both internally and with the environment. The Moon sign represents the 'prison of the soul' pattern - a negative core-belief residing in the unconscious that interferes with rational conscious behaviour. This pattern needs to be transmuted, healed and balanced.

Mortality: The state of being subject to death. ♄♇, 8H.

Mother: Nurture a child/ children. Spx. ♋☽, 4H.

Motor Nerves: Sends motor signals from the central nervous system to the muscles of the body. Ajna. ♊☿ (♀≈♅) > ♂.

Motor Neurone Disease - see Amyotrophic Lateral Sclerosis, ALS.

Mould: Growth of fungus on damp or decaying material. [♋☽,♓♆].

Mouth: The opening in the head, through which food and liquid is ingested. Thr. ♉♀.

Movement: Body movement, especially involving the hips, thighs, legs - governed by Sagittarius and Jupiter. Gemini and Mercury rule upper body movement. ♐♃.

1   Bailey, Alice: Education in the New Age, 146.
2   Bailey, Alice: Esoteric Astrology, 399.

Mucous: Slimy substance secreted by mucous glands for lubrication, protection. ♋ ☽ (♓ ♆).

- Mucous, Thick, Excessive: (See Cystic Fibrosis). This can be caused by an infection. Link mucous [and excessive]. ♋ ☽ [♃].

Multiple Personalities/ Split-Personalities/ Obsession: This is now known as Dissociative Identity Disorder (see that section). However, esoterically, they are different conditions.

Type 1. The ownership of a physical body by two or more persons. Occurs mainly with females who are emotionally powerful, weak intellectually, and who have a great dislike for physical incarnation. They are born with a weak connection between the etheric web and physical body. Obsession can occur in the following ways. The etheric web stretches, permitting entry by an entity from the emotional plane. Or, the consciousness thread from soul to brain becomes disconnected and is picked up by an entity. This enables that entity to express itself via the nerves and communication apparatus. To observers, it appears as a different personality. A less common occurrence is due to wrong meditation, which renders the self completely negative and open to invasion.

Type 2: Men are more prone, those who are weak mentally, but powerful physically and emotionally. When asleep and in the emotional body, an entity invades the physical body, preventing reentry by the rightful owner.

Sometimes, with wise assistance, and an effort to become positively grounded, ownership can be re-established. Otherwise, only a new incarnation will bring relief. Link the consciousness thread [and foreign entity]. ♊ ☿ [♏ ♂ ♇].

Last century, these two American women were diagnosed with multiple personality disorder.

(1) Chris Costner Sizemore (4 Apr 1927, 15:00, Colliers, SC). Her life story and situation were made famous in the movie, The Three Faces of Eve. ☿ ♓ [□ ♂ ♊].

(2) Shirley Ardell Mason (25 Jan 1923, 03:00 Dodge Center, MN). Her sessions with her psychiatrist gave rise to the 1973 book, and the 1976 movie, Sybil. ☿ ℞ [⚻ ♇ ♋ 8].

Multiple Sclerosis: (See Autoimmune Disease). The immune system attacks the central nervous system. It destroys the protective covering (myelin sheath) of nerve cells, then the nerves. This causes a loss of body control. Sagittarius and Jupiter for 'movement' may link in. Link the nervous system [immune attack > and loss]. ♊ ☿ (♀ ♒ ♅) [♂ ☉ > ♄ ♇].

(1) Annette Funicello (22 Oct 1942, 20:10, Utica, NY). ♅ ♊ [☌ ♄ ♊ 12].

(2) Jacqueline du Pre (26 Jan 1945, 11:30, Oxford, Eng). ☿ ♑ coruler 6H [☌ ♂ ♑ > both disposited by ♄ ♋].

(3) Mary Whitehouse (4 Oct 1911, 15:00, Montclair, NJ). ☿ [□ ♇ ♊].

Mumps: Swelling of the parotid/ salivary glands, caused by a virus. Link parotid glands [and virus]. Jupiter may link in for swelling. Thr. ♉ ♀ [♂ ♅ ♆].

(1) Vincent Astor (15 Nov 1891, 03:30, New York, NY). A bout with mumps (♉), left him sterile (♏). ☽ ♉ [⚻ ♂ ♎ coruler 6H]. ♀ [☍ ♆ > □ ♃ ♓ 5]. He was denied children - ♅ ♏ r5H, disposited by ♇ 8.

Murder: Unlawful premeditated killing of one human being by another. Link life [and murder]. ☉, Asc [♏ ♂ ♇].

These two ladies were murdered by the Manson Family.

(1) Abigail Folger (11 Aug 1943, 17:27, San Francisco, CA). ☉ 8 [□ ♂].

(2) Sharon Tate (24 Jan 1943, 17:47, Dallas, TX). ☉ [☍ ♇ 1].

Muscles: Convert stored energy to heat, to energy, and into motion (kinetic energy). ♂.

- Muscle Wasting, Weakness: Shrinking/ loss of muscle tone caused by a disease or lack of use. Link muscle [and wasting]. ♂ [♄ ♆].

- Muscular Dystrophy: Genetic disease that causes progressive weakness and loss of muscle mass. Link genetic > muscle [wasting]. ♒♅ > ♂ [♄ ♆].

(1) Dick Tinkham (24 Jun 1932, 08:25. Hammond, IN). Tinkham died from muscular dystrophy at age 86. ♂ [♆♍].

(2) Ralph Braun (18 Dec 1940, 05:00, Winamac, IN). Was diagnosed at age 6 and started using a wheelchair at 14. He lived until 2013. ♂12 [♆♍ mp ♂/♇].

(3) Rona Barrett (8 Oct 1936, 04:15, New York, NY). Had the disease as a child, but lived an active life, surviving into seniorhood. ♂12 [wide ☌♆♍12]

Mutation: The action or process of mutating. [♅].

Myasthenia Gravis: A rogue immune system attacks nerves that communicate with the muscles, so they weaken. Link nerves > muscles [immune attack > weaken]. Ajna. ♊ ☿ (♀♒♅) > ♂ [♂☉ > ♓♆☽].

(1) Giuliana Pavarotti (9 Jan 1967, 01:55, Modena, Italy). Was diagnosed with myasthenia gravis at age 17. ☿♑ [□♂♎12 > ∠♆].

Myelitis: Inflammation of the spinal cord. Link spinal cord [inflame]. Ajna. ♊ ☿ [♂☉].

(1) Juventino Rosas (25 Jan 1868, 02:00, Ixtlahuacan, MX). Celebrated Mexican composer and violinist. He contracted myelitis and died while on tour in Cuba. ☿♒ [☌☉♂]. ♂ rules the 12H and ☿ the 8H.

Myeloma: This disease is a type of bone marrow cancer. Link bone marrow [and the cancer formula]. Base. ♋☽ [(♋☽ >♄♇) > ♃☉].

(1) Sam Walton (29 Mar 1918, 21:00, Kingfisher, OK), the founder of WalMart died from multiple myeloma. ☽♏12 [(□♄). ☽ Yod: ⚻♃8, ⚻☉5].

Myocardium: The middle muscular layer of the heart wall. Hrt. ♌☉ > ♂.

- Myocardial Infarction - see Heart Attack.

- Myocarditis: Inflammation of the middle layer of the heart wall. It can be caused by a viral infection or an autoimmune attack. Link the heart [and inflammation]. Hrt. ♌☉ [♂☉].

(1) Norman Chaney (18 Oct 1914, 15:45, Cambridge, MD). The American child actor died from myocarditis at age 21. ☉♎ [□♆♌].

Myopia: Nearsightedness. Near objects appear clear, objects farther away blurry. Happens if the eyeball grows too long from front to back, or problems with the cornea or lens. Link vision [short-sighted / blurry]. Ajna. ☉☽ [♄/♆].

(1) August Muller (4 Mar 1864, 23:00, Monchengladbach, Ger). A German ophthalmologist whose pioneering work in the manufacture of contact lenses led him to be able to correct his own severe myopia. ☉♓ [⚻♄].

Mystical Vision: (See Delusion, Guidance, Stigmata). The process of visioning the many symbols that veil the soul. The mystical approach is the right way for many, provided it does not extend to hallucination and fanaticism. ♓♆.

Myxedema - see Hypothyroidism.

N

Nails: Tough covering protecting the upper end of each finger and toe. Base. ♑ ♄.

Narcissism: Excessive admiration of oneself and one's physical appearance. Ajna. [♀ ♅].

Narcolepsy: Overwhelming daytime drowsiness, sudden attacks of sleep. Psychologically, a powerful emotional nature that likes to daydream, a lack of interest in life, and a consciousness thread that unplugs suddenly because of the consequent weak grasp on life. Link the self / the consciousness thread [emotional, weak grasp]. Ajna. ☉ Asc / ☿ [☽ ♓ ♆].
Narcolepsy could run in families. These three examples are related.
(1) Astro.com 4811 (28 Nov 1913, 07:30, Conway, KS). ☉ Asc [☌ ☽ ⚼ ♆].
(2) Astro.com 7296 (20 Aug 1933, 04:30, Los Angeles, CA). Asc > ☌ ☿ [Asc ☌ ☽ 1].
(3) Astro.com 12077 (29 Jan 1952, 15:30, Santa Monica, CA). Asc ♋ [☍ ☿ , △ ☽ ♓].

Narcotics: Drugs/ substances consumed to pleasure the mood. [♓ ♆].

Nasal, Nasal Cavity: Relating to the nose. Ajna. ♈ ♂ ♏.

- **Nasal Congestion:** Nasal passages become swollen with excess fluid and mucous. Link nasal [congested > mucous]. Ajna. ♈ ♂ ♏ [♄ > ♋ ☽].

- **Nasal Septum**: The cartilage and bone in the nose that divides the nasal cavity into a right and left side. Ajna. ♈ ♂ ♏ > ♄.

Naturopathy: A system of alternative medicine. ♍ ☿ > ♅.

Nausea: A queasy sensation including an urge to vomit. Spx [♋ ☽].

Nearsightedness - see Myopia.

Neck: Body part between the head and the shoulders. Thr. ♉ ♀.

- **Neck, Stiff**: Can be caused by muscle and ligament issues, injuries or arthritis, or having a 'stiff-neck' attitude. Link neck [stiff]. ♉ ♀ [♄].

Necrophilia: Sex with corpses. Link sex [dead, corpse]. ♏ ♂ ♇ [♄ ♇,8H > ♄ ♇ (☽)].
(1) Astro.com 39667 (17 Sep 1970, 02:00, Bellville, Sth. Africa). Serial killer who had sex with dead boys. ♅ r8H [⚼ ♄ ♉/♏]. ♇ [qd ☽].
(2) Ted Bundy (24 Nov 1946, 22:35, Burlington, VA). ♇12 [☌ ♄]. ♂ coruler 8H [☌ ☽].

Necrosis: (See Gangrene). Death of cells through disease or injury. Bone - and skin necrosis (gangrene), are the common types. The Sun and Moon are related to cell life and may be involved. Link bones/ skin - or the organ affected [and death]. ♑ ♄ [♏ ♇].
(1) Vertus Hardiman (9 Mar 1922, 02:20, Montgomery, IN). In 1928, he was "treated" with radiation in an experiment. It led to life-long health issues, and severe progressive bone necrosis. Asc □ ♄ [□ ♇ ♋].

Negative Core Beliefs: (See the Moon - Psychology). These are unresolved emotional hurts from past lives - triggered again in childhood; residing in the unconscious. [☽ sign].

Neocortex - see Triune Brain Theory.

Nephritis, Bright's Disease, Kidney Disease: Inflamed kidneys impair filtering, resulting in high levels of waste in the blood. Rulers for blood may link in. Link kidneys > filtering [inflamed/ impaired]. Base. ♎♀ > ♓♆♃ (♋☽) [♂☉/ malefics].

These four examples are from Heinrich Daath's, Medical Astrology.

(1) HD p92. (17 Apr 1878, 12:35, Suffolk, Eng). ♀♓8 [□♂/ qd ♅♌1 coruler 6H].

(2) HD p93-2. (9 Aug 1836, no time). ♀♋ [□♄♎ > ♄□♆♒].

(3) HD p93-3. (4 Jan 1884, 13:15). ♀♒ r6H > ∠☽♓ [♀☍♃♌].

(4) HD p93-4. 25 Oct 1833, 7:45, Hematite, MI). ♀♎ r12H > ☍☽♓ [♀☌♄♎].

Nephrons: Filtering units in the kidneys - about a million in each one. They filter the blood, return needed substances to the blood, and remove waste. ♎♀.

NEPTUNE. ♆.

Signs it rules: It is the exoteric ruler of Pisces, and the esoteric and hierarchy ruler of Cancer.

House it rules: the 12H.

Rays: Neptune's personal force is the 6th ray of Idealism and Devotion. This is the force of the emotional-astral plane, which at its lowest deludes and glamourises. At its highest Neptune is a representative of the Heart of the Sun, the heart of God.

Body: Neptune shares rulership of the solar plexus chakra, influencing the digestive organs. It corules body secretions, liquids and the circular fluid highways (bloodstream and lymphatic). Neptune is also related to the life aspect that is carried in the blood and which vitalises the body. Via Pisces, it governs the feet and toes. Additionally, Neptune is related to sleep - consciousness slips onto the astral plane at night.

Disease: When afflicted, Neptune can represent trouble with waterway circulation, such as the bloodstream and the lymphatic system. Also, with neurodegenerative diseases such as dementia and Alzheimer's, which are due to brain fluid atrophy.

As the afflictor, Neptune weakens, dilutes, subtly undermines, it twists and distorts, makes insidious and barely detectable, unhealthy changes. It represents diseases that are hard to detect or to diagnose. It can represent carcinogenicity - the ability or tendency to alter the genetic structure of healthy cells so they become cancerous. It is the primary representative of viruses, which are stealthy, insidious and debilitating. Viruses try to evade detection by the immune system so they can infect cells. When successful, they rapidly reproduce and spread through the bloodstream like a tidal wave swamping the body.

Psychology: Negative Neptune represents emotionalism, delusion, glamour, escapism and evil perversions. Positive Neptune represents the finer emotions such as sadness, sorrow, grief, hurt, anguish, anxiety, joy, hope, serenity, ecstasy, bliss, idealism and devotion. Esoterically, Neptune represents the attempts of the soul to render the emotional body more sensitive and to refine emotional expression.

NERVOUS SYSTEM (NS): It is the instrument of consciousness. [1] The consciousness thread extends from the soul and anchors in the centre of the head. From there consciousness controls the brain, and induces awareness through the body via the nervous system. [2] The 3rd ray creates and uses the nervous system, the brain, and the five senses. [3]

1 Bailey, Alice: Education in the New Age, 18.
2 Bailey, Alice: Education in the New Age, 92.
3 Bailey, Alice: Esoteric Psychology I, 251.

Gemini-Mercury are the prime rulers of nerves and are presented as the rulers in all sections for the nerves. Sub-rulers are Venus (because of its rulership of the ajna), Aquarius and Uranus. Any of these could substitute for Gemini or Mercury. ♊ ☿ (♀ ♒ ♅).

Below is a map of the Central Nervous System and associated nerve systems.

CNS: it is the central driving force of nerve sensitivity. ♊ ☿.

CNS > Peripheral NS: branches off from the spinal cord to all parts of the body. ♊ ☿.

CNS > Peripheral NS > Autonomic NS: regulates involuntary processes such as heart rate and respiration. ♊ ☿.

CNS > Peripheral NS > Autonomic NS > Sympathetic NS: activates the fight-flight response. ♊ ☿ > ♂.

CNS > Peripheral NS > Autonomic NS > Parasympathetic NS: restores the body to a state of calm. ♊ ☿.

CNS > Peripheral NS > Autonomic NS > Enteric NS: controls digestion. ♍ ☿.

- **Nerve Fluid:** Clear, colourless, watery fluid that flows in and around the brain and spinal cord. ♋ ☽.

- **Nerve Synapse:** The junction points for the transmission of electric nerve impulses between two nerve cells, or between a neuron and a muscle cell. Ajna. ♊ ☿, ♒ ♅.

- **Nervous Twitches, Tics, Spasms:** Compulsive and repetitive sounds and movements that may be difficult to control. Link nerves [twitches]. Ajna. Spx. ♊ ☿ (♀ ♒ ♅) > [♅].

- **Nervy**: Easily agitated or alarmed; nervous. Link nerves > emotions [unstable]. Spx. ♊ ☿ > ♋ ☽ ♂ [♂ ♅].

- **Neuralgia: Neuritis, Neuropathy:** Neuralgia is nerve pain. It is caused by either *neuritis* (inflammation, injury, infection - ♂ ♅ ♆); or *neuropathy* (damage, degeneration, nerve dysfunction - ♄ ♇). Link nerves [pain > and either neuritis / or neuropathy rulers]. Ajna. ♊ ☿ (♀ ♒ ♅) [♂ ♅ > ♂ ♅ ♆ / ♄ ♇].

These are neuritis examples.

(1) Ralph Nader (27 Feb 1934, 04:52, Winsted, CT). Nerve pain caused him to involuntarily shed tears so he took to wearing sunglasses. ☿ ℞ [☌ ♂ ♓].

(2) Rossetti D. G. (12 May 1828, 04:30, London, Eng). ☿ 12 r6H [□ ♅ ♒]. ♀ coruler of 6H and 12H [☍ ♂].

(3) Salman Khan (27 Dec 1965, 10:45, Indore, India). ☿ ♐ [□ ♅ r12H].

(4) Thea Von Harbou (27 Dec 1888, 10:30, Tauperlitz, Ger). ☿ [∠ ♂ ♒ 12].

- **Neurodegenerative Disease:** CNS cells stop working or die. It may be genetic, be caused by a tumour, a stroke, or aging and cell hardening. Examples are Alzheimer's, Ataxia, Huntington's Disease, Parkinson's Disease and Motor Neuron Disease. Link nerves [and degeneration]. Ajna. ♊ ☿ (♀ ♒ ♅) [♄ ♇].

- **Neurons**: Nerve cells. Ajna. ♅ ♒ (♊ ☿).

- **Neurotic, Neuroses:** Outdated term for mental, emotional, physical reactions that are drastic and irrational. Ajna. Spx. ♊ ☿, ☽ ♂ [♂ ♅].

- **Neurotransmitters:** A signalling molecule secreted by a neuron to affect another cell across a synapse. Ajna. ♅ ♒ (♊ ☿).

Nicotine: The chief active constituent of tobacco. [♓ ♆].

- **Nicotine/ Cigarette Addiction**. (See Triune Brain - Limbic System). Nicotine is the addictive substance in cigarettes. It stimulates the adrenals, which release adrenaline, giving good feelings. Addictions involve the Limbic System, the desire or emotional brain. Link the Limbic System [and nicotine addiction]. Thr. Spx. ♉ ♀ (♋ ☽ ♂) [♓♆].
(1) Leonard Bernstein (25 Aug 1918, 13:00, Lawrence, MA). He smoked several packs of cigarettes a day and died of a heart attack brought on by complications from lung cancer and emphysema. ♀ r6H [☌ ♆].

Nightmares: (See Dreams). When we sleep, consciousness withdraws into the astral body, onto the astral plane. The lower level of this plane is the dumping ground of all men's fears and traumas. Dark things exist there, including ancient racial evil. If the sleeping consciousness wanders down to this level for whatever reason, "nightmares", bad dreams, can be experienced. This level is related to "the underworld", ruled by Scorpio, Pluto and the 8H. So, people with any of these prominent in their nature/ in the chart; can be susceptible. If so, all psychic work, past-life retrieval work, should be avoided. This can open a channel to that level. Link sleep [and nightmares]. Spx. ♓♆ 12H, ☽ [♏♇ 8H].
(1) Arthur Conan Doyle (22 May 1859, 04:55, Edinburgh, Scot). ☽ [☍ ♄ r8H, □♇♉12].
(2) Barbara Rare (30 Jun 1944, 14:04, Gisborne, NZ). ♆ [□ 8H stellium]. [♇☌MC].
(3) Courtney Love (9 Jul 1964, 14:08, San Francisco, CA). ☽ [∠♇]. ♆♏ [⚻♂8].
(4) John Berryman (25 Oct 1914, 11:00, McAlester, OK). ☽ ♑ [☍♆8]. Asc [☍♇].

Nodules: A growth (Jupiter) of abnormal (Uranus) tissue. [♃ > ♅].

Noradrenaline: Adrenal medulla hormone that helps quick defensive reactions. ♏♂♇.

Nose: Face protuberance through which we breathe and smell. Ajna [1]. ♈ ♉ ♂ (♄).

- **Nose Broken.** Link nose/ bone [broken]. ♈ ♉ ♂ (♄) [♂ ♅].
(1) Joe Meredith (10 Apr 1938, 21:30, Mount Vernon, TX). ♈ ♄ [□♂].

- **Nosebleeds**: Bleeding from the nose. Ajna. [♈♂].

Nourishment: The food necessary for good growth and health. Spx. ♋ ☽.

Nucleus Accumbens: Part of the limbic system, related to motivation, reward and addiction. Thr. ♉ ♀.

Numb: Deprived of the power of physical sensation. [♄].

Nurture: Care for and protect someone/ something while they are growing. Spx. ♋ ☽.

Nut Allergy - see Peanut Allergy, Food Allergies.

Nutrition: The taking in and use of food and other nourishing material by the body. Spx. ♍ ☿, 6H; ♋ ☽.

1 Bailey, Alice: Esoteric Healing, 45.

O

Obese: Fatness. There may be genetic, behavioural, metabolic and hormonal influences, but obesity usually occurs when more calories are consumed that are burnt up. Comfort-eating is associated with emotional neediness and low self-esteem. Cancer and the Moon rule both food and the emotions. Link food/ emotions, desire [with excess]. Thr. Spx ♋ ☽/♂ ♉ [♃].

(1) Chris Farley (15 Feb 1964, 15:34, Madison WI). The American comedian was an obese child and adult. He loved lots of food. ☽ ♓ [♀ ♈ mp ☽/♃].

(2) Clarice Zion (16 Aug 1888, 11:00, London, Eng). With the inclusion of the 8H of sex, and 2H of values, it is possible that sexual abuse and consequent self-devaluing drove the circumstances that led to her obesity. ☽ ♐2 [disposited by ♃. ♃ ☍ ♆8].

(3) Theo Morrell (22 Jul 1886, 14:00, Munzenberg, Ger). Morrell loved eating and socialising with friends. ☽5, the house of pleasure [wide ☍ ♃ ♎11 house of friends].

Obscure Diseases: These are diseases that are hard to diagnose or find. [♓♆].

Obsession, Obsessed: (See Multiple Personalities). Fixated about someone or something. Consciousness being invaded by and taken over by a foreign entity. Spx ♊ ☿ [♏♇].

Obsessive Compulsive Disorder, OCD: Driven by a compelling emotion or desire to perform repeated rituals (R7-Uranus), in order to stave off an imagined disaster. Link the emotions [and compulsion]. Spx. ♋ ☽ ♂ [♏♂♇, 8H].

(1) Astro.com 37914 (26 Aug 1958, 14:30, Brighton, Australia). ☽ ♑1 [⚻ ☿ ☌ ♇8].

(2) Howie Mandel (29 Nov 1955, 10:00, Toronto, Ontario). ☽ [□♇8].

(3) Rafael Nadal (3 Jun 1986, 18:20, Manacor, Spain). The tennis great performed his rituals on court, in the full gaze of the public. ☽6 [☍♇♏12].

Obstetrics: Branch of medicine and surgery concerned with childbirth and midwifery. ♋ ☽.

Obstructs: Interferes with free movement/ development/ expression, flow. [♄♇/ ♃].

Occlusion: The blockage or closing of an opening, blood vessel, or hollow organ. [♄].

Odour: To stink, putrefy, have a strong or unpleasant smell. [♂(♆)].

Oedema: Build-up of fluid in the body causing swelling. Medicines and pregnancy can cause it, or a disease such as heart failure, kidney or liver disease. Link the organ affected [fluid > swell]. ♋ ☽, ♓♆ [♃ (♓♆)].

(1) Andrew Dezorzi (14 Feb 1956, 22:30, Sydney, Australia). ☽ ♓ [⚻♃].

(2) Ferdinand Hodler (14 Mar 1853, 05:00, Bern, Switzerland). The Swiss artist died from pulmonary oedema. ☿ ♈ unaspected [disposited by ♂ ♓ coruler 8H, ♂ ☌ ♆ ♓].

(3) Joelle (3 Feb 1953, 15:00, Westchester, NY). The American singer died of pulmonary oedema. ☿8 lungs [☌ ♂ ♓, ☍ ☽]. ♅ ♋12 r8H [⚹♃].

(4) Johny Weissmuller (2 Jun 1904, 18:00, Timisoara, Romania). The Tarzan movie star died from pulmonary oedema. ☿ r8H [∠♆♋8].

Oesophagus: The upper part of the alimentary canal. The tube that runs from the throat (Taurus) to the stomach (Cancer); through which food passes. Thr. Spx. ♉ ♋.

– **Oesophageal Ulcer** - see Peptic Ulcer.

Oestrogen: Sex hormone responsible for the development and regulation of the female reproductive system and secondary sex characteristics. Sac. ♋ ☽ , ♀ .

Ointment: Smooth oily substance that is rubbed on the skin for medicinal purposes. ♄ .

Old Age: The latter part of normal life. ♄ .

Olfactory Bulbs: (See Anosmia, Hyposmia). Rounded masses of tissue containing nerve cells that enable us to smell. There is one above each nasal cavity. They are considered part of the Limbic system. Thr. ♉ ♀ .

Olfactory Nerves: Connect the olfactory bulb to the brain. They enable the sense of smell. Ajna. Thr. ♉ ♀ > ♊ ☿ .

Oncologist: Medical practitioner qualified to diagnose and treat tumours. ♍ ☿ , 6H.

Online Scammers: Those who commit fraud by using the internet or modern social media. R3 [♊ ☿ ♅, ♆].

Operation: A surgical procedure. ♂ (♈♏).

Ophthalmology: Branch of medicine concerned with the study and treatment of disorders and diseases of the eye. Ajna. ♍ ☿ > ☉.

Opiates: Drugs relating to or containing opium that dull the senses. [♆].

- **Opiate Addiction**: Addicted to an opiate drug. Link emotions/ desire [to opiates]. Thr. Spx. ♋ ☽ , ♂ ♆, ♉ [♓♆].

(1) Brett Whiteley (7 Apr 1939, 06:10, Longueville). The Australian artist died from an opiate overdose. ☽ ♏8 [⚹♆♍6].

Optic Nerve: The nerve that carries messages from the retina to the brain. Ajna. ☿ ♅.

Optician: Person qualified to detect and treat eye diseases. ♍ ☿ .

Orchitis: Inflammation of a testicle. Sac. ♏♂ [♂ ☉].

Organ Transplant - see Transplant.

Orthopaedic: A branch of medicine that cares for the musculoskeletal system. Base. ♄ ♂.

Oscillation: Movement back and forth in a regular rhythm. This is the action of the 4th ray of agitation and conflict, which is carried by the Moon and Mercury. R4. ☽ ☿ .

Ossicle bones: Three tiny bones located within the middle ear. Ajna. ♊ ☿ .

Ossification: Bone formation. Base. ♑ ♄ .

Osteo: Relating to the bones. Base. ♑ ♄ .

- **Osteoarthritis** - see Arthritis.

- **Osteogenesis Imperfecta:** Brittle bone disease. An inherited (genetic) bone disorder, which causes multiple bone breaks - sometimes from the slightest pressure. Saturn rules both bones and brittle, and with Uranus, rules crystallisation. Saturn and Pluto carry R1 which 'hardens'. Mars for fractures, ♅ ♆ ♒ for genetic. Link genetic > bones [brittle > fractures]. Base. ♒ ♅ > ♑ ♄ [♄ > ♂ ♅].

(1) Michel Petrucciani (28 Dec 1962, 15:00, Orange, FR). French pianist and composer who was born with this disease. He suffered literally hundreds of bone fractures during his life. Aquarius, the 'universal' sign (with Mars), can indicate 'breaks everywhere'. ♄♒ [qd ♂℞ r12H, coruler 6H].

- **Osteomalacia**: Softening of the bones. Link bones [weaken]. Base. ♑♄ [♓♆, ☽].

(1) Maxime Lalanne (27 Nov 1827, 21:00, Bordeaux, Fr). Struggled 10 years with osteomalacia. ♄♋12 [☍♆♑6].

- **Osteomyelitis**: Inflammation of bone, and/ or bone marrow, usually due to an infection. Link bone/ bone-marrow [infection / inflammation]. Base. ♑♄/ ♋☽ [♂♅♆/ ♂☉)].

(1) Eduard Fraenkel (17 Mar 1888, 01:00, Berlin, Ger). At age ten, the German-British academic suffered from an attack of osteomyelitis in his right arm. It deformed his right hand. ♄♋ [□♂♎℞ r12H].

- **Osteopathy**: A branch of medicine concerned with the physical manipulation of the body's muscle tissue and bones. Base. ♍☿ > ♑♄♂.

- **Osteoporosis**: Bones become weak, brittle, due to a lack of calcium. Saturn rules both bones and calcium. Link bones [weak/ brittle > break]. Base. ♑♄ [♓♆ /♄ > ♂].

(1) Ann Richards (1 Sep 1933, 06:00, Lakeview, TX). ♄♒6 [⚻♆♍ > □♂].

(2) Carole Hemstreet (6 Jul 1938, 06:21, Los Angeles, CA). ♄♈ [⚻♆♍ > □♂♋12].

(3) Joseph Bernardini (2 Apr 1928, 02:00, Columbia, SC). ♄♐ [△♆ > ♆☍♂].

(4) Lois Rodden (22 May 1928, 00:27, Lang, Saskatchewan). ♄♐ [⚻♇☌☽♋ lack of calcium > ☽□♂♈].

Otosclerosis: Abnormal hardening of body tissue (sclerosis), in the ears (oto). The middle-ear bones cannot vibrate, which means sound is unable to travel through the ear and hearing is impaired. Link ears > tissue [hardening, loss]. Ajna. ♊☿ > ♋☽, ♑♄ [♄♇].

(1) Frankie Valli (3 May 1934, 09:00, Newark, NJ). Lead singer of the 1960s group, The Four Seasons. ☿ coruler 12H [☌♅ > ♅□♇♋1].

Ovaries: Female reproductive organ in which ova or eggs are produced. Sac. ♋☽.

- **Ovarian Cancer:** The Moon and Cancer rule both the emotions and ovaries. Investigate emotional repression as a psychological cause. Link the ovaries [and the cancer formula]. Sac. ♋☽ [(♋☽ >♄♇) > ♃☉].

These three ladies died from ovarian cancer.

(1) Alice Pearce (16 Oct 1917, 21:15, New York, NY). An American actress. ☽♏ [(□♆ > ☌♄) > ♄⚹♃].

(2) Patsy Ramsey (29 Dec 1956, 14:00, Parkersburg, WV). Mother of murdered child, JonBenet. With that horror happening, it is not surprising that she should develop trouble in a child-related organ. ☽ [(☌♄♐) > ♃ disposits ♄].

(3) Sandy Dennis (27 Apr 1937, 19:17, Hastings, NE). An American actress. ♇♋ representing repressed emotions and the diseased ovaries [☍♃♑].

- **Ovarian Cyst:** A cyst in the ovaries. Link the ovaries [and cyst]. Sac. ♋☽ [☽♃].

(1) Anne Elliot (7 Jul 1946, 07:00, Melbourne, Australia). In 1978, the Australian astrologer suffered a ruptured ovarian cyst. Experts believe a cyst is more likely to rupture during strenuous exercise or sexual activity. ☽ [☌♃ > ∠♂ for the rupture].

- Ovulation: Release of an egg from an ovary during the menstrual cycle. Sac. ♋ ☽ .

Overbuilding of Cells: (See Cancer). Abnormal increase in cell production. Negative R2, which flows through Jupiter and the Sun, overbuilds. R2. [♃ (☉)].

Overdose: Commonly refers to overdose of a drug. Spx. [♆ ♓].

Over-emotional: Excessive, out-of-control emotional expression. Esoterically, "fever in the emotional body." [1] Spx. ♋ ☽ [♂ ♅].

Overgrowth: Abnormal increase in growth - cells, tissue, bones, body parts. [♃].

Overweight: (See Obese). Carrying more weight than is normal for the height and build of a person. [♃].

Oxygen, Oxygenation: The life-supporting component of the air, carried into the body by the breath. The Sun rules oxygen, while Mercury represents the process of oxygen being passed into the blood via the lungs. As well as keeping us alive, oxygenation cleans the blood currents. [2] Thr. Hrt. ☉ > ☿ .

- Oxygen Deprivation: (See Choked, Smother, Strangled, Suffocation). Being deprived of air. Scorpio rules suffocation. Link oxygen [deprived of]. Thr. Hrt. ☉ ☿ [♏ ♄ ♇].

---

1   Bailey, Alice: Esoteric Healing, 314.
2   Bailey, Alice: Light of the Soul, 219.

P

Pacemaker: Device implanted in the chest to help control the heartbeat. ♅.

Paediatricians: Medical specialists who care for babies and children. ♍ ☿ > ♋ ☽, 5H.

Paedophilia: Abnormal, unhealthy sex attraction to children. To find this attitude, look at aspects from Uranus (or Mars), to the rulers of children - the Sun, the 5H, the ruler of the 5H. Pluto is the prime ruler for predatory sexual behaviour. Neptune rules deviants. Link sex attitudes > children [deviant, predatory]. Sac. ♅ ♂ > 5H (♌ ☉) > [♆ ♇].
(1) Gabriel Matzneff (12 Aug 1936, 23:30, Neuilly sur Seine, Fr). ♅ ♉ 12 [△ ♆ ♍ 5].
(2) Jean Martin (10 Jan 1936, 10:00, Mohon, Fr). ♅ ♉/♏ [□ ♇ ♋ 5]. ☉ [☍ ♇ 5].
(3) Lorenzo Artico (6 Jun 1967, 12:30, Milan, Italy). ♂ ♎ [☍ ♄ 8 r5H]. ♅ 1 > □ ☉ [☌ ♇].

Paget's Disease: Replacement of old bone tissue with new is disrupted. Symptoms are bone deformities, broken bones, pain. Link bones [deformities/ broken] Base. ♑ ♄ [♄/ ♂ ♅].
(1) Ludwig Van Beethoven (16 Dec 1770, no time). Based on an autopsy description, researchers speculate that Ludwig had Paget's disease. If so, it may have contributed to his well-known deafness. When Paget's disease affects the skull, it can significantly damage hearing. His chart shows it is a possibility. The 'growth' planet Jupiter is afflicted in Capricorn. ♄ [⚼ ♃ ♑ > △ ☿ ♐ for the ears].

Pain, Acute: A temporary sharp pain that comes on quickly. [♂].

Pain, Chronic: Persistent pain that lasts weeks to years. [♂ > ♄].

Palate: The roof of the mouth and floor of the nose. Thr. ♉ ♀.

Palliative Care: Treatment to offset the pain and agony of dying. ♍ > ♃, ♓ ♆, 12H.

Palpitations: Feeling that the heart is racing or fluttering. ♌ ☉ [♅].

Palsy: (See Paralysis). A form of paralysis, with tremors. Ajna. [♄ > ♅].

Pancreas Gland: It is the physical body anchorage of the solar plexus chakra. The organ has a dual function. (i) It is a digestive organ, secreting digestive enzymes. (ii) It has an endocrine function via the Islets of Langerhans cells, which secrete insulin and glucagon into the blood to control blood sugar levels. Spx. ♋ ☽ (♎ ♀).

- Pancreatic Cancer: Link the pancreas [and cancer formula]. Spx. ♋ ☽ (♎ ♀) [(♋ ☽ > ♄ ♇) > ♃ ☉].

These examples have Pluto in Cancer, which can represent repressed emotions as well as the diseased (♇), pancreas (♋).
(1) Bob Gibson (9 Nov 1935, 13:45, Omaha, NE). ♇ ♋ 6 [△ ♃ ♐].
(2) Marv Brown (15 Aug 1930, 05:00, Leonard, TX). ♇ ♋ 12 [wide ☌ ♃ ♋].
(3) Ruth Bader Ginsburg (15 Mar 1933), no time). ♇ ♋ [⚹ ♃ ♍ ℞].

- Pancreatic Juice: A digestive juice secreted by the pancreas. Spx. ♋ ☽.

- Pancreatitis: An inflamed pancreas. Link pancreas [inflammation] Spx. ♋ ☽ , ♀ ♎ [♂ ☉].
(1) Stuart Roosa (16 Aug 1933, 23:00, Durango, CO). He suffered from pancreatitis and died from complications of the disease. ♇♋ [□ ♂ ♎6 r12H].

Pandemics: (See Epidemics). Worldwide occurrence of an infectious disease. Jupiter, Sagittarius, 9H for global. Rays 4 & 7 [☽ ☿ ♅].

Panic Attack, Anxiety Attack: A sudden episode of intense fear and anxiety. Some scientists have linked this condition to an activated 'flight-flight' syndrome. This fits with esoteric science which links the sympathetic nervous system (that activates flight-flight), to the emotional solar plexus chakra (R6: Mars, Neptune). But unlike animals that return to normal activity when the physical danger has passed, humans can embed terror-related incidents in the unconscious (12H-Pisces, Moon, Pluto). These feelings and fearful images can be brought into the present consciousness by incidents and sounds.

In the chart, examine the 12th of the unconscious, and the 8th of major emotional traumas. See if there are malefics on the Asc and other angles of the chart, which can contribute to the hypervigilant and fast-reactions of the fight-flight reaction. Look for afflicted, fearful emotions - especially concerning Mars. Link emotions [fear > attack]. Spx. ♋ ☽ , ♂ ♆, 8H, 12H [♄ ♇ > ♂ ♅].

These charts, all had a malefic on an angle - Pluto four times and Neptune twice. Such people are born with a sense that unseen danger lurks, making them hyper-vigilant

(1) Adele (5 May 1988, 08:19, Tottenham, Eng). The British singer said, "I have anxiety attacks, constant panicking on stage, my heart feels like it's going to explode." The 5H rules entertainment. ♆♑, ☍Asc [☌ ♅ ♄ ♑6].
(2) Ally Sheedy (13 Jun 1962, 05:57, New York, NY). ☽ [∠♇☌IC].
(3) Florence Henderson (14 Feb 1934, 05:00, Dale, IN). ♇♋ ☍ Asc [⚼ ♂].
(4) Naomi Judd (11 Jan 1946, 18:45, Ashland, KY). ♂♋12 [☌ ♄]. ☽ [□♇☌Asc].
(5) Adam Richard (10 Jan 1971, 05:00, Melbourne, Australia). ☽6 [□♇☌MC].
(6) Sara Benincasa (25 Oct 1980, 04:08, Somerville, NJ). The Moon is alone in the top half of the chart; all other planets are in the first 3 houses. This indicates a hyper-vigilant emotional nature, especially with Neptune on the IC. ☽ [⚻♆☌IC].

Paralysis: (See Catalepsy, Paraplegic, Polio, Quadriplegic). Inability to move. A 1st ray *destroyer* problem caused by nerve trauma. Most common causes are strokes or injuries to the spinal cord. Link nerves [trauma/ paralysis > movement]. Ajna. ♊ ☿ (♀♒♅) [♂ ♅/ ♄♇ > ♐♃].

Paranoia: Unrealistic distrust of others or a feeling of being persecuted. Spx. [♏♇].

Paraplegic: The paralysis of the legs and lower body due to spinal cord damage. Link the nerves [paralysis > impaired movement]. Ajna. ♊ ☿ (♀♒♅) [♂ ♅/♄ ♇ > ♐♃].
(1)Dimitri Ghion (3 Apr 1963, 16:35, Nivelles, Belgium). ♅12 [wide ☌♇ > ⚻♃].
(2) Eric Lindmann (25 Jan 1975, 12pm, St Etienne, Fr). ♅♏6 [disp. ♇6 > ⚼ ♃].
(3) Joe Bousquet (19 Mar 1897, 23:00, Narbonne, Fr). ☿ ♓ [□♇♊ r12H > qd ♃♍℞].
(4) Karl Kassulke (20 Mar 1941, 04:36, Milwaukee, WI). ☿ ♓ [⚻♇6. ☿ disp. by ♃].
(5) Larry Flynt (1 Nov 1942, 21:10, Salyersville, KY). ♅♊ [☌ ♄ ♊12 > ♄ ∠♃].

Parasite: Organism that lives in a host. [♏♂ ♇, ♍].

Parasomnia: Sleepwalking and sleep talking. This is due to abnormal behaviour of the nervous system during sleep. Some scientists believe the brain's limbic region (the desire brain) remains awake, while the rest of the brain associated with wakefulness is inactive. During sleep, something alarms the limbic system (Taurus-Venus). This activates a fight-flight reaction (Scorpio-Mars), to get away from/ fight off/ save a situation. Link the limbic system [sleep > fight-flight]. Spx. ♉ ♀ [☽ ♆ > ♏♂♇].

(1) Barbara Rare (30 June 1944, 14:04, Gisborne, NZ). Can scream out loud in fear or anger, or get out of bed to grapple with an 'assailant'. All without waking. There are also nightmares. ♀♋ [□♆ > ∠♂, ⚻♇☌MC].

(2) Jennifer Aniston (11 Feb 1969, 22:22, Los Angeles, CA). The actress said, "I've been woken up by house alarms going off that I've set off." ♀♈6 [⚼ ♂ ☌ ♆♏].

Parathyroids: Four pea-sized glands on the thyroid, whose hormone (PTH), regulates calcium levels. Thr. ♉ ♀ (♄).

Parkinson's Disease: A disorder of the central nervous system that causes jerky movements and tremors. Link nerves [and tremors]. Ajna. ♊ ☿ (♀♒♅) [♅].

Fox developed the condition at age 30, Ali around age 40, Connolly at 71.

(1) Billy Connolly (24 Nov 1942, 04:30, Glasgow, Scotland). ☿ [☍ ♅ ♊].

(2) Michael J. Fox (9 Jun 1961, 00:15, Edmonton, Alberta). ☿ [∠♅].

(3) Muhammad Ali (17 Jan 1942, 18:35, Louisville, KY). ♀ ☌ ☿ ♒6 [♀ □ ♅ ♉].

Paroxysms: A sudden attack or outburst of emotion. Spx. ♋ ☽ ♂ [♂ ♅].

Past Life Prison Patterns: (See Moon - Psychology). Negative core-beliefs. Spx. [☽ sign].

Patella: The kneecap. Base. ♑ ♄.

Pathogen: Any organism/ agent/ germ that can cause disease. [♂ ♅ ♆].

Pathology: The science of the causes and effects of diseases. ♏♇.

Peanut Allergy: (See Food Allergies). The immune system mistakenly identifies peanut proteins as something harmful. Emotional hyper-sensitivity underlies allergies. Link digestion [emotions/ food > immune reaction]. ♋ ☽ , ♍ [♋ ☽ > ♂ ☉].

(1) Serena Williams (26 Sep 1981, 20:28, Saginaw, MI). The tennis great did not outgrow her peanut allergy, indicating hyper-sensitivity to an aspect of life still exists within. ☽6 [mp ♂/♇6].

Pellagra: A condition in which, a lack of niacin (a B vitamin) in the diet, results in dermatitis, diarrhoea, and mental disturbance. Link nutrition/ or food [and deficient]. Spx. ♍ ☿ 6H/ ♋ ☽ [♑ ♄].

Pelvis, Pelvic Girdle: Basin-shaped bony structure that supports the spinal column and protects the abdominal organs. Base. ♐ ♃.

- Pelvic Organ Prolapse - see Prolapse.

Penis: Male genital organ. Sac. ♏♂.

Pepsin: Stomach enzyme that digests proteins. Spx. ♍ ☿.

Peptic Ulcer - see Ulcer.

Pericardium: A thin fluid-filled sac covering the surface of the heart. Hrt. ♌☉ > ♋ ☽.

- Pericarditis: Swelling/ irritation of the pericardium that causes chest pain and a high temperature. Link pericardium [pain/ swelling]. Leo-Sun may link in for the heart. Hrt. ♋ ☽ [♂/♃].

Periodontitis - see Gingivitis.

Periods - see Menstruation, Menstrual Cycle.

Peripheral NS - see Nervous System.

Peristalsis: Constriction/ relaxation waves of the muscles of a canal that push contents forwards. ☽ ☿.

Peritoneum: The serous membrane that lines the abdominal cavity. Spx. ♋ ☽.

- Peritonitis: Bacterial infection of the peritoneum. Without treatment it can lead to sepsis and death. Link the peritoneum [and infection]. Spx. ♋ ☽ [♅ ♂ ♆].
These two men died from the disease.
(1) Friedrich Ebert (4 Feb 1871, 12pm, Heidelberg, Ger). ☽ [wide ☌ ♅ ♋; ♅ qd ♄ 8H].
(2) Rudolph Valentino (6 May 1895, 15:00, Castellaneta, Italy). Heart-throb of the silent screen movie period. He died of peritonitis at age 31. ☽ [□ ♂ ♋, r8H].

Permanent Atoms: These are five energy-centres, located on the 1st subplane [1] of each of the five planes of human evolution - atma (spiritual), buddhi (intuition), mental, emotional and physical. Around them the various sheaths or bodies are built. They are memory banks, carrying from life to life our DNA, all that we have ever been or experienced in past lives - spiritual, mental, emotional and physical. ♒ ♅.
Here are supportive quotes:

> In these atoms the past memory of the personal self is stored; these are in the nature of "memory cells." [2]
>
> All consciousness, all memory, all faculty is stored up in the permanent atom. [3]
>
> The physical permanent atom, is governed by Aquarius, [4] and the seventh ray. [5]

Pernicious Anaemia: (See Autoimmune Disease). A decrease in red blood cells, endangering health. It is caused by an autoimmune attack upon the mucosal lining of the stomach, inhibiting the body's ability to absorb vitamin B12, which is needed to form red blood cells. Link the blood [immune attack > inhibiting]. Hrt. ♂ ♃ ♒ [♂ ☉ > ♄ ♇].
These 3 died from the disease.
(1) Alexander G. Bell (3 Mar 1847, 07:00, Edinburgh, Scot). ♆ ♒ 12 [∠ ♂ r8H > ☌ ♄ ♓ 12].
(2) Edwin Peary (6 May 1856, 12:04, Cresson, PA). ♃ ♆ ♓ 8 [☍ ♂ ♎ ℞ > □ ♄].
(3) Marie Curie (7 Nov 1867, 12:00, Warsaw, Poland). ♃ ♒ [□ ♂ > □ ♄].

Personality, Self-consciousness: The ego, the sense of self, of "I." ♌ ☉.

Perspiration: Process of sweating. ♋ ☽.

Pervert, Perverts, Perverted: A person whose sexual behaviour is regarded as abnormal and unacceptable. Turning something good or healthy into something bad or unhealthy. [♓ ♆].

1 Bailey, Alice: Treatise of Cosmic Fire, 344.
2 Bailey, Alice: Esoteric Astrology, 303.
3 Bailey, Alice: Treatise of Cosmic Fire, 693.
4 Bailey, Alice: Esoteric Astrology, 303.
5 Bailey, Alice: Treatise on White Magic, 373.

Phalanges: Any one of the small bones of the fingers/ toes. Thr. Base. ♊/ ♓.

Pharmacies: Shops that prepare drugs according to a doctor's prescription. ♆.

Pharmacologist: Someone trained in the science of drugs. ♍ ☿ > ♆.

Pharynx: The throat. It is part of the respiratory and digestive systems. Thr. ♉ ♀.

- Pharyngitis: Inflammation of the pharynx, causing a sore throat. Thr. ♉ ♀ [♂ ☉].

Phlebitis, Thrombophlebitis: Inflammation of a vein. On its own it is not considered dangerous, but untreated there is a risk of developing other conditions like deep vein thrombosis. Link veins [inflammation]. Hrt. ♀ [♂ ☉].

(1) Richard Nixon (9 Jan 1913, 21:35, Yorba Linda, CA). In 1974, he suffered from phlebitis, which led to blood clots. ♀ ♓6 [⚹♂ > □ ♄ for blood clots].

Phlegm: A type of mucous made in the chest. Typically, it is not excessive unless an illness is contracted. Thr. ♋ ☽.

- Phlegm Thick in Airways: Due to an illness or irritation, phlegm is coughed up from the respiratory tract. Link airways [phlegm]. Thr. ♊ ☿ [♋ ☽].

Phobia: (See Panic Attack, Agoraphobia, Arachnophobia). Anxiety disorder defined by a persistent and excessive fear of an object or situation - "something is going to get me." A fear of 'scary, creepy, crawly, bitey, germy, bloodsucking things' is particularly related to Scorpio and Pluto. Examine the emotions, the 8th - 12th houses, malefics on angles. [Link emotions [fear/ scary things] Spx. ♋ ☽ ♂ [♄/ ♏♇, 8H, 12H].

(1) Fear of darkness: Coco Chanel (19 Aug 1883, 16:00, Saumur, Fr). ☽ ♓ [□ ♄ ☌ ♇].

(2) Fear of germs: Howie Mandel (29 Nov 1955, 10:00, Toronto, Ontario). ☽ [□♇8]. ♂♏, ☌MC [⚹♇8].

(3) Fear of heights: Gordon Liddy (30 Nov 1930, 06:00, Brooklyn, NY). ♀♏ ☌♏ Asc [∠♄ > △♇♋8].

Phosphorus: Mineral needed for the growth and repair of all tissues and cells, for normal bone and teeth structure. ♄.

Physical Body - see Body, Physical.

- Physical Body Power: Known variously as physical life force, vital energy, and animal life. This power is anchored in the sacral chakra. [1] ♂.

- Physical Disability: Impairment of the body that makes it difficult to participate in normal daily activities. Link physical body (or organ affected) [and disability]. ☽ ♂ ♄, Asc, 1H [♄ ♇].

- Physical Matter: The physical matter from which the body is made, is governed by Saturn and Capricorn, [2] and the Moon and Cancer. The Moon is the mother of forms. [3] ♋ ☽, ♑ ♄.

Piles - see Haemorrhoids.

Pimples: Skin swelling that may be filled with pus due to clogged/ inflamed oil glands or bacteria. [♈ ♂].

Pineal Gland: The endocrine gland located in the centre of the brain, is the anchorage

1 Bailey, Alice: Esoteric Healing, 45.
2 Bailey, Alice: Esoteric Astrology, 173.
3 Bailey, Alice: Light of the Soul, 302.

of the crown/ head chakra. Reacting to signals from the hypothalamus, it controls the 24-hour circadian sleep-wake cycle. Absence of light stimulates the production of the hormone melatonin, which regulates the sleep–wake cycle. The pineal maintains and regulates homeostasis during sleep by fine tuning body functions such as sleep, blood pressure and hormone levels. Light activates the pineal to produce serotonin, the neurotransmitter responsible for mood levels. Sunlight/ serotonin, helps us feel better.

At the physical level, Aries-Mars govern the pineal. Pluto is also a ruler and is associated with the functions of sleep and death. Spiritually, the pineal is the seat of the intuition, of the soul. Cwn. ♈ ♂ ♇.

PISCES. ♓.

Rulers: The exoteric rulers are Neptune and Jupiter. Pluto is both the esoteric and the hierarchy ruler. Pluto has the ultimate evolutionary task - to cut away all ties to the material world (symbolised by the cord connecting the two fishes in the Pisces symbol), freeing the earth-bound soul.

Rays: Pisces carries R2 of Wisdom and R6 of Devotion & Idealism; and R1 via Pluto. Pisces energy is emotional, watery, diffuse and adaptive. But with the presence of the 1st ray, it gives its spiritually advanced people the power to rule.

Body: Pisces is related to the base chakra, which rules the feet. But it is also related to the heart chakra via Neptune, which rules the bloodstream; and to the throat chakra, which rules the lymphatic system. It governs the sleep state, body fluids and cyclic waterways - the lymphatic system and blood stream.

Disease: When planets are afflicted in Pisces, or when Pisces rules the 6H, it indicates trouble mainly with the waterways in the body, and/ or with the intestines that are governed by its opposite sign Virgo. As an afflictor - because the 2nd ray flows through Pisces, when dysfunctional it can cause the overstimulation of cells. When this happens, cells pile together and overbuild, resulting in fatness and more insidiously, tumours and cancer.

Psychology: Ray 6 flows through Pisces, the force of the emotional plane. It represents the ocean of emotions and attempts to escape it through mind-altering substances such as alcohol or drugs. At its highest, Pisces represents devotion to the highest spiritual ideals, and giving one's all in selfless service. Its higher keynote is, 'I leave my Father's house, and turning back, I save.' Ray 2 gives wisdom.

Pituitary Gland: At the base of the brain, the pituitary anchors the ajna chakra. It is related to the development of higher intellectual comprehension and the expression of "love wisdom." [1] Scientists say the pituitary body is the master gland, because it appears to direct most endocrine activities - importantly, to maintain homeostasis, balance and stability in the body. Problems with its hormones can cause inferior moral and intellectual development, excessive growth or dwarfism, and abnormal function of ovaries and testes. Ajna. ♀ (☿).

- Pituitary Cancer: (See Brain Cancer, Glioblastoma). Rare cancers found mainly in older people. Link the pituitary [to the cancer formula]. Ajna. ♀ ☿ [(♋ ☽ > ♄ ♇) > ♃ ☉].

- Pituitary Cyst: A cyst in the gland. Link the pituitary [and cyst]. Ajna. ♀ ☿ [♋ ☽ ♃].

- Pituitary Deficiency - see Hypopituitarism.

- Pituitary Overproducing - see Hyperpituitarism.

- Pituitary Tumour - see Brain Tumour - Benign.

1 Bailey, Alice: Light of the Soul, 80.

Placenta: Organ that develops in the uterus during pregnancy to provide oxygen and nutrients to the foetus. Sac. ♋ ☽ .

Plagues - see Epidemics/ Plagues.

Plant Poisons: (See Poison - Vegetable Kingdom). Plants that when touched or eaten can be harmful and fatal. [1] [♆, ♀ ♃].

Plaque: Is a build-up of waste or bacterial products. It occurs in the arteries as cholesterol and as a bacterial film on teeth. [♃ ♅].

Plasma: Fluid part of blood and lymph whose main role is to take nutrients, hormones and proteins to where they are needed; then remove cell waste. Hrt. ♋ ☽ (♓ ♆).

Pleurae: Tissue that covers the lungs and lines the interior wall of the chest cavity. ♋ ☽ .

- Pleurisy: An infection inflames the pleurae, resulting in pain when breathing. Left untreated, pleurisy can lead to serious complications. Link the pleurae/ airways [and infection]. Thr. ♋ ☽ / ♊ ☿ [♂ ♅ ♆].

The following aristocrats died from pleurisy and associated complications.

(1) Prince Aage of Rosenborg (10 Jun 1887, 13:00, Copenhagen, Denmark), died of pleurisy ♄ ♋ [∠ ♂, r8H].

(2) Hildegard of Bavaria (10 Jun 1825, 10:00, Wurzburg, Ger). ☽ ∠ ☿ [☽ □ ♆ ♑ > ♂ ♇ 8].

PLUTO. ♇.

Signs it rules: It is the exoteric ruler of Scorpio, and esoteric and hierarchy ruler of Pisces.

House it rules: The 8H.

Rays: Pluto carries the 1st ray of Will and Power, the force of life and death, demonstrating the destructive power of this force.

Body: Pluto is related to the crown chakra, presiding over sleep and death. It also corules the base chakra and is related to the adrenals, the will-to-survive/ fight-or-flight syndrome and atomic life. Via Scorpio, Pluto is related to elimination of body waste, and to sex.

Disease: When afflicted, the sign Pluto is in, can indicate serious trouble with the part of the body ruled by that sign. Or, it can indicate trouble in the organs governed by Scorpio. More often it is the afflictor. As the Arrow of Death, Pluto transforms - forcing a major psychological or life-style change; and sometimes through physical death. Its diseases are relentless. They age, harden and crystallise. Any health issue under a hard Pluto aspect could be life-threatening, indicating (serious) medical intervention is required.

Psychology: In younger people, hard Pluto transits usually indicate psychological transformations are underway. Its negative effect gives a powerful and selfish will, arrogance, cruelty, destructiveness and ambition for power. In the advanced spiritual person, 1st ray power is used for the higher good.

Pneumogastric Nerve - see Vagus Nerve.

Pneumonia: An infection (bacterial, viral, fungi) that inflames air sacs in the lungs, which fill with fluid and pus. Link lungs [infection > fluid/pus]. Thr. ♊ ☿ [♂ ♅ ♆ > ♋ ☽ ♆].

(1) Isabella of Bavaria (31 Aug 1863, 18:00, Munich, Ger). ☿ 8 [♂ ♆ > qd ☽ r6H].

(2) Marie of Hohenzollern (17 Nov 1845, 08:00, Sigmaringen, Ger). ☿ ♐ [□ ♂ ♓].

(3) Max Reinhardt (9 Sep 1873, 01:00, Vienna, Austria. ☿ r12 [□ ♂ > ⚷ ☽].

---

1   Bailey, Alice: Treatise of Cosmic Fire, 1072.

Podiatry: Branch of medicine devoted to the study and treatment of foot and ankle problems. ♍ > ♓♒.

POISONS, TOXINS. (See Food Poisoning). Substances capable of causing illness or death when ingested, bitten, stung by, or touched. Neptune is the prime ruler for all types of poisoning. Link body part/s affected, or eat/ drink [and poison]: [animal poison ♂ (♆♇)], [mineral poison ♄ ♅♇ (♆)], [vegetable poison ♆ (♇)].

Animal Kingdom poisons including parasitic: Fish, snakes, spiders, frogs, mosquitos, etc., poisons usually injected by stings and bites. Mosquito bites kill more humans than all other animals and at the top of the list is malaria. Mars is a ruler of the animal kingdom [1] and is the representative for bites and stings. [♂ (♆♇)].

(1) Lenny Henry (29 Aug 1958, 03:00, Sedgley, Eng). Got malaria in 1997, when he visited the Amazon. (See Malaria). These parasites infect red blood cells. ☉ [☌♇].

Mineral Kingdom poison: Lead, mercury, arsenic, asbestos, radium, plutonium, silica, strychnine, uranium, etc. The mineral kingdom is ruled by rays 1 and 7. [♄ ♅♇ (♆)].

(1) Marie Curie (7 Nov 1867, 12pm, Warsaw, Poland), died of aplastic pernicious anaemia due to years of exposure to radium. ☉♏ [☍♇♉]. ♃♒ [□♄].

These three drank arsenic to die.

(2) Astro.com 1326 (15 Oct 1939, 23:16, Marmet, WV). ☽ drank [qd ♅ r8H].

(3) Pyotr Tchaikovsky (7 May 1840, 06:35, Votkinsk, Russia). ♆ drank [⚹♄6 r8H].

(4) Thomas Chatterton (20 Nov 1752, 06:14, London, Eng). ☽6 drank [⚻♇1].

Vegetable Kingdom poison: Cyanide, hemlock, deadly nightshade, some mushrooms/ fungi, etc. Neptune is the "informing life" of the kingdom. [2] [♆ (♇)].

(1) Alan Turing (23 Jun 1912, 02:15, London UK). The British mathematician committed suicide by injecting an apple with cyanide and taking a bite. ☽ ate [□♆♋ cyanide].

(2) Socrates (20 May 0467, no time. Astro.com). The Greek philosopher was forced to kill himself by drinking hemlock. ☽ drank [□♆♍ – if he was born at night].

Polio, Poliomyelitis: (See Paralysis). A viral attack on the nervous system, causing paralysis. Link nerves [virus > paralysis]. Ajna. ♊ ☿ (♀♒♅) [♆♂♅ > ♄♇].

(1) President Franklin D. Roosevelt (30 Jan 1882, 20:45, Hyde Park, NY). He was paralyzed from the waist down by polio. ☿ ♒6 [disposited by ♅12 > ☿ □♇♉].

Polyps: Abnormal cell growth, mostly benign. [♃].

Pons: Part of the central nervous system located at the base of the brain. Ajna. ♊ ☿.

Ponzi Scheme - see White-collar Crime.

Possession - see Multiple Personalities.

Post Nasal Drip/ Catarrh: Mucous from the nose/ sinuses, drips down the back of the throat. Link the throat > sinuses [mucous]. Thr. ♉ ♀/ ♋ ☽ [♋ ☽].

Post Traumatic Stress Disorder, PTSD: A terrifying event which was experienced in the past, resurfaces when triggered, causing a panic attack. The 8H for emotional trauma and the 12H for buried memories, may be implicated. Link self [emotional > trauma]. Spx. ☉, Asc [♋ ☽ ♂ > ♄♇].

1 Bailey, Alice: Esoteric Psychology I, 245.

2 Bailey, Alice; A Treatise on Cosmic Fire, 1072.

(1) Daniel Cotnoir (21 Jun 1972, 22:41, Fitchburg, MA). American Iraq War veteran, who suffered from PTSD. Waking from sleep when a bottle came flying through his window, before he was fully alert, he grabbed his gun and started shooting into people outside his house. ☉♋ [□♇8].

Postpartum Blues: New mothers who experience mood swings, crying spells, anxiety and depression. Link self [depressed > emotions]. Spx. ☉, Asc [♑♄ > ♋☽♂].

(1) Chrissy Teigen (30 Nov 1985, 06:10, Delta, Utah). ☉ [☌☿♄ ⚻ ☽♋].

(2) Diana, Princess (1 Jul 1961, 19:45, Sandringham, Eng). Diana's emotional difficulties have been widely reported. ☉♋ [qd ♄♑].

(3) Drew Barrymore (22 Feb 1975, 11:51, Culver City, CA). ☉♓ [⚼ ☽♋ > ☽☌♄].

Potassium: Mineral whose main role is to help maintain normal levels of fluid inside our cells. ♋☽.

Potency Issues - see Impotent.

Prana: The life/ vitalising principle emanating from the Sun. Prana, the life force and vitality, are synonymous terms. [1] ☉.

Predator: Just as animals stalk their prey, so do human predators ruthlessly stalk people to use and / or exploit them. [♏♇].

Pregnancy: The period in which a foetus develops inside a woman's womb. Sac. ♋☽.

Premature Ejaculation: In men, premature orgasm and emission of semen just before or shortly after beginning sexual intercourse. Link sex [and premature]. Sac. ♏♂ ♀ [♂♅].

Premenstrual Syndrome (PMS), Premenstrual Dysphoric Disorder (PMDD): Debilitating symptoms experienced after ovulation and before menstruation - mood swings, tender breasts, food cravings, fatigue, irritability and depression. Link menstruation [depression, fatigue]. Sac. ♏♂ (♋☽) [♄ (♇)].

(1) Bridget Malcolm (3 Nov 1991, no time). ♂ [☌♇♏].

(2) Dixie D'Amelio (12 Aug 2001, no time). ♂ [☌♇].

(3) Zara Larrson (16 Dec 1997, no time). ☽♋ [☍♂♑, ⚼♇].

Prescription Medicine: Prescribed by doctors. ♍ > ♄.

Pressures: Puts pressure on. [♄♇].

Prison of the Soul: (See Moon - Psychology). A pattern of unconscious, self-defeating beliefs/ behaviours. R6, Spx. [☽ sign].

Procreate - see Reproduction.

Progeria: Genetic mutation that causes rapid aging/ accelerated dying. Ray 1 carried by Saturn and Pluto is the aging, hardening, dying force. Link self/ life [genetic mutation > aging]. Ajna. ☉, Asc [♒♅ > ♑♄ (♇)].

(1) Adalia Williams (10 Dec 2006, 15:17, Austin, TX). ☉8 [□♅ > ☌♇8].

(2) Hayley Okines (3 Dec 1997, 14:50, St Leonards, Eng). ☉ [⚹♅♒ > ☌♇].

(3) Megane Durel-Zoubida (9 Jan 1993, 00:04, Paris, Fr). ☉♑ [☌♅ > ☉ disp. by ♄].

(4) Peedie Snipes, 10 May 1977, 17:15, Burlington, NC. The Sun has no aspects, indicating immediately, trouble with vitalisation and life. ☉8 [♄ mp ☉/♅]. Asc [☌♇12].

1 Bailey, Alice: Letters on Occult Meditation, 245.

Progesterone: Hormone that stimulates the uterus to prepare for pregnancy. Sac. ♋ ☽.

Prolapse: Bulging or dropping of the womb (♋), bowel (♏), or bladder (♎♏); because of weak pelvis muscles. Link organ involved [weak > muscles]. Organ [♓♆, ♃ ♀ > ♂].

Promiscuity: Having many casual, sexual relationships. Sac. Sex [casual]. ♏ ♀ ♂ [♊ ♐, ♅].

Prostate Gland: Male sex gland that releases a fluid component of semen. Sac. ♏♂♇.

- Prostate Cancer: Generally, the psychological cause is repression of desire. This can happen in celibates who have not yet learnt to transmute desire naturally. For others, sex may not be available. In aged men, it may be a consequence of not being able to attain an erection and/ or have sex. Mars can represent both the prostate and desire/ emotion. Link the prostate [and the cancer formula]. Sac. ♏♂♇ [(♋ ☽ > ♄ ♇) > ♃ ☉].

These three men died from the disease.

(1) Carl Pauling (28 Feb 1901, 22:00, Portland, Oregon). ♂℞ r6H [(⚼ ♄ ♑) > ♄ ☌ ♃].

(2) Frank Capra Jr. (20 Mar 1934, 17:44, Los Angeles, CA). ♇♋ [(∠♆ > qd ♄) > □ ♃].

(3) Pierre Trudeau (18 Oct 1919, 08:03, Outremont, Quebec). The charismatic PM of Canada. ♂ r6H [(☌ ♄) > ♄ ∠☉12].

- **Prostate Enlarged**: Caused by hormonal changes as a man ages. Sac. ♏♂♇ [♃].

Prosthesis: Artificial body part. ♆.

Protective: To protect someone or something. ♋ ☽.

Proteins: They are made up of chemical building (♃), blocks (♄), called amino acids. These are needed for the growth and maintenance of cells and tissues, and make up hair, nails, bones and muscles. Ray 3, carried by Saturn and Capricorn rules cells [1], protein and the physical form. [2] ♄ ♃.

Protozoa: These are groups of single-celled microscopic animals that feed on organic matter. ♏♇.

Psoriasis: Skin rash with itchy, scaly patches. Link skin [rash]. Base. ♑ ♄ (♋ ☽) [♂].

(1) John Updike (18 Mar 1932, 15:45, West Reading, PA). Suffered from psoriasis in childhood. ♄6 [∠♂].

Psychiatry: Medical branch designed to diagnose, prevent, treat mental disorders. ♍ ☿.

Psychics, Psychism: Lower clairvoyants. Those who 'see' through their solar plexus centre onto the astral plane of delusion, who use lower psychic powers. [♓♆].

By training the intellect to think, by refusing to use the lower powers and by rejecting all contacts or messages that feed the ego and the sense of being superior or special - this will eventually close the solar plexus centre and the open door to the astral plane. It will also atrophy that part of the inner mechanism that has made these powers available.

Psychological: Related to the mental and emotional state of a person. ♊ ☿ ☽.

- Psychoanalysis: A method of explaining and treating mental and emotional disorders by having the patient talk freely about himself, troubles, emotions. ♍ ☿ > ♏♇.

- Psychological Disorder: Wide range of conditions that affect mood, thinking and behaviour. ☿ ☽ [malefics].

1 Bailey, Alice: Treatise on White Magic, 195.
2 Bailey, Alice: Destiny of the Nations, 118.

- **Psychological Trauma:** (See Post Traumatic Stress Disorder). Emotional-mental shock and distress, sometimes denial; due to seeing or being part of, a terrible event or major abuse. Link emotions [and shock/ denial]. ♋ ☽ ♂ [♅/ ♄ ♇].

- **Psychopath**: (See Sociopath). Personality disorder with cunning and sly (♄), violent and often cruel (♂ ♇), extremely selfish (☉), narcissistic social behaviour (♀ ♅). Link the self [narcissism > cruel/ cunning]. Thr. Spx. ☉, Asc [♀ ♅ > ♂ ♇/ ♄].

NB. It is important to remember that two people can have the same astrology. But while the spiritually advanced person will use the forces positively, the narcissistic and selfish person will use them for personal profit and gain - as did the following.

(1) Charles Manson (12 Nov 1934, 16:40, Cincinnati, Oh). Psychopathic murderer, who led his followers (the Mason Family), on a murder spree in the 1960s. ☉♏ [☌ ♀ > □ ♄].
(2) Marvin Lemons (15 Jun 1935, 00:01, Danville, VI). American sexual psychopath and necrophiliac. Asc [☌ ♄ 12 > ♄ ⚻ ♀ ♌6].
(3) Thomas Hamilton (10 May 1952, 08:50, Glasgow, Scot). Scottish psychopath and suspected paedophile. Asc [☌ ♅ 12 > ♅ □ ♄].
(4) Yves Gamonet (15 May 1933, 04:00, Sarreguemines, Fr). French psychopath. Asc [☌ ♅ ♈12 > □ ♇].

- **Psychotherapy**: Treatment of mental disorder through psychology. ♍ ☿.

- **Psychotic**: Mental disorder characterised by a disconnection from reality. [♆].

Ptomaine Poisoning: (See Food poisoning). Most usually caused by eating food that is contaminated by bacteria. Link food [poisoned]. ♋ ☽ [♂ ♅ ♆].

Puberty: Period when adolescent boys and girls reach sexual maturity. ♀ ♂.

Pubic Bone, Pubis: One of the three main bones that make up the pelvis. The others are the ilium and ischium. Sac. ♏♐.

Pubic Crabs: Small parasites that cling to pubic hair and suck blood for nourishment. [♏♂ ♇].

PULMONARY: Relating to the lungs. ♊ ☿ (☉).

- **Pulmonary Artery Circulation:** The system of blood vessels between the heart and lungs, through which deoxygenated blood is pumped to the lungs for oxygenation. The artery carries blood from the right side of the heart to the lungs. Thr. Hrt. ♊ ☿ > ♃ ♒ ♅.

- **Pulmonary Embolism/ Thrombosis:** A blocked lung artery. The most common cause is a blood clot (thrombosis). The clot travels upwards from a deep vein and gets wedged in a lung artery. Untreated, it can kill. When chronic, this condition comes under the category 'Chronic Obstructive Pulmonary Disease.' Link lungs > artery [clot]. Thr. Hrt. ♊ ☿ > ♃ ♒ ♅ [♄ ♇].
(1) Gerrie Kneteman (6 Mar 1951, 05:45, Amsterdam, Netherlands. A Dutch cyclist who died from a heart attack, the result of a pulmonary embolism. ☿ > ☌ ☉ ♃ ♓ [☉ qd ♄ 8].

- **Pulmonary Fibrosis**. Connective tissue in the lungs is damaged and scarred, making it difficult to breathe. Link airways [harden/ scar]. Thr. ♊ ☿ [♑ ♄ ♇).
(1) Jerry Lewis (16 Mar 1926, 12:15, Newark, NJ). ☿ r12H [⚼ ♄].

(2) John Connally (27 Feb 1917, 02:00, Floresville, TX). ☿ ♒ [⚼ ♇ ♋ r12H].
(3) Peggy Solomon (14 Aug 1908, 08:00, Philadelphia, PA). ☿ [⚻ ♅ ♑ r6H].

- Pulmonary Hypertension in the Lungs. Either high blood pressure causes blood clots to form in the lungs; or blood clots (embolisms) in the lungs cause the high pressure. Either way, untreated, lung arteries are damaged so blood-oxygenation cannot occur, limiting airflow. The right heart ventricle is also damaged. Link lungs > blood [clots > high pressure]. Thr. Hrt. ♊ ☿ > ♂ ♃ ♒ [♄ ♇, ♃ > ♄ ♇].
(1) Paula (28 Apr 1974, 06:30, Port Kembla, Australia). In 2022, she collapsed, was rushed to hospital and diagnosed with pulmonary embolisms and hypertension. ☿ ♈ 12 > ⚹ ♂ ♋ r12H [☌ ♄ ♋, ♄ □ ♇]. Positive aspects in the progressed chart helped an amazing recovery.

- Pulmonary Silicosis. (See Poison - Metal-Mineral). A long-term lung disease caused by inhaling unsafe levels of silica dust usually over a period of many years. This can occur for example, in industries that produce kitchen bench tops made of stone. Once inside the lungs, the dust particles settle and work their harm - hardening and scarring lung connective tissue (fibrosis). It is a ray 1 progressive, fatal disease. Link airways > connective tissue [harden/ scar]. Thr. ♊ ☿ > ♑ ♄ [♄ (♇)].

- Pulmonary Tuberculosis. (See Tuberculosis). A bacterial infection that destroys lung tissue. Sufferers cough up the bacteria, which spreads to infect others. The following examples died from the disease. Link the lungs [and infection]. Thr. ♊ ☿ [♅ ♂ ♆].
(1) Albert Samain (3 Apr 1858, 09:00, Lille, Fr). ☿ coruler 12H [mp ♅ 12 /♆].
(2) Leo Karl of Austria (5 Jul 1893, 08:30, Pula, Croatia). ☿ 12 [☌ ♂ 12, □ ♅ r6H].
(3) Mathilde of Bavaria (17 Aug 1877, 21:00, Munich, Ger). ☿ 6 [☍ ♂ ♓ ℞, 12].
(4) Wilhelm Franz of Austria (10 Feb 1895, 20:15, Pula Croatia). ☿ ♓ 6 [□ ♆ ♊].

Pulse: Rhythmical throbbing of the arteries as blood is propelled through them. Hrt. ♃.

Pupils: Black hole in the centre of the eye that allows light to strike the retina. Ajna. ♈ ☉.

Purpura: (See Schonlein Purpura). A rash of purple spots due to small blood vessels leaking blood into the skin, joints, intestines or organs. It can be caused by a disease, bruising from trauma, ageing, medication side effects or drawing of blood.

Purge: Remove something unwanted. ♏ ♇.

Pus: Dead white cells that form around an infection. The Moon is the primary ruler of decay, and Cancer and the Moon rule white cells and pus. [♋ ☽]. [1]

Putrefy: Decomposition of organic matter. [♋ ☽ , ♏ ♇].

Pyelitis: Inflammation of the mucous membrane of the pelvis and kidney chambers. Link mucous membrane > pelvis/ kidneys [inflammation]. ♋ ☽ > ♐ ♃ / ♎ ♀ [♂ ☉ fire signs].

Pyloric Valve: A muscular valve that holds food in the stomach until it is ready for the next stage in digestion. Spx. ♂.

Pylorus: First part of the small intestine that connects to the duodenum. Spx. ♍ ☿.

Pyorrhea - see Gingivitis.

1 In Heindel's Astro-Diagnosis, he gave several examples where pus formed during the Moon's influence.

Q

Q Fever - Quintan Fever, Trench fever: Bacterial infection primarily transmitted by human body lice with flu-like symptoms. There is fever, headaches, dizziness and severe pains in the legs. Called "trench fever," it infected armies in the early 20th Century wars. But now, it is a re-emerging pathogen among impoverished populations. Link airways [infection]. ♊ ☿ [♅♂♆].

Quadriceps Muscles: A group of muscles at the front of the thigh. ♐ ♂

Quadriplegic: (See Paralysis). This is paralysis of all four limbs due to a 'broken neck.' Spinal cord damage anywhere between C1 and C8. The higher the injury, the more dangerous the effects. Jupiter and Sagittarius could link in for impaired movement. Link spine/ nerves [trauma > paralysis]. ♌ ☉ ♄ / ♊ ☿ (♀ ♒ ♅) [♂ ♅ > ♄ ♇].

(1) Christopher Reeve (25 Sep 1952, 03:12, Manhattan, NY). Was paralysed in a horse-riding (♐) accident. ♅ coruler 6H [⚻ ♂ ♐ > □ ♄].

(2) John Callahan (5 Feb 1951, 02:45, Portland, OR). Paralyzed in a car accident. ☉3 transport [⚼ ♄ > ♄ □ ♅]. ♀ neck [☌ ♂ broken, qd ♇ ♌ paralysed].

(3) Larry Flynt (1 Nov 1942, 21:10, Salyersville, KY). He was shot. ☉ [☌ ♂ > □ ♇ ♌ r6H].

(4) Mark Buoniconti (29 Sep 1966, 17:08, Boston, MA). He broke his neck playing football. ♀ [☌ ♅ > ☌ ♇]. His spine ♄ [was injured ☍ ♅ > and he was paralysed ☍ ♇].

(5) Perry Cross (24 Mar 1975, 07:00, Taree, Australia). He broke his neck playing football. ☉12, r5H of sport [∠ ♂ ♒ > ☍ ♇6].

Quinine: A bitter crystalline compound present in cinchona bark, used as a tonic. ♂. [1]

Quinsy, Peritonsillar Abscess: (See Tonsillitis). An abscess that forms between a tonsil and wall of the throat. The condition is not common today because of early medical intervention. Link tonsils [and abscess]. ♉ ♀ [♋ ☽].

(1) Michel de Montaigne (28 Feb 1533, 11:30, 44N53, 00E01, France). French writer and Renaissance man, he died of quinsy. ♀8 [□ ☽ ♉].

Quiver: To shake slightly; tremble. [♅].

1 Mars rulership given in Bills, Rulership Book, 224.

R

Rabies: (See Animal Attacks). A deadly virus spread to people from bites of infected animals, such as dogs, bats, coyotes, foxes, skunks and raccoons. It infects the central nervous system, causing muscle spasms, paralysis and mental confusion. Once symptoms appear, it is nearly always fatal. Link the self/ or nerves [infection > spasms/ paralysis]. ☉, Asc, ♊ ☿ [♆♂♅ > ♂♅/ ♄♇].
(1) George Reeves (3 Jan 1826, no time). A Colonel in the Confederate States Army, he was bitten by a rabid dog while trying to protect a child. He died from the infection. ☿ [☌♆ > □♇].

Radioactive Substances: In esoteric teachings, these substances - along with chemicals, metals and minerals; are viewed as living subhuman units of the mineral kingdom. This kingdom is governed by 7th ray, [1] which is carried by Uranus. The 1st ray (carried by Pluto) is also related to radioactivity. R1 and R7, ♅♇.

- Radiation Poisoning: Cells are damaged due to exposure to high doses of toxic radiation. Links cells [to radiation]. ☉ ☽ [♅♇].
(1) Alexander Litvinenko (4 Dec 1962, no time). He was poisoned with Polonium which had been placed in his tea by Russian agents. ☉ [□ ♅♇].
The following died from radiation poisoning during laboratory work.
(2) Cecil Kelley (16 Oct 1920, no time). ☉♎ [♂ for poison, is mp ☉/♅].
(3) Harry Daghnian (4 May 1921, no time). ☉ [☉ ☿ mp ♅/♇].
(4) Marie Curie (7 Nov 1867, 12pm, Warsaw Poland). A few of her books and papers are still so radioactive that they are stored in lead boxes. ☉♏ [☍♇♉].

- Radiation Therapy to treat Cancer: This therapy kills cancer cells or slows their growth by damaging their DNA. This brings it under the rule of Pluto. Uranus which governs radical new treatments could be associated. ♇♅.

Radium: Chemical element dangerous for health with prolonged exposure. [♇♅].

Radius: One of the two bones (other is the ulna) that make up the forearm. ♊ ☿.

Ramsay Hunt Syndrome: (See Paralysis). A facial nerve is damaged by a virus, causing paralysis in the face and hearing loss. The condition is like Bell's palsy, but is more dangerous and enduring. Link the face/ nerves [virus > paralysis]. Ajna. ♈/♊ ☿ [♆♂♅ > ♄♇].
(1) Justin Bieber (1 Mar 1994, 00:56, London, Ontario). In 2022, the entertainer announced on Instagram he had this problem. ☿ ♒℞ [☌ ♂ r12H, □♇☌Asc].

Rape: Forced, violent, sexual intercourse on an unwilling partner. Mars is the prime ruler of rape, Uranus and Pluto are substitute rulers. Link the self [rape]. R6, Sac. ☉ Asc [♏♂♇]. These are female rape victims.

---

1 Bailey, Alice: Esoteric Psychology I, 369.

(1) Astro.com 10536 (30 Mar 1947, 13:49, Los Angeles, CA). This was an American rape victim. ☉♈ [disposited by ♂8, ♂□♅].

(2) Astro.com 13171 (31 Aug 1957, 08:50, Chicago, IL). This American teenager was raped by her stepfather at age 15. ☉ [☌♂♇].

(3) Astro.com 14827 (13 Dec 1981, 12:23, Westfield, MA). At age 3, she was raped by a 13-year-old boy, who was the son of her in-home care provider. ☉ [□♂6, r8H].

Rash: Temporary outbreak of red, scaly or itchy patches of skin. Rashes can cover just one part of the body or spread all over it. Link skin [and rash]. Base. ♑♄ (♋☽) [♂].

RAYS, THE SEVEN: These are the seven basic forces of nature, from which all things are made. They flow through the constellations, signs, planets, to humanity and all living things. They give rise to seven different psychological types and disease groups, all which display the energy traits of the parent ray.

- **Ray 1** (R1)**:** The 1st Ray of Will and Power is the energy expression of the power of God, the 'spirit' aspect in the "Spirit-Soul-Body" trilogy. It is the most powerful force in the universe, ruling creation, life and death.

Astrology: R1 flows directly through Aries, Leo, Capricorn, Vulcan and Pluto. Indirectly through Saturn (via Capricorn), Uranus (because its R7 force is the lower pole of R1); and through Taurus, Virgo and Scorpio via their rulers Vulcan and Pluto.

Chakras-glands: Flows primarily via the crown and pineal, and the base and adrenals.

Body: R1 governs life and death, respiration - the breath, sleep, and instils the will to be, to live and to survive. Via the base chakra, R1 vitalises the kidneys, urinary tract, the spinal column and skeleton.

Disease: When imperfect, this energy crystallises, hardens, restricts reduces, atrophies and ages. It is relentless and unstoppable, and when chronic, its diseases move inexorably towards death - whether rapid or lingering. The prime ruler for the hardening and aging effect of R1 is Saturn. The prime representative for R1's destructive effect is Pluto. But any of the planets mentioned, or planets in the signs mentioned; could represent a R1 disease

- **Ray 2** (R2)**:** The 2nd Ray of Love and Wisdom is the love-energy expression of God, of the 'soul' aspect in the "Spirit-Soul-Body" trilogy. This means it deals with relationships, feelings and consciousness - of ourselves, of others and of the world around us. Its job is to help us become sensitive, caring people - like our souls, and like Christ.

Astrology: R2 flows directly through Gemini, Virgo, Pisces, the Sun and Jupiter. Indirectly through Leo (via the Sun) and Sagittarius (via Jupiter).

Chakras-glands: R2 flows via the heart and thymus.

Body: R2 governs growth and the body's vitalisation via the heart and cardiovascular system.

Disease: When imperfect, R2 overstimulates. Excess energy pours in, more than the body can handle. The result is multiplication of atoms, inappropriate growths such as tumours and cancer, and extra body parts.

- **Ray 3** (R3)**:** The 3rd Ray of Intelligent Activity - or the Mind of God; is the force of the 'body' aspect in the "Spirit-Soul-Body" trilogy. While ray 1 governs breathing and life, and ray 2 governs consciousness and vitalisation; ray 3 generally governs the body - cells and structure, digestion and reproduction. However, on an individual level, R3 (or any of the rays), can potentially vitalise any of the soul, personality, mind, emotional, physical bodies.

Astrology: R3 flows directly through Cancer, Libra, Capricorn, Saturn and the Earth. Indirectly through Gemini and Sagittarius via the Earth. The prime rulers for the intelligence aspect of R3 are Saturn and Mercury (because Mercury rules the 3rd sign Gemini).

Chakras-glands: R3 flows via the throat and thyroid, also the sacral and gonads for reproduction.

Body: Vitalises the brain, the central nervous system and the five senses, which are created by the activity of the 3rd ray. [1] It is the intelligence aspect of the endocrine system, and vitalises the breathing apparatus, the gastrointestinal tract, the lymphatic system, reproduction, the physical body mass, and kundalini fire that is housed in the base chakra.

Disease: When malfunctioning, the intelligent functioning of body systems can go awry. Wrong messaging is given. Particularly in organs and systems governed by the throat chakra (primarily governed by R3), such as the thyroid and the intelligence of the endocrine system. Energy imbalance means there may be excessive energy and smothering in one direction, and energy-starvation in another.

- Ray 4 (R4): The 4th Ray of Harmony through Conflict is aligned with the 2nd Ray of Love and Wisdom, which means it deals with relationships and their eventual harmonising - after a period of conflict.

Astrology: R4 flows directly through Taurus, Scorpio, Sagittarius, the Moon and Mercury. Indirectly through Cancer, Gemini, Virgo, via their rulers the Moon and Mercury - which are the prime carriers of this force.

Chakras-glands: R4 is a secondary ajna chakra force (after R5).

Body: R4's influence is mental-emotional, influencing mental perception and moods.

Disease: The combative force of ray 4, is responsible for devitalisation, emotional swings, allergic reactions, mucous build up - and on a global level, epidemics and pandemics.

- Ray 5 (R5): The 5th ray of Concrete Mind and Science is allied with ray 3 of Intelligence and is the primary the force of the lower concrete mind and its thoughtform building capabilities.

Astrology: R5 flows directly through Leo, Aquarius, Sagittarius and Venus; and indirectly through the signs Venus rules - Taurus and Libra. The prime carriers of this force are Venus and Aquarius.

Chakras-glands: Flows via the ajna and pituitary.

Body: R5's influence is mainly mental. It can affect neural flows and connections in the brain.

Disease: When imperfect, R5 has much to do with many modern psychological disorders.

> In the activity of this energy which demonstrates primarily upon the fifth or mental plane will be found eventually the source of many psychological disorders and mental trouble. Cleavage is the outstanding characteristic—cleavage within the individual or between the individual and his group, rendering him anti-social. Other results are certain forms of insanities, brain lesions and those gaps in the relation of the physical body to the subtle bodies which show as imbecilities and psychological troubles. [Also] migraine, which is caused by a lack of relationship between the energy around the pineal gland and that around the pituitary body. [2]

---

1   Bailey, Alice: Esoteric Psychology I, 251.
2   Bailey, Alice: Esoteric Healing, 302.

- Ray 6 (R6): The 6th Ray of Devotion and Idealism is closely aligned with the 2nd Ray of Love and Wisdom, which means it deals with human relations, particularly the emotional life - consequently, it is the causal force behind most diseases at an individual level.

Astrology: Flows through Virgo, Sagittarius, Pisces, Mars, Neptune. Indirectly through Aries, Cancer, Scorpio - signs ruled by Mars and Neptune, the primary carriers of this force.

Chakras-glands: R6 flows via the solar plexus and pancreas glands.

Body: It influences the sympathetic nervous system, body fluids and waterways (the astral plane is the 'water' plane).

Disease: This energy when virulent via Mars, is acidic and burns. This causes trouble with the digestive organs, and manifests as wrong-desire through the sacral. When virulent via Neptune, diseases are hard to see, find and treat. There is escapism, drug and alcohol abuse.

- Ray 7 (R7): The 7th Ray of Ceremony, Order and Magic is the lower extension of ray 1 - it carries power. R7 is one of the relationship rays. Its higher function is to unite spirit and matter, and part of this task is to bring us consciously into a right-relation with the soul.

Astrology: R7 flows directly through Aries, Cancer, Capricorn and Uranus. Indirectly through Aquarius and Libra - signs ruled by Uranus, the primary carrier of this force.

Chakras-glands: Flows via the sacral and gonads, also through the throat.

Body: Vitalises the organs of the sacral chakra - the etheric body, DNA, sex and reproduction.

Disease: R7 brings together life and matter upon the physical plane and when this process is imperfect, the result is activity of germs and bacteria within the medium which best nurtures them. Its force is largely responsible for infections and contagious diseases. The task of ray 7 is to establish balance and rhythm. Failure results in arrhythmia, seizures, spasms, wild and uncontrolled growth, and problems with circulation and blood quality.

Raynaud's Disease: Fingers and toes feel numb/ cold in response to cold. Mainly because of the build-up of fats on artery walls. Link fingers/ toes [cold]. Hrt. ♊ ☿ / ♓ ♆ [♄].
(1) Alison Levine (5 Apr 1966, no time). Despite having suffered from this disease since her 20s, she is a renowned mountain climber. ☿ ♓ [♂ ♄ ♓].

Recreational drugs: Chemical substances taken for enjoyment. ♆.

Rectum: Final section of the large intestine, terminating at the anus. Thr. Spx. ♏ ♂ ♇.

Recuperative Power: The power to recover health and strength after an illness or injury. R2, Hrt. ☉ ♃ ♂.

Red Blood Cells: Haemoglobin gives the red colour to red blood cells. Hrt. ☉ ♂.

Redness: Flesh showing a red colour. ♂.

Reduces: Lessens the amount of. The force of R1 reduces. [♄ (♇)].

Reflux: A digestive disease. Stomach acid/ bile irritates the food pipe lining. Spx. ♋ ☽ [♂].

Refuse: Rubbish. [♄].

Regulating, Balancing: Of organs/ systems in the body. ♎ ♀.

Reincarnate: Rebirth. To incarnate again, re-clothe or re-embody in flesh. An Eastern spiritual-wisdom fundamental. The real 'man' is the soul - a spark of God, on a journey from ignorance to enlightenment; from chaos to the Divine. To acquire the necessary experience and wisdom, the soul reincarnates repeatedly on Earth. The Asc.

Relapse: Deterioration after a period of health improvement. [♄].

Remission: Decrease or disappearance of signs and symptoms of cancer. ♃.

Renal - see Kidneys.

- **Renal Failure** - see Uraemia.

Repetitive Strain Injury, Repetitive Stress Syndrome (RSI): Aches and pains in mainly the arms, shoulders, wrists and hands, from doing repetitive movements. Link arms, shoulders, wrists, hands [and repetitive]. ♊ ☿ [☿ ♅[1]].
(1) Leon Fleisher (23 Jul 1928, 22:20, San Francisco, CA). American pianist and conductor who developed paralysis of his right hand. One diagnosis was for Carpal Tunnel Syndrome, a pinched nerve in the wrist (see that entry). Another was for RSI. ☿ coruler 6H [□ ♅].

Repress: Subdue someone or something by using superior force to smother. [♄ ♇].

Reproduction, Human: Sexual intercourse that results in fertilization and production of offspring. The reproduction region is vitalised by the sacral chakra. R3, Sac. ♋ ☽ ,♏ ♂.

Reptilian Brain - see Triune Brain.

Respiration, Respiratory system - see Breath.

Restless Legs Syndrome (RLS): A condition characterised by an irresistible urge to move the legs, typically in the evenings, during sleep. Link legs [and restless]. ♐ ♒ ♃ [♂ ♅].
(1) Jon Stewart (28 Nov 1962, no time). American talk-show host, calls his restless legs "Jimmy Legs." ☉ ♐ [□ ♅]. ♃ [☍ ♅].
(2) Keith Olbermann (27 Jan 1959, no time). American talk-show host, said being active reduces RLS symptoms. ♃ [☍ ♂ ♉].

Restlessness: Inability to rest or relax. [♂ ♅].

Restricts: Reduces freedom of movement/ development/ expression, flow. [♄].

Retard: Delay or hold back in terms of progress or development. [♄]

Retina: Tissue at the back of the eye that turns light into electrical signals. Via the optic nerve these signals travel to the brain which converts them into images. Ajna. ☉, ☿ ♅.

Rheumatic Fever: Streptococcal bacterial infection causing fever inflammation and pain in joints, impairing mobility. Link joints [and infection/ pain]. Jupiter may link in for impaired mobility. Base. ♑ ♄ [♅ ♂ ♆/ ♂].
(1) Ann Toth (3 Aug 1940, 06:01, Niagara Falls, Canada. ♄ r6H [□ ♂ ♌ 1> ♄ ☌ ♃].
(2) Bill Paxton (17 May 1955, no time). ♄ [□ ♇ ♌].
(3) Bobby Darin (14 May 1936, 05:28, Manhattan, NY). ♄ [☍ ♆ ♍, ∠ ♅ ♉ 12 > □ ♃].
(4) Patsy Cline (8 Sep 1932, 23:05, Winchester, VA). ♄ ♑ [☍ ♂ ♋ r6H, □ ♅ ♈ > ♅ ⚼ ♃].

Rheumatoid Arthritis, Rheumatism: An autoimmune disease. The immune system attacks the joints and joint linings, causing pain and impairing mobility. Sagittarius and Jupiter may link in for mobility. Link joints [and immune attack]. Base. ♑ ♄ [♂ ☉].
(1) Anna Marchesini (18 Nov 1953, 18:45, Orvieto, Italy). ♄ ♏ [mp ♂/☉6].
(2) Christiaan Barnard (8 Nov 1922, 20:00, Beaufort West, South Africa). The surgeon who transplanted a baboon's heart into a human. ♄ [□ ♇ ♋/♑ > ♇ △ ☉6].

1 Rulerships by Bills, The Rulership Book, 118.

(3) David Icke (29 Apr 1952, 19:15, Leicester, Eng). ♄12 [☍☉].

(4) James Coburn (31 Aug 1928, 20:15, Laurel, NE). ♄♐ [Tsq. ☍♂, □☉6].

Rhinitis, Allergic: (See Allergies). Stuffy nose, sneezing. Can be caused by acid reflux. Thr. ♈♂/ ♏ [♋☽].

Ribs: The skeleton generally is ruled by Capricorn-Saturn, but each region-ruler governs the bones in its part of the body. Hence Gemini for the upper ribs [1]. ♊.

Rickets: Softening/ weakening of bones usually due to inadequate vitamin D. The Sun rules vitamin D and may link in. Link the bones [and weak]. Base. ♑♄ [♓♆, ☽].

(1) Joseph Pilates (9 Dec 1883, 00:30, Gladbach, Ger). Inventor of the Pilates fitness method. He was a sickly child and suffered from asthma, rickets. ♄ [☍♀♑; ♀□♆ r6H].

Rigidity: Hardness, unable to be changed or adapted. The force of R1 'hardens'. [♄♇].

Rigor Mortis: Stiffening of joints and muscles a few hours after death. [♄♇].

Ringworm: A highly contagious fungal (Cancer, Moon), infection of the skin. Link skin [fungal > infection]. Spx. Base. ♑♄ (♋) [♋☽,♓♆ > ♂♅♆].

(1) Frank Rice (13 Sep 1915, 13:00, Albuquerque, NM). Had a ring worm on his face at 10. ♄♋ [♂♂♋].

Road Rage Attack: Tension in the world shows in many ways in society. An example is a road rage attack, which can include shouting, excessive use of a horn, obscene gestures, using the car as a weapon, or an actual physical attack. Link transport [and vehicle/ rage]. If there is a physical attack, include the self, the body (☉, Asc, 1H). ☿, 3H [♂].

(1) Jim Hodgson (8 Sep 1947, 01:55, Hawkwell, Eng). His car was rammed, then he was assaulted, ending up in hospital with a fractured skull. ☉ [♄♇ mp ☉3/ ♂12]. The surgeon said he survived because he had a thick (ray 3) skull.

Rubella (See Measles). Virus that causes a fever and a red rash. Although it shares some signs and symptoms of measles - such as the red rash; rubella is caused by a different virus. Although it is considered not to be as infectious or as severe as measles, it remains dangerous. [♂♆♅]

The following children became deaf after catching Rubella. For this effect of the infection, link the ears [infection > deafness]. ♊☿ [♂♆♅ > ♄]

(1) Astro.com 14169 (19 Oct 1966, 16:31, Phoenix, AZ). ☿ [♂♆♏ > ♓♇6, ♇☍♄12]

(2) Astro.com 14474 (9 Jan 1971, 08:23, Phoenix, AZ). ☿♐ [□♄ r12H; ♄☍♅8]

Rupture: Breaking or bursting open/ apart suddenly. [♂♅ (♇)].

---

1   Heindel, Astro-Diagnosis, 17.

S

SACRAL CHAKRA (Sac): (See Chakras and Etheric Web).

Consciousness: This is the sexual/ desire force centre. Although most people are focused in a higher centre, the sacral remains powerful because desire still drives most people.

Ray and Astrology energies: The governing rays are the 7th of Ceremony, Order, Magic, which flows via Uranus for sex attitudes; and the 6th of Devotion and Idealism, which flows via Mars for desire and sex. Scorpio governs this centre, and so does Sagittarius, which "provides the energy for the use of the creative powers of the physical life." [1]

Body rulership: This 6-petal lotus enters the spine around vertebrae L5 and S1, anchoring in the gonads. It vitalises the etheric web, genes - DNA, sex and reproduction.

Diseases: All problems with the sex organs and reproduction, genetic or congenital diseases.

Sacral Vertebrae: The sacral region is at the bottom of the spine, in the Sagittarius region and lies between the fifth segment of the lumbar spine (L5) and the coccyx (tailbone). Problems to these vertebrae are indicated by afflictions to Sagittarius and Jupiter. Sac. ♐♃.

Sacroiliac Joint: Links the pelvis and lower spine. Saturn for joints. Sac. ♐♃.

Sacrum: Bony structure located at the base of the lumbar vertebrae, that is connected to the pelvis. There are five fused vertebrae (S1–S5). Sac. ♐♃.

Sadism, Sadistic: Deriving perverted pleasure from inflicting pain, suffering, humiliation on others. Link self [and sadistic]. R6. Spx. Sac. ☉, Asc [♏♂♆].

(1) Marquis de Sade (2 Jun 1740, 17:00, Paris, Fr). The depraved French noble from whom the term 'sadism' derived. He spent most of his life in prison for staging sexual orgies that embraced crimes of sadomasochistic violence. Asc ♏ [☌♇♏12, qd ♂♈6].

SAGITTARIUS. ♐.

Rulers: Exoteric ruler is Jupiter, the esoteric ruler is the Earth, the hierarchy ruler is Mars.

Rays: Carries R4 of Conflict, R5 of Science, R6 of Devotion; also, R2 via Jupiter and R3 via the Earth. Energy is fiery, versatile and expansive.

Body: Sagittarius governs the sacral chakra, physical power, the hips, thighs, buttocks and locomotion.

Disease: When planets are afflicted in Sagittarius, or when Sagittarius rules the 6H, it indicates trouble with mobility, and/ or with nerves, which are governed by its opposite sign Gemini. As an afflictor - in conjunction with its ruler Jupiter, it can indicate problems of excess, with drink or food, of obesity and associated problems that impair the liver or mobility. Horse-riding accidents are also a danger.

Psychology: The keynote for average man in this sign is 'Let food be sought.' This can manifest as drinking or gluttony at one end of the scale, to serious criminal, sexual abuse at the other. This is due to Sagittarius' relation to the sexual sacral chakra. Sagittarius people are multitalented - artistic, intelligent and devotional. Their task is to direct people to a

1 Bailey, Alice: Esoteric Astrology, 191.

higher and finer path in life. Its higher keynote is, 'I see the goal, I reach that goal, and then I see another.'

Salivary Glands, Saliva: Discharge saliva - a digestive juice; into the mouth. Spx. ♋ ☽.

Salmonella Poisoning - see Poisons, Food Poisoning.

Salt: A mineral composed primarily of sodium chloride. ♄.

Sanitation: Steps taken to purify living conditions, to be hygienic. ♍ ☿, 6H.

Sarcoma/ Cancer: A sarcoma is a type of cancer that begins in the bones and soft tissues, and can occur in various parts of the body. Link bones /soft tissue [and the cancer formula]. ♑ ♄/♋ ☽ [(♋ ☽ >♄ ♇) > ♃ ☉].
(1) Robert Urich (19 Dec 1946, 21:40, Toronto, Ohio). In 1996, he began treatment for a synovial sarcoma. He went into remission but died in 2002. ☽ ♏ [(□ ♇12) > ☽ ☌ ♃].

SATURN. ♄.
Signs it rules: Saturn is the exoteric ruler of Capricorn, and of Aquarius (though this influence is fast fading). It is the esoteric ruler of Capricorn, and the hierarchy ruler of Libra.
House it rules: The 10H.
Rays: Carries the 3rd ray of Intelligence and Activity, the primary force in nature that governs the 'body' aspect of all living things. It also carries R1 of Will and Power, and R7 of Order, via Capricorn.
Body: Governs the throat chakra, the parathyroids, and is related to the thyroid gland and the intelligent functioning of the endocrine system. It corules the base chakra, vitalising the dense physical body, bones, skeletal structure, spine, skin, hair and teeth.
Disease: Afflicted, Saturn can represent trouble with the parts and organs it rules. Its sign points to a part of the body that may have a genetic or chronic weakness, which is underdeveloped or impaired in some way. As the afflictor, Saturn causes cold and deprives. It represents the hardening, crystallising, atrophying, ageing, calcifying, drying, contracting and stiffening effect of the 1st ray; and slow forming, chronic, enduring diseases.
Psychology: Its function is to teach us to act intelligently and responsibly, to make correct decisions according to the Law of Karma. When debased, we see avarice, greed, hard-heartedness, manipulation, deviousness, dishonesty, ruthless ambition and abuse of power. Positively, it produces intelligent, professional leaders who shoulder huge responsibilities.

Scabies: A contagious, intensely itchy skin condition caused by a tiny, burrowing mite. Link skin [and parasite]. Base. ♑ ♄ (♋ ☽) [♏ ♂ ♇].
(1) Rebecca Zeni (23 Nov 1922, no time). She died in 2015. An autopsy found she died of septicaemia due to crusted scabies - mites were living under her skin. ♄ [□ ♇ ♋/♑].

Scabs: A crusty protective tissue covering, which forms over damaged skin. ♄.

Scalded: To burn the skin with very hot liquid or steam. Link the skin or the body part burnt [and burn]. The Moon or Neptune could link in for liquid and steam; so could the 1H for the appearance or face. ♑ ♄ (♋ ☽) [♈ ♂ ☉].
(1) Amy Rodden (23 Nov 1949, 00:45, Palo Alto, CA). Burnt on the arm. ☿ [☌ ☉ ♐ r12H].
(2) Astro.com 44299 (23 May 1942, 10:04, Sydney, Austl). The face. ♀ ♈ (face) [□ ♂ 1].
(3) Cassandra Peterson (Elvira) (17 Sep 1951, 09:00 Manhattan, KS). She had severe burns over 35% of her body. ♄ 12 [∠ ♂ ♇ ♌].

Scales: Visible peeling or flaking of outer skin layers. Base ♑ ♄ (♋ ☽) [♂].

Scalp: The skin on the top of the head where hair grows. Cwn ♈ ♂.

Scapula: Triangular bone at the back of the shoulder. Thr. ♊.

Scar: Tissue growth where skin has healed after an injury. Base [♑ ♄ (♇)].

Scarlet Fever: A bacterial infection that attacks the throat. A distinguishing red rash develops. Link throat [and infection]. Thr. ♉ ♀ [♅ ♂ ♆].
These aristocrats died of the disease. An extra step for death (8H) has been added.
(1) Caroline Matilda (11 Jul 1751, 06:00, London, Eng). ♀ ♍ [∠♆12 r8H].
(2) Princess Henrietta (30 Oct 1797, 08:00, Bayreuth, Ger). ♀ r6H [□ ♅ > ♅ ⚹ ♄8].

Scheuermann's Kyphosis: Like scoliosis, except the curvature of the spine is front to back, not sideways. (See Scoliosis).

Schizophrenia: (See Mental Illness). Serious mental illness that interferes with a person's ability to think clearly, manage emotions, make decisions and relate to others. It is due to the level of psychological development. Link the self/ mind [emotionalism > malefic that describes the nature of the disorder]. Spx. ☉, Asc / ♊ ☿ [♋ ☽ ♂ ♆ > malefic].
(1) Vincent Van Gogh (30 Mar 1853, 11:00, Zundert, Neth). Asc ♋, □ ☿ [∠♆ ♓ > ☿ ☌ ♇ (for deep introspection, thinking dark thoughts)].

Schonlein Purpura, Henoch - Schonlein Purpura, IgA Vasculitis: Inflames small blood vessels so they bleed. A purplish rash is distinctive (typically on the lower legs and buttocks), abdominal pain, aching joints. Most common in children under 10. Link blood vessels [inflamed, bleed, pain > aching joints]. ♒ ♅ [♂ ☉ > ♑ ♄].
(1) Damion Mckinnon (10 Feb 1971, Auckland, NZ). Had an attack around age 7 and was hospitalised. The condition recovered on its own and never returned. ☉ ♒ [□ ♄ 12].

Sciatic nerve: A peripheral nerve that provides motor function and sensations in the legs. Ajna. Base. ♐ ♃ (♊ ☿).

- Sciatica: Pain radiating along the sciatic nerve. Link the sciatic nerve [and pain]. Ajna. Base. ♐ ♃/ ♊ ☿ [♂].
(1) Emmy Goring (24 Mar 1893, 13:30, Hamburg, Ger). ♃ ♈ [mp ♂ ♉/ ☉ ♈].
(2) Jim Hodgson (8 Sep 1947, 01:55, Hawkwell, Eng). ☿ r12H [mp ♂/♃ r6H].
(3) Whoopi Goldberg (13 Nov 1955, 12:48, New York, NY). The American actress suffers debilitating sciatica pain, even using a walker to help her move around. ♃ [♂ ♎ mp ♀ ♐/♃].

Sclera: White outer coating of the eye. Ajna. ☉.

Scleroderma, Systemic Sclerosis: The autoimmune system makes too much collagen in connective tissue, which thickens and hardens. Muscles shorten, constricting organs. In time, mobility is seriously impaired. Sagittarius and Jupiter may link in for loss of movement. If Saturn is chosen to represent connective tissue, it can also double up as a ruler of hardening. Link the connective tissue [immune attack > thickens/ hardens]. Base. ♑ ♄ [♂ ☉ > ♃/ ♄ ♇].
(1) Alice Lon (23 Nov 1926, 10:00, Kilgore, TX). The American dancer and singer suffered for several years from the disease, dying in 1981. ♄ ♏ [☌ ☉ r8H > ⚼ ♇ ♋].

(2) Paul Klee (18 Dec 1879, 04:00, Münchenbuchsee, Switzerland). The Herman artist was diagnosed with the disease in 1935, dying 5 years later. ♄ ♈ [mp ♂ ♉ r6H / ♃].

(3) Tylyn John (31 Jul 1966, 02:33, Encino, CA). The ex-Playboy bunny was diagnosed in 1999, and has been living with the disease for over 20 years. ☽ ♑8 [☍♃ ♋/♑ > ♃ ☌ ♂ r6H].

Scoliosis: Abnormal sideways curve of the spine. Link the spine [twisted]. ♌ ☉ ♄ [♅ ♆].
(1) Astro.com 35997 (20 Oct 1942, 20:05, Danville, IL). ♄1 [☌ ♅12, via the Asc].
(2) Eugenie, Princess (23 Mar 1990, 19:58, London, Eng). ☉6 [□ ♅ ♑].
(3) Rowena Wallace (23 Aug 1947, 08:10, Coventry, Eng). ☉12 [⚹ ♅ r6H].
(4) Shailene Woodley (15 Nov 1991, 21:06, Upland, CA). ☉ [∠ ♅ ♑6].

SCORPIO. ♏.

Rulers: Mars is both the exoteric and esoteric ruler; the hierarchy ruler is Mercury.
Rays: Carries R4 of Harmony through Conflict. Via its rulers, Scorpio also expresses R6 (Mars) and R1 (Pluto). Scorpio energy is emotional and watery, but more fiery, intense and concentrated than other water signs due to the fixed nature of the sign, and the presence of R1 and fiery Mars.
Body: Scorpio corules the solar plexus chakra (the elimination of excretion), and the sacral chakra (sex, reproduction - the ovaries and testes). It is also related to the base chakra and the adrenal medulla 'fight or flight' reaction. Scorpio also rules death.
Disease: When planets are afflicted in Scorpio, or when Scorpio rules the 6H, it indicates trouble with sex, with reproduction, with body elimination - and/ or with the throat, which is governed by its opposite sign Taurus.

Being a fixed-water sign, as an afflictor, Scorpio can bring sluggish, damp conditions that are slow-moving and chronic. Scorpio people are prone to inner conflict, which grinds down vitality, undermining the immune system and rendering the body open to infection. They also tend to hold onto the past, to old issues and hurts. The reflex action of this upon the body, thickens body fluids causing phlegm. Anger and vengeance (other Scorpio traits), poison the blood, which erupt as nasty skin conditions and ulcers.
Psychology: Scorpio's task is to teach emotional control and balance. As part of this process, it endows its people with heroism and courage then guides them into emotionally wrenching and traumatic experiences, which forces them to draw upon these higher qualities. Its higher keynote is, 'Warrior I am, and from the battle I emerge triumphant.'

Scrofula: Tuberculosis infection of the neck lymph nodes. Link neck > lymph [infection]. Thr. ♉ ♀ > ♓♆, ♋ ☽ [♅ ♂ ♆].
(1) Astro.com 11652 (7 Aug 1950, 09:43, Pauls Valley, OK). ♀ > □ ♆ r6H [♆ □ ♅].

Scrotum: Pouch below the penis containing the testes, epididymis etc. Sac. ♏♂.

Scurvy: Vitamin C deficiency. This weakens collagen, the tissue that connects muscles and bones, resulting in muscle fibre atrophy and haemorrhage. It is a nutritional problem. Link food/ nutrition [deficient]. ♋ ☽/ ☿ ♍ 6H [♑ ♄ ♇].

(1) Arnold Spencer-Smith (17 Mar 1883, no time). He was on Ernest Shackleton's 1914-17 Ross Sea voyage. With limited nutrition, he died of scurvy. ☿ ♓/♍ [□ ♇].
(2) James Blunt (22 Feb 1974, no time). After an all-meat diet for a few weeks, the British singer developed signs of scurvy. ☽ ☿ ♓/♍ [⚻ ♇ ♎, extreme nutritional imbalance].

Sebaceous Cyst: Small, non-cancerous bump under the skin. Base. [♋ ☽, ♃].

Sebaceous Gland: Small oil-producing gland present in the skin. Base. ♋ ☽.

Secretions: Secreting body fluids. ♋ ☽.

Sedative: A tonic that promotes calm or induces sleep. ♆.

Seizures: Sudden, uncontrolled electrical disturbances in brain nerves. Link nerves [and seizures]. Ajna. ♊ ☿ (♀♒♅) [♅♒].
(1) Marina LeBlanc (8 Feb 2004, 14:50, Los Angeles, CA). At age 8 months, she suffered seizures due to a neurological disorder. ☿♒ [♅ mp ☿/♀].
(2) Maureen Reagan (4 Jan 1941, 03:21, Los Angeles, CA). In 2001, she began to have mild seizures and was diagnosed with two brain tumours. ☿ [⚼ ♅ ♉6].

Selenium: Trace mineral that helps make DNA, protect against cell damage, infection. ♌♒.

Self (The), Self-consciousness: Self-awareness. Greater insight about oneself and one's place in the world. This development awakens the ajna centre. [1] The Sun is the prime ruler of consciousness and of the personality. Additionally, the ascendant can represent 'the self.' Venus and Mercury as rulers of the intelligence and of the ajna, can substitute. R2. ☉, Asc (☿ ♀).

Self-harm: (See Cuts, Cutting). Deliberate causing of pain or injury to oneself.

Semen: The male reproductive fluid containing sperm. Sac. ♏♂.

Seminal Vesicle: Male sex glands that produce semen. Sac. ♏♂.

Senile Decay: (See Dementia). Decline (largely mental), as in old age. R1 [♑ ♄ (♇)].

Senses, The 5: Sight, taste, touch, hearing and smell - they are part of the peripheral nervous system. The senses collect information about our environment, which is passed to the brain and then interpreted by the mind. We make sense of this information based on previous experience. The Tibetan Master Djwhal Khul said that the mind is the sixth sense. [2] The 3rd ray "creates and uses the nervous system, brain and the five senses." [3] Gemini, the 3rd sign, is related to R3. Ajna. Thr. ♊ ☿.

Sensual: Preoccupied with the senses or appetites. ♀ ♂.

Separative: Causing, or expressing separation. [R5, ♒♅ (♀)].

Sepsis, Septicaemia: The bloodstream is invaded by a bacterial infection. Untreated it can kill. Link blood [and infection]. ♂ ♃ ♒ [♅ ♂ ♆].
These 4 examples died from sepsis, so an extra link for death has been added.
(1) Brian Dennehy (9 Jul 1938, no time). ♃♓℞ [qd ♆♍ > ⚻♇].
(2) Colin Weir (24 May 1947, 16:20, Edinburgh, Sc). ♃♏℞ r6H [⚻♅. ♂8 disposits ♃].
(3) David Leland (6 Jan 1932, 19:30, Alassio, Italy). ♃♌℞ [⚻♂6 > ♂☍♇12].
(4) Patty Duke (14 Dec 1946, 22:39, Manhattan, NY). ♃♏ [⚻♅ r6H > □♇12].

Serial Killer: Person who commits a series of murders, usually for sexual gratification. An 'astral maniac' (see that entry). However, while that type of mania can be harmless, the hunger in this type has turned very dark. Look for that darkness in the chart (♏♇, 8H,

1 Bailey, Alice: Esoteric Psychology II, 415.
2 Bailey, Alice: From Intellect to Intuition, 95.
3 Bailey, Alice: Esoteric Psychology I, 251.

12H). Taurus or Venus, rulers of 'the appetite' may be involved. They also rule the limbic system / the emotional brain and addictions. This explains why Venus may be tied in with this type of pattern. An addiction - *love of killing,* develops. So, look for Venus-Mars links. Link the astral nature [love > of killing]. Thr. Spx. R6. Sac. ♂♆ [♀ > ♏♂♇, 8H].

(1) David Berkowitz, the Son of Sam (1 Jun 1953, 16:52, Brooklyn, NY). He pleaded guilty to eight shootings. ♂8 [mp ♀♈6 /♇].

(2) Dennis Rader, BTK (9 Mar 1945, 14:47, Wichita, KS). ♂♒8 [☉☿ mp ♀♈/♂].

(3) Harold Shipman (14 Jan 1946, no time). Felt in control when killing. ♂♋ [☌♄ ☍♀♑].

(4) Peter Sutcliffe, the Yorkshire Killer (2 Jun 1946, 20:30, Bingley, Eng). He has 5 planets in the 8H, including Mars and Pluto. He was a deviant killer. ♂8 [mp ♀8/ ♆].

(5) Ted Bundy (24 Nov 1946, 22:35, Burlington, VT). Kidnapped, raped and murdered dozens of young men. ♀♏℞ [□♇12].

Serotonin: Pineal gland hormone that acts as a mood stabilizer. Cwn. ♀.

Serous Membranes: Epithelial membranes that are moist and line cavities. The outer lining of organs and body cavities of the abdomen, chest and stomach. Base. ♋☽.

SEX, SEXUAL ACTIVITY: Specifically sexual intercourse. The sacral chakra controls sex, and Scorpio and its ruler Mars generally rule sexual desire and the sex act. Venus is also a representative of sex. Sac. ♏♂♀.

- Sex Attitudes: Uranus, carrying R7 (and governing the sacral), governs sex attitudes and the developing world-wide mental interest in sex. [1] ♅

- Sexual Energy: The energy called upon during sex via the hips, thighs and thrusting. Scorpio is sex, Sagittarius gives power to. Sac. ♏♐.

- Sex Organs and Glands: The sacral chakra controls the sex life and sex organs. Sac. ♏♂, ♀.

- Sexual Desire: The 6th ray of desire playing through the sacral chakra. Sac. ♏♂♀.

- Sexual Development - see Puberty.

- Sexual Difficulties: Such as frigidity, low libido, inability to achieve an erection, an orgasm. Often such difficulties are the result of sexual abuse. Link sex [deficient, inhibited]. Sac. ♏♂♀ [♑♄].

- Sexual Preferences: Are governed by ray 7, carried by Uranus. [2] R7. Sac. ♅.

- Sexual Violations, Perversions: Such as sexual sadism. Sac [♏♂ > ♅♆].

- Sexually Transmitted Disease, STD: (See Herpes, Gonorrhoea, Syphilis). An infection transmitted through sexual contact. It can be either bacterial/ viral/ or parasitic. Link sex [and STD]. Sac. ♏♂♀ [♂♅♆,♇].

Shatters: Break or cause to break suddenly and violently into pieces. [♅].

Shingles: Reactivation of the chickenpox virus in the body, causing nerve pain and rash. Link nerves [virus > rash, pain]. Ajna. Base. ♊☿(♀♒♅) [♂♅♆ > ♂].

(1) David Letterman (12 Apr 1947, 06:00, Indianapolis, IN). In February 2003, the American talk show host suffered from a painful bout of shingles. ☿♓12 [□♅♊ > ☌♂♈12].

1 Bailey, Alice: Esoteric Psychology I, 262.
2 Bailey, Alice: The Rays and the Initiations, 571.

Shins: Front of the leg below the knee. Base. ♅.

Shocks: A sudden, strong, upsetting effect in the body. [♅].

Shoulders: Part of the body where the arm joins the body. Thr. ♊ ☿.

Shrinks: To contract, grow smaller. [♄].

Sickness: Being unwell. [♄].

Sight, Vision: Ability to see the world around us, via the eye organs and eye nerves in the head. The Sun is the primary ruler of vision, and rules specifically the right eye. The Moon is a substitute ruler and rules the left eye.

The physical eye came into being in response to the light of the sun. [1]

Uranus and Mercury rule the retina and optic eye nerves and can also substitute for vision. The 3rd Ray rules sight. [2] Ajna. ☉ ☽ (☿ ♅).

- Short-sighted: Unable to see far. Neptune may link in for the gradual fading of vision. Gemini can represent eye nerves. Link vision [loss, fading]. Ajna. ☉ ☽ (☿ ♅) [♑ ♄ (♆)].
(1) Alfred Tennyson (6 Aug 1809, 00:05, Somersby, Eng). ☽ ♊ 12 [qd ♄ 6].
(2) John Kipling (17 Aug 1897, 01:50, Rottingdean, Eng). ☉ [□ ♄ coruler 6H].
(3) Louis Hillesum (25 May 1880, 22:00, Amsterdam, Neth). ☉ ♊ [☌ ♇ ♉]. ☽ 12 [⚼ ♆].

Sigmoid Flexure: End part of the bowel. Stores faecal waste for elimination. Spx. ♏ ♂ ♇.

Silicosis - see Pulmonary Silicosis, Poison - Mineral Kingdom.

Simmonds' Disease: Destruction of the anterior lobe of the pituitary gland. Causes emaciation, premature aging. Link the pituitary [and destruction]. Ajna. ☿ ♀ [♄ ♇].

Sinews - see Tendons.

Sinuses: These are small, air-filled cavities behind the cheekbones and forehead. They produce mucous that usually drains into the nose through small channels. Thr. ♋ ☽.

- Sinusitis: Inflammation of a nasal sinus. Thr. ♋ ☽ [♂ ☉].
(1) Marilyn Miller (1 Sep 1898, 09:30, Evansville, IN). She had a long history of sinusitis infections. ☽ ♓ [□ ♂ r6H].

Sjogren's Syndrome: (See Autoimmune Disease). The immune system attacks healthy cells, which produce saliva and tears. Symptoms are dry eyes and dry mouth. The relation between repressing the emotions (holding back tears), and the condition, is easy to see. Link tears, saliva [immune attack > atrophy]. ♋ ☽ [♂ ☉ > ♄ (♇)].
(1) Venus Williams (17 June 1980, 14:12, Lynwood, CA). The tennis champion was stoic in the face of challenges faced in her career. But it took its toll. ☿ ♋ [⚻ ♆ > ♆ □ ♄ 12].

Skeletal Dysplasia - see Dysplasia.

Skeleton: The structural frame that supports the body. R3, Base. ♑ ♄.

Skin: The largest organ of the body. With the hair, nails, oil glands and sweat glands, it is part of the Integumentary System - the body's outer covering. One of its main functions is protection from external threats such as bacteria, chemicals and temperature. It is generally ruled by R3, the base chakra, Saturn and Capricorn. Cancer - Moon (related to soft tissue, that envelop and protect); are substitute rulers. Base. ♑ ♄ (♋ ☽).

1 Bailey, Alice: Treatise on White Magic, 213.
2 Bailey, Alice: Esoteric Psychology I, 133.

- **Skin Allergy:** (See Eczema). Reaction of the skin to an allergic substance. Link skin [allergy]. Base. Spx. ♑ ♄ [♋ ☽, ♅].

- **Skin Cancer:** Basal and squamous cell carcinomas are the two most common types. Melanoma, the third most common type of skin cancer, begins in the melanocytes. Though exposure to ultraviolet radiation from the sun and tanning lamps are thought to be leading causes of skin cancer; the cancer formula still applies. This because not everyone exposed gets the disease. For those who do, perhaps being exposed to damaging radiation is a life metaphor for feeling exposed to the harsh light of judgment and criticism. Link the skin [to the cancer formula]. Base. ♑ ♄ [(♋ ☽ > ♄ ♇) > ♃ ☉].

- Skin cancer: Basal.

(1) Diane Keaton (5 Jan 1946, 02:49, Los Angeles, CA). ♄ ♋ [(☌ ♂ ℞ r6H) > □ ♃].
(2) Ewan McGregor, (31 Mar 1971, 20:10, Perth, Scot). ♂ ♑ [□ ☉ 6].
(3) Hugh Jackman (12 Oct 1968, no time). ♄ [(⚻ ♆ ♏) > ☍ ☉ ♎].
(4) Melanie Griffith (9 Aug 1957, 23:49, NY, NY). ♄ [mp ☽/♃]. Jupiter is ☌ the 6H cusp.

- Skin cancer: Melanoma.

(1) Colin Bloomfield (22 Feb 1982, 19:30, Montford Bridge, UK). ♄ [(☌ ♂ ♇ ♎) > ♄ ⚼ ☉].
(2) John Bunch (1 Dec 1921, 04:00, Tipton, IN). ♄ [(□ ☽ ♑) > ♄ ☌ ♃ 12].
(3) Terry Melcher (8 Feb 1942, 12pm, New York, NY). ♄ 12 [(☍ ☽ 6♏, ♄ ☌ ♂) > □ ☉].

- **Skin, Dry:** Skin drier than normal. Base. ♑ ♄ (♋ ☽) [♄].

- **Skin Infection, Eruptions:** Infection of the skin. Base. ♑ ♄ (♋ ☽) [♂ ♅ ♆].

- **Skin Lesion:** An area of abnormal tissue. Link tissue [and abnormal]. Base. ♋ ☽ [♅].

- **Skin Rash:** Temporary red, bumpy, scaly, itchy patches of skin. Base. ♑ ♄ (♋ ☽) [♈ ♂].

Skull: Bone framework enclosing the brain. Cwn. Base. ♈ ♄.

- **Skull Injuries:** Accidents, injuries to the skull. Link skull [injury]. Cwn. Base. ♑ ♄ [♂ ♅].

Sleep: When we fall asleep, consciousness withdraws to the astral plane, bringing sleep under the domain of Neptune (a ruler of that plane), its sign Pisces, and the 12H that represents the 'unconscious.' The Moon governs 'night-time' and is also a ruler of the 'unconscious.' Pluto - associated with the pineal gland physically, governs death and sleep, which is temporary death on the physical plane. Cwn. ♓ ♆, ☽ ♇, 12H.

- **Sleep Apnoea:** Breathing repeatedly stops and starts, because muscles in the back of the throat relax too much to allow normal breathing. It increases the risk of sudden death, especially in the ill or elderly. Sleep is associated with the 12H. The rulers of sleep (☽ ♆) may link in. Link breathing [with cessation of]. Thr. ♊ ☿ [♄ ♇].

(1) Linda Ronstadt (15 Jul 1946, 17:39, Tucson, AZ). ☿ r6H [☌ ♇ 8].
(2) Rosie O'Donnell (21 Mar 1962, 10:00, Commack, NY). ☿ ♓ [☍ ♇ r6H].
(3) Shaquille O'Neal (6 Mar 1972, 08:00, Newark, NJ). ☿ 12 [☍ ♇ 6].

- **Sleep Disorder** - see Sleep, Insomnia, Narcolepsy, Nightmares, Sleepwalking.

- **Sleep Walking** - see Parasomnia.

Small intestine - see Intestines, Small.

Smallpox: Deadly air-borne, highly contagious viral disease. Millions have died from it through history - more than 300 million people since 1900. Death is by systemic shock due to body-wide infection and toxins in the blood. Pus-filled blisters leave disfiguring scars. Link blood [infection > shock/ trauma, death]. Thr. Base. ♂♃♒ [♆♂♅ > ♅/♇].
These aristocrats died from the disease.
(1) Johanna Gabriele (4 Feb 1750, 20:30, Vienna, Austria). ☉♒ [☌♅ r6H > ⚹♂ r8H].
(2) Henriette, Princess (14 Aug 1727, 11:25, Versailles, FR). ☉♌ [□♅1 > ∠♀ r8H].
(3) Karl Joseph (1 Feb 1745, 09:15, Vienna, Austria). ☉☿♒ [⚻♆ > ☿□♇♏8].
(4) Maria Josepha (19 Mar 1751, 12:30, Vienna, Austria). ♅♒8 r8H [⚻♆☌Asc].

Smell Sense: (See Senses, Anosmia, Hyposmia). The senses are part of the peripheral nervous system. Ajna. Thr. ♊ ☿ ♀.

Smelly: Having a strong or unpleasant odour. Venus is sweet, Mars is not. [♂ (♆)].

Smoking: Inhaling toxic smoke via cigarettes, cigars or vaping. [♆].

Smother: R3 carried by Saturn, smothers. [1] So does Scorpio. [2] [♏♇, ♄].

Snake Bite: The bite of a snake, especially a venomous one. [♏♂♇].
(1) Joseph Slowinski (15 Nov 1962, no time). He was killed by a snake bite. ☉♏ [□♂♌].

Sneeze: A sudden blast of air expelled from the mouth and nose, caused by an irritation in nose/ mouth mucous membranes. Thr. [☿ > ♂].

Snoring: When air cannot move freely, tissues in the neck vibrate. Thr. ☿ > [♅].

Social Anxiety Disorder - see Panic Attacks.

Social Diseases - see Sexually Transmitted Diseases.

Sociopath/ Antisocial Personality Disorder: (See Psychopath). There is no empathy or remorse, no regard for social rights and wrongs. Driven powerfully by their emotions and desires, behaviour is aggressive, violent, selfish and impulsive. Link self [social > selfishness, violence]. Thr. Spx. ☉ Asc [♎♀ > ♂♅].
(1) Gary Lee Sampson (29 Sep 1959, 00:44, Weymouth, MA). ☉♎ [♀☌♇ > ∠♅].
(2) Nick Nolte (8 Feb 1941, 10:40, Omaha, NE). T-square ☉♒ [□♅♉1 > ♀☍♇].
(3) Richard Tingler (2 Dec 1940, 12pm, Portsmouth, Ohio). ☉ [qd ♅♉ > ♀□♇].

Solar Angel: A member of the Kingdom of Souls, which controls the evolution of humanity. Everyone has a Solar Angel, a spiritual guide and mentor. ♀.

Solar Fire: Love energy streaming from the heart of the Sun. R2, ☉♃.

SOLAR PLEXUS CHAKRA (Spx): (See Chakras and Etheric Web).
Consciousness: This is the emotional chakra, and because most people are dominated by their emotions, it is the most potent centre in humanity.
Ray and Astrology energies: Ray 6 of Devotion and Idealism flows through this centre via Mars and Neptune. The Moon and Cancer are related.
Body rulership: This 10-petal lotus enters the spine around T12 and L1, anchoring in the pancreas gland. It vitalises the digestion organs - the stomach, liver, gallbladder, pancreas, duodenum, intestines; and the sympathetic nervous system.

1 Bailey, Alice: Esoteric Healing, 300.
2 Bailey, Alice: Esoteric Astrology, 98.

Diseases: It is related to the many mental and physical disorders caused by powerful and unstable emotions. Physically, problems with digestive organs - especially the stomach and pancreas; and trouble with the bloodstream: sepsis, blood poisoning and skin eruptions.

Somnambulism, Sleepwalking - see Parasomnia.

Soporific: Tending to induce drowsiness or sleep. ☽ ♆.

Sore Throat: Raw or painful throat. Thr. ♉ ♀ [♂].

Sores: A sore can be a blister, bump, lesion, wound, or ulcer. Base. Spx. [♂].

Sound Therapy: Healing through sound and music. The correct note when sent forth "Can destroy and eliminate corrupt tissue and cause new tissue to be built in." [1] Thr. ♊ ☿ (♍).

Spasms, Spasmodic, Spastic, Spasticity: Sudden, involuntary movements. Ajna [♅].

Speech, Organs of Speech: Ability to express thoughts vocally. Thr. ♊ ☿ .

Sperm: Male reproductive cell. Sac. ♏♂.

Sphincter Muscles: Ring-shaped muscles that relax or tighten, to allow the flow of fluids in one direction. There are over 50 in the body. ♂.

Spine, Spinal Column, Backbone, Vertebral Column: The line of bones down the centre of the back that provides support for the body and protects the spinal cord. Generally ruled by Leo, the Sun and Saturn. Vertebrae sections are co-ruled by signs governing back sections, from Taurus to Sagittarius. Base. ♌☉♄.

- Spina Bifida: (See Incontinence). A birth defect. The spine which normally protects the spinal cord and nerves, does not form properly and close as it should. This can damage nerves. Include ♊ ☿ if nerves are damaged. Link congenital > spine [incomplete]. Base. ♋☽ > ♌☉,♑♄ [♄].

(1) Edwin Meese (2 Dec 1931, 03:29, Oakland, CA). ☽ [⚼ ♄ for spine and incomplete development].

(2) Florence Henderson (14 Feb 1934, 05:00, Dale, IN). ☽ coruler 6H > ☌ ☉ [☌ ♄].

(3) Jean Driscoll (18 Nov 1966, 09:15, Milwaukee, WI). ☽ [∠♄ > ⚼ ♅ for nerve damage].

(4) Linda Martel (21 Aug 1956, 03:30, St Peter Port, Guernsey). ☽ [□ ♄].

- Spinal Arthritis, Stiffening: Ageing and deterioration of spinal vertebrae. [♑ ♄].

- Spinal Cord. An extension of the brain that carries messages to and from the brain via the network of peripheral nerves. Ajna. ♊ ☿ .

- Spinal Curvature - see Scoliosis.

- Spinal Fluid - see Cerebrospinal Fluid.

- Spinal Fractures - see Broken Back.

- Spinal Meningitis - see Meningitis.

Spleen: The organ of vitality, of prana or physical sun force. ♌☉.

Split Personality - see Multiple Personalities.

Sprain: Wrench or twist the ankle, wrist, or other joint violently, causing pain and swelling. Link joint [wrench, sprain] ♑ ♄ (♊ ☿ wrists, ♒ ♅ ankles [♂ ♅].

1 Bailey, Alice: Esoteric Psychology I, 125-126.

Sputum: Mucous that is coughed up from the lower airways. Thr ♋ ☽ [♂].

Squint: A permanent deviation in the direction of the gaze of one eye. Ajna. ☉ ☽ [♄ ♅].

St. Vitus' Dance - see Sydenham's Chorea.

Stabbed: Being stabbed by a knife or other sharp implement. Link the self/ life [and stabbed]. ☉, Asc [♂].

These four women were stabbed to death.

(1) Abigail Folger (11 Aug 1943, 17:27, San Francisco, CA). Heiress to the Folger Coffee fortune ☉8 [□ ♂ ♉/♏].

(2) Giulia Pasini (8 Jul 1994, 19:30, Castel san Pietro, Italy). ☉ r8 [∠♂].

(3) Sharon Tate (24 Jan 1943, 17:47, Dallas, TX). The beautiful, pregnant actress killed by the Manson family. ☉ [☍ ♇1 murder, substituting for Mars].

(4) Valerie Percy (10 Dec 1944, 17:25, Oakland, CA). ☉ [☌ ♂6].

Stagnate: Cease to flow or move, become inactive or dull. [♄].

Stalk, Stalker, Stalking: Person who harasses or persecutes someone with unwanted and obsessive attention. [♏♂♇].

Starch: A complex carbohydrate, long chains of simple sugar called glucose. ♀.

Starve, Starvation: Suffering or death caused by lack of food. Link life > food/ nourishment [starvation]. Spx. ☉, Asc > ♋ ☽ [♄ (♇)].

(1) Kurt Godel (28 Apr 1906, no time). In 1977, mentally unstable, the mathematician refused to eat and starved to death. ☉ [mp ♄/♆♋].

Stem Cells: The body's raw materials. Cells from which all other cells with specialized functions are generated. They mostly live in bone marrow, where they divide to make new blood cells. Once mature, they leave bone marrow and enter the bloodstream. ☽.

Stenosis: Narrowing or constriction of the diameter of a bodily passage or orifice. [♄].

Sterile, Sterility, Sterilization: (See Barren). Inability to produce offspring. Sterilization is a medical procedure to prevent reproduction. ♋ ☽, 5H [♄ ♇ (♂ for sterilization)].

(1) Erna Kronshage (12 Dec 1922, 21:00, Senne II, Ger). A victim of the Nazis in 1943 she was forcibly sterilized. ☽ [□♇♋].

Sternum: The breastbone. Hrt. ♋ ☽.

Stiff, Stiffens: To make stiff or stiffer. [♑ ♄].

- Stiff Person's Syndrome: A neurological disorder. The disease targets the muscles, causing them to spasm and stiffen. Link nerves > muscles [spasm/ stiff]. Ajna. ♊ ☿ > ♂ [♅/♑ ♄].

(1) Celine Dion (30 Mar 1968, 12:15, Charlemagne, Quebec). In 2022, the singer announced she was cancelling a tour because she had this condition and it affected her ability to sing. ☿ ♓ [☉ ♄ r6H mp ☿/♂].

Stigmata: (See Delusion). In Catholicism, wounds and scars which appear in locations corresponding to the crucifixion wounds of Jesus - hands, wrists and feet. Esoterically, these are considered to be cases of mystical delusion shaping and influencing the power of thought. Here is what the Tibetan Master says of mystical delusion. (Comments by the author are in square brackets).

> When the focus of the life is in the astral body.. the constant cultivation of the vision (whatever that might be [Author: in this case the suffering crucifixion of Christ]), absorbs the mystic's whole attention.. This powerful dream (built year by year through aspiration, worship and longing) [Author: can end up obsessing the mystic]. Sometimes he died of the ecstasy induced by his identification with his vision [Author: killed by his delusion]. [1]

The emotional devotee is obsessed by the vision of Christ suffering, and because of the great and fundamental law that "energy follows thought," that suffering appears on the physical body as scars and blood. Link the self/ the mind/ emotions [delusion > obsession]. Spx. ☉ Asc/ ♊ ☿/ ♋ ☽ ♂ [♓♆/ ♇].

(1) Anna Emmerich (8 Sep 1774, no time). Born into a poor farming family, she joined the Augustinian nuns. She had weak health, religious ecstasies and stigmata. ☉ [☌♆♍]. ☽ [Tsq. □♇, □♂♋].

(2) Catherine Benincasa/ St. Catherine of Siena (25 Mar 1347, no time). A Dominican mystic. "Her biographer implied that she was subject to hystero-epileptic attacks" (Britannica). ☉ ☿ [⚹♆]. ☽ [☍♂♓ > ⚻♇].

(3) Elena Aiello (10 Apr 1895, 10:00, Montalto Uffugo, Italy). She was born into a devout Italian family She "received the stigmata every Good Friday." [2] ☽♏ [⚼♆12 > ♆☌♇].

(4) Marthe Robin (13 Mar 1902, 17:00, Chateuaneuf-Galaure, Fr). French Roman Catholic mystic and stigmatist. ☉♂♓ [□♆♇].

(5) Resl von Konnersreuth (9 Apr 1898, 01:00, Konnersreuth, Ger). Born into a poor village family, she joined a religious order and developed stigmata. ☉ [⚹♆☌♇6].

The remedy for delusion. "Gently and gradually develop.. a cycle of doubt, leading even to a temporary agnosticism. The encouraging of a normal physical life, with its ordinary interests, the fulfilling of its obligations and responsibilities. The result would be a rapid establishing of the desired equilibrium." [3]

Stillborn: Death or loss of a baby before birth or during delivery. In the baby's chart, link congenital / life [and death]. Sac. ♋ ☽/ ☉ Asc [♏♇, 8H].

(1) Astro.com Duncan (3 Aug 1914, 10:30, Bellevue, Fr). ☽ ♑ [☍♇].

(2) Jesse Presley (8 Jan 1935, 04:00, Tupelo, MS). Elvis' twin. ☽ [☌ ♄]. ☉ [☍♇♋8].

---- Gladys Presley (25 Apr 1912, no time). The mother of Jesse Presley. Her chart shows the loss of a child, a loss connected with pregnancy. ☽ [□ ♄ for an incomplete foetus].

(3) Rodden baby (20 Jul 1956, 05:32, Castro Valley, CA). ☽ [⚻♅♌ r8H].

Stimulants: Drugs that speed up messages travelling between the brain and body, which raise levels of physiological or nervous activity. ♂ ♅.

Stomach: Organ that is part of the digestive system. Spx. ♋ ☽.

- Stomach Cancer: Because repressed emotions are the root cause of cancer, often the disease will strike the stomach. Link the stomach to the cancer formula. Spx. ♋ ☽ [(♋ ☽ >♄♇) > ♃☉].

These men died from this disease. The Moon is able to represent both the emotions and the stomach.

---

1 Bailey, Alice: Esoteric Psychology II, 600.

2 https://aleteia.org/2018/07/06/this-saint-bore-the-stigmata-every-good-friday-for-38-years/

3 Bailey, Alice: Esoteric Psychology II, 602.

(1) David Marr (27 Dec 1933, 10:55, Houston TX). ☽ [(□ ♄ 12) > ⚻ ♃ 8].
(2) Jaques Anquetil (8 Jan 1934, 10:30, Mont St. Aignan, Fr). ♇ ♋ r8H [□ ♃].
(3) John Wayne (26 May 1907, 05:00, Winterset, Iowa). ☽ ♏ 6 [(disp. by ♇) > ☽ △ ♃ ♋].
(4) Roy Disney (10 Jan 1930, 11:50, Los Angeles, CA). ♇ ♋ [☍ ☉]. Malevolent cells.

- Stomach Cramps: Painful cramping in the stomach. Spx. ♋ ☽ [♂ ♅].

- Stomach Ulcer: Open sore that develops on the inside lining of the stomach. Spx. ♋ ☽ [♂ ♅].
(1) Eugene Atget (12 Feb 1857, 18:00, Libourne, Fr). ☽ [⚼ ♅ r6H].
(2) George Clooney (6 May 1961, 02:58, Lexington, KY). ☽ ♑ [☍ ♂ ♌, ♌ r6H].
(3) Natsume Soseki (9 Feb 1867, 16:30, Tokyo, Japan). ☽ ♈ [□ ♂ ♋ 12℞].

Stone: (See Kidney Stones). Abnormal mineral salt concretion commonly found in the gallbladder, kidney, bladder. [♄ ♅].

Strangled, Strangulation: (See Asphyxia and Suffocation). Squeezing/ constricting the neck causing death. Link life and/ or throat [and killed]. Thr. ☉ Asc / ♉ ♀ [♏ ♂ ♇, 8H]. These homicide victims were strangled.
(1) Daniel Croteau (27 May 1959, 06:12, Springfield, MA). ☉ 12 ☌ ☿ ♉ [□ ♇].
(2) Enrique Linares (15 Jul 1938, 15:45, Gomez Palacio, MX). ☉ 8 [☌ ♂ ♇ 8].
(3) Karyn Kupcinet (6 Mar 1941, 18:28, Chicago, IL). ☉ 6 [♅ ♉ mp ☉/♇].

Streptococcus Bacteria: Common bacteria found on and in the body. [♅ ♂ ♆].

- Strep Throat: Bacterial infection that can cause a sore, scratchy throat. Link throat [and infection]. ♉ ♀ [♅ ♂ ♆].
(1) Alois Alzheimer (14 Jun 1864, 04:00, Marktbreit, Ger). ♀ 12 [♇ ♉ mp ♀/ ♂ ♆].
(2) Paul Anderson (17 Oct 1932, 05:30, Toccoa, GA). ♀ ♍ [☌ ♆ ♍].

Stress: Reaction in the body when under pressure or threatened. Persistent unrelenting stress is a R1, Saturn or Pluto type of force. In such a case, the consistent and ongoing increase in heart rate, and the elevated levels of stress hormones and of blood pressure, can increase the risk for hypertension, heart attack, or stroke. Stress of a shorter duration could be triggered by other planet transits. Hrt. Spx. [♄ ♇].

Stretch, Stretches: Flexibility or looseness of muscles, joints. ♃.

Stye: A red, painful lump near the eyelid. Some are pus-filled. Link eyelids [infection > pus]. Spx. ♈ ♂ [♂ ♅ ♆].

Stroke: Damage to the brain due to interruption of blood supply. Can be caused by a blocked artery (ischemic stroke - ♄), or a burst blood vessel (haemorrhagic stroke - ♂ ♅). Link the brain/ blood flow [blocked / or ruptured]. Cwn. ♈ ♋ [♒ ♅, ♓ ♆ > ♑ ♄/ ♂ ♅].
(1) Arno Schmidt (18 Jan 1914, 14:30, Hamburg, Ger). ♂ ♋ r6H [⚻ ♅ ♒].
(2) Margaret, Princess (21 Aug 1930, 21:22, Glamis, Scot). ♅ ♈ 1, r12H [wide □ ♄ ♑].
(3) Rahsaan Kirk (7 Aug 1935, 16:45, Columbus, OH). ♂ ♏ [☍ ♅ ♉].
(4) Thelonius Monk (10 Oct 1917, 21:15, Rocky Mount, NC). ☽ ♂ ♌ [☌ ♄ / ☍ ♅ ♒].

Strychnine: (See Poison - Mineral Kingdom). A highly toxic, colourless, bitter, crystalline alkaloid used as a pesticide. [♄ ♇, ♅]

Stunt: Prevent from growing or developing properly. [♄].

Stupor: A state of near-unconsciousness or insensibility. Ajna [♄].

Stutter/ Stammer: Difficulty talking because of the continued involuntary repetition of sounds. Thr. ♊ ☿ [♅].

Subclavian Veins: Under the collarbone, they move oxygen-poor blood from the upper body back to the heart, and lymph back to the bloodstream. Hrt. ♀, ♊ [1].

Subconscious Mind: Part of the mind that stores forgotten thoughts/ memories. ☽, 12H.

Submandibular Glands: Salivary glands. Thr. ♋ ☽.

Substance Abuse: Misuse of alcohol and other drugs. Spx. [♆♓].

Subverts: To pervert, or corrupt. [♆, ♇].

Sucrose: Compound which is the chief component of cane or beet sugar. ♀ ♃.

Sudden Infant Death Syndrome, SIDS, Cot Death: (See Incarnate). The sudden, unexplained death of a healthy baby. The ascendant governs the new incarnation, so look for close afflictions to it, from malefics that have links to death. They could represent an early demise. Link, self, incarnation [and death]. ☉, Asc [♂ ♅ > ♏ ♂, 8H].

(1) Astro.com 14634 (17 Nov 1974, 12:55, Esslingen, Ger). Asc 10♒ [□ ♂13♏, coruler 8H]. The Asc is applying to Mars by 3 degrees - which makes it possible the death occurred at 3 months.

(2) Astro.com 14696 (26 Aug 1977, 10:24, Canberra, Australia). Asc 25 ♏ [⚻♂8 > ∠♇]. The baby died either at 2 months or 14 months. It was probably 2 months - the Asc semisquare to Pluto, is applying by around 2 degrees.

(3) Astro.com 14749 (1 Feb 1979, 06:57, Schwabisch Hall, Ger). Asc 20♑ [□♇8 19♎]. Transit Pluto was retrograde at birth. The baby died (at 3 months), when Pluto - still retrograde, reached 17♎ - 3 degrees off the exact square to the Asc.

(4) Astro.com 15049 (25 Dec 1985, 17:45, Remscheid, Ger). Asc [⚻ ♅6, r8H]. At birth, the Asc was separating from Uranus by 1 degree, 37 minutes.

The message for carers is - if there are malefics closely aspecting the ascendant, be extra vigilant in those few early months after birth. Especially in the period the aspect is exact.

Suffering: Undergoing pain, distress, or hardship. [♄].

Suffocation: (See Asphyxia). Starved of oxygen. Thr. ♊ ☿ [♏♂♇].

Sugar: A simple carbohydrate, sweet crystalline substance from plants. ♀ ♃.

- Sugar Addiction, Craving: Dependence on sugary foods and drinks. ♀ ♃ [♆].

Suicide: (See Euthanasia). Injuring oneself with the intent to die. Link life [and death]. ☉, Asc [♏♂♇,8H].

(1) Michael Blosil (4 May 1991, no time). Jumped off a building. ☉ [☍♇♏].

(2) Rudolf, Crown Prince of Austria (21 Aug 1858, 22:15, Laxenburg, Austria). Unhappy with the role he was born into, he committed suicide with his mistress. ☉ [□♂].

-Suicidal Thoughts: Thinking about killing oneself. It is usually accompanied with depression. Thr. Spx. ♊ ☿ [♂].

Sulphur: A mineral chemical element essential for good skin, hair, nails and DNA. ♄ ♂.

---

1 Gemini, Daath.

SUN. ⊙.

Signs it rules: The Sun is the exoteric ruler of Leo, the esoteric ruler of Leo (unveiling Neptune), and the hierarchy ruler of Leo (unveiling Uranus).

House it rules: The 5H via Leo.

Rays: Its personal force is the 2nd ray of Love and Wisdom, the energy of soul or consciousness. R2 is the major building force in nature. The Sun also carries R1 of Will and Power via Leo.

Body: Governs the heart chakra, the heart, the spine and eyes - particularly the right eye, the constitution, vitalisation, the spleen, and generally rules the cardiovascular (circulatory) system (heart, arteries, capillaries, veins, blood and bloodstream).

Disease: When afflicted, the Sun indicates trouble with the cardiovascular system, with vitality and lowered resistance to disease. The Sun sign often points to a part of the body that will suffer if vitality or immunity should falter. As the afflictor, it represents burns, scalds, high temperatures, fevers, autoimmune attacks. The 2nd ray that flows through the Sun produces overstimulation and an over-production of atoms that show as growths, tumours, cancer, organs that are too big etc.

Psychology: The 2nd ray of Wisdom, the 'consciousness' or sentient ray that the Sun carries; enables us to develop a sense of 'self'. The Sun represents personality consciousness, the power of the individual "I" - and its ability or inability, to dominate the environment. When afflicted, the Sun can represent egoism and megalomania.

Sunburn: Skin that is inflamed, blistered, peeling due to overexposure to the sun. [⊙ ♂].

Sunstroke, Hyperthermia: Body temperature above F104/ C40 degrees). It can result in brain damage and organ failure. Base [⊙ (♂ ♌ ♅)].

Supernumerary Body Part: Most commonly due to a congenital disorder, a deviation from the body-building plan. [R2, ♃ ♅].

Suppress: To put down by weight of force. [♄ ♇].

Surgery: Treatment that cuts open the body to remove/ repair damaged parts. Mars is the traditional ruler. Ultra-modern surgical techniques may include Uranus. ♂ (♅).

Survival Instinct: Instinctive, defensive reactions to stay alive. Spx. Base. ♂.

Sutratma: It is our connection with God, with the divine, the "direct stream of life from the monad," [1]. Synonyms are "Life Thread and Silver Cord," [2] "Thread Soul and life current." [3] It carries within itself the life stream and consciousness thread. The life stream anchors in the heart, the consciousness thread anchors in the head. [4] ⊙.

Swallow: To ingest food/ drink from the mouth to the stomach via the oesophagus. Thr. ☽ ♉.

Sweat: Moisture that is exuded through skin pores due to heat, physicality, fever or fear. ♋ ☽.

Swell, swelling: Body part that grows larger/ rounder because of an accumulation of fluid. [♃ (♓ ♆)].

---

1   Bailey, Alice: Education in the New Age, 26-27.
2   Bailey, Alice: Education in the New Age, 32.
3   Bailey, Alice: Treatise on White Magic, 495.
4   Bailey, Alice: The Rays and the Initiations, 450.

Sydenham's Chorea/ St. Vitus Dance/ Rheumatic Chorea: It is a neurological disorder with rapid, jerking movements primarily of the face, hands and feet. It is caused by a bacterial infection that triggers an abnormal immune system response - healthy brain tissue is attacked instead of the bacteria. Link the brain/ nervous system [infection > jerky movements]. Ajna. ♈ ♂ (♋ ☽) / ♊ ☿ [♅ ♂ ♆ > ♅].

(1) Andy Warhol (6 Aug 1928, 06:30, Pittsburgh, PA). At age 8, he caught rheumatic fever which was followed by Sydenham's chorea. ☽ ♈ [☌ ♅ ♈ coruler 6H].

Sympathetic Nervous System (SNS): Part of the peripheral system, the network of nerves primarily known for activating the body's 'fight-or-flight' response. It is vitalised by the solar plexus chakra and the 6th ray. Ajna. Spx. R6, ♂ ♆.

The builders of the astral plane represent this (SNS) system. [1]

Synapse: A junction between two nerve cells, through which nerve signals pass from one cell to the next. ♅, ♊ ☿.

Synesthesia: An evolutionary advancement. Blending of the senses. The stimulation of one sense simultaneously produces sensation in a different sense. The most common form of synesthesia is coloured hearing: sounds, music or voices seen as colours. Link senses [evolutionary advancement]. Ajna, Thr. ♊ ☿ (♀) [♅].

(1) Billie Eilish (18 Dec 2001, 11:30, Los Angeles, CA). She said she has coloured hearing. ☿ [∠ ♅ ♒]. ♀ [⚹ ♅ ♒].

Synovial Joint: The joint found between bones that move against each other - shoulder, hip, elbow, knee, ankle. Base. ♑ ♄.

- Synovial Fluid: A fluid in the cavities of synovial joints. Base. ♋ ☽.

- Synovial Membranes: Are moist membranes that line cavities, secreting synovial fluid into joint cavities to aid free movement. Base. ♋ ☽.

- Synovitis: Inflammation of a synovial membrane. ♋ ☽ [♂ ☉].

Synthetic Drugs: Either illegal or prescription, are created using man-made chemicals rather than natural ingredients. ♆.

Syphilis: (See Indigenous Disease, Sexually Transmitted Disease). A sexually transmitted bacterial disease, which untreated, can be lethal. From the 1400s to the early 20th century, mercury was used to treat the disease and it did slow down its ravages. Link sex [and bacterial infection]. Sac. ♏ ♂ ♇ [♅ ♂ ♆].

(1) Charles Baudelaire (9 Apr 1821, 15,00, Paris, Fr). ♂ ♇ [□ ♆ ♅, ♅ r6H].
(2) Henri Toulouse-Lautrec (24 Nov 1864, 06:00, Albi, Fr). ♇ ♉ 6 [∠ ♅ 8].
(3) Niccolo Paganini (27 Oct 1782, 10:30, Genoa, Italy). ♂ ♎ [□ ♅]. ♇ ♒ [⚻ ♅].
(4) Paul Gauguin (7 Jun 1848, 10:00, Paris, Fr). ♂ [□ ♅ ☌ ♇].

1 Bailey, Alice: Treatise of Cosmic Fire, 634.

T

Tachycardia: Rapid heartbeat. Untreated, it can be life-threatening. Link the heart [and rapid beat]. Hrt. ♌☉ [♂♅].

(1) Miley Cyrus (23 Nov 1992, 16:19, Nashville, TN), revealed in her memoir that she struggles with tachycardia. ☉♐ [∠♅, △♂ r12H].

Tapeworm: A parasitic flatworm that attaches to the wall of the intestine where it feeds. Link intestines [and parasite]. Spx. ♍☿ [♏♂♇].

(1) Jimmy Carruthers (5 Jul 1929, 07:00, Sydney, Australia). Carruthers was carrying a 30-foot-long tapeworm. ♂♍ [∠♇♋].

(2) Kingi Mckinnon (27 Jul 1943, no time). The parasite was picked up on a farm, when he was a child. ♆♍ [⚼♂ ♉/♏].

Tarsus bones: Cluster of seven bones in each foot. Base. ♓♆.

Tartar - see Plaque.

Taste Sense: (See Senses). Sense that distinguishes between sweet, sour, bitter and salty via the tongue. The senses are part of the peripheral nervous system. R3, Ajna. Thr. ♊☿.

- **Taste Problems** - see Ageusia, Hypogeusia.

TAURUS. ♉.

Rulers: Exoteric ruler is Venus, the esoteric ruler is Vulcan, the hierarchy ruler is Vulcan.

Rays: Carries R4 of Harmony through Conflict; R5 via Venus and R1 via Vulcan. Taurus energy is earthy, concentrated and slow to move.

Body: Taurus rules the throat chakra, the neck and all within it, including the upper digestive tract, the tonsils and the thyroid gland.

Disease: Planets afflicted in Taurus, or when Taurus rules the 6H of health, indicate trouble in the throat region, and/ or in the organs of its polar-opposite sign, Scorpio (reproduction and elimination). As an afflictor, Taurus troubles have to do with unregulated desire, with gluttony that can lead to weight gain and associated diseases. One consequence is diabetes, a disease of wrong inner desires.

Psychology: Taurus carries the 4th ray of conflict, and its people struggle with inner and outer conflict. It governs the transmutation of sex and desire into spiritual aspiration. To achieve this, people must be aware about how they use desire. The higher keynote is, 'I see and when the eye is opened, all is light;' then take steps to refine their appetites/ desires.

T-cells: Are types of white blood cells that form part of the immune system, and help protect the body from infection. There are two types: Helper T-cells and Killer T-cells. The Moon rules white blood cells, the Sun rules cell life, Mars represents the killing action of T-cells. Hrt. ☽ (☉,♂).

Tears, Tear Ducts: (See Sjoren's Syndrome). Salty liquid that flows from the eye when it is hurt or because of a strong emotion. ♋☽ (♆).

Teeth: Hard, bony enamel-coated structures used for eating. Upper jaw teeth are ruled by Aries, lower teeth by Taurus. Thr. Base. ♑ ♄.

- Teeth Decay: This occurs when bacteria in plaque turns sugars from food and drink into acid, which attacks the teeth. Link teeth [bacteria > acid]. Thr. ♑ ♄ [♅ > ♂].

- Teeth Grinding: Grind, gnash or clench teeth. Thr. ♄ [♂ ♅].

Tempered, Bad: Easily annoyed or angered, surly. Spx. [♂].

Temples: The temples lie at the side of the face, just behind the eyes, between the forehead and ear. Cwn. Base. ♈ ♂.

Tendons: Strong bands of tissue that connect a muscle with its bony attachment. Base. ♑ ♄.

Tension: Mental or emotional strain which takes its toll on the body, undermining health. Link mental/ or emotional [and strain]. ☿ / ☽ [♄].

Terrorist, Terrorism: Violence and intimidation used in pursuit of political aims. Base. [♏ ♂ ♇].

Testes/ Testicles/ Male Gonads: Male reproductive organs. Sac. ♏ ♂.

- Testicular Cancer: The testes are ruled by Scorpio and Mars. Link the testes to the cancer formula. Sac. ♏ ♂ ♇ [(♋ ☽ > ♄ ♇) > ♃ ☉].
(1) Scott Hamilton (28 Aug 1958, 09:00, Toledo, OH). In 1997, the American champion Olympic figure skater was treated for testicular cancer. ♂ [(□ ☽ > ☽ ☍ ♇) > ♇ ☌ ☉12].

- Testiculitis, Epididymitis: Infection, inflammation - usually bacterial, of the epididymis. It causes pain and swelling. Link epididymis [infection/ inflamed]. ♏ ♂ [♂ ♅ ♆/ ♂ ☉].

Testosterone: Hormone that stimulates sexual development. Sac. ♂.

Tetanus: Serious bacterial infection of the nervous system. It causes painful muscle spasms and can lead to death. Link the nervous system [and infection]. Ajna. ♊ ☿ [♅ ♂ ♆].

Thalamus: An information relay station. Ajna. ♊ ☿.

Therapy: Treatment intended to relieve or heal a disorder. ♍ ☿.

Thighs: Part of the leg above the knee. Base. ♐ ♃.

Third eye: The eye of the soul. It is the etheric correspondence of the pineal gland, and when activated (at a spiritually advanced stage), the soul can see into the physical world and our human consciousness can see into higher spiritual realms. Ajna. ☉ ♅.

Thoracic Duct: Largest vessel of the lymphatic system. Thr. ♋ ☽, ♓ ♆.

Thoracic/ Dorsal Vertebrae. Middle section of the spine, starting at the base of the neck and ending at the top of the pelvis. Located in the Leo-Sun region, it consists of 12 vertebrae (T1-T12). Leo, the Sun and Saturn are all rulers of the spine. Problems to these vertebrae are indicated by afflictions to Leo and the Sun from malefics that represent the various causes. Hrt. ♌ ☉.

Thread of Life: The stream of life emanating from the Universal Life (God), anchoring in the heart. There the life principle is found. From the heart, life pervades the entire physical body through the medium of the blood stream. Hrt. ☉.

THROAT: The passage from the mouth to the stomach and lungs. Thr. ♉ ♀.

- Throat Cancer: (See Cancer). Link the throat to the cancer formula. Thr. ♉ ♀ [(♋ ☽ > ♄ ♇) > ♃ ☉].

Halen is in remission, Genet and Sydney died from the disease.

(1) Eddie Van Halen (26 Jan 1955, 01:05, Amsterdam, Neth). ♀ [(♄ mp ♀/ ♇12) > ∠☉].

(2) Jean Genet (19 Dec 1910, 19:45, Paris, Fr). ♀ ♑/♋ [(☍♇) > ♂ ☉].

(3) Sylvia Sydney (8 Aug 1910, 15:00, Bronx, NY). ♀ ♋8 [(☽ > □♇) > ♀ □♃].

- Throat, Sore: Pain, scratchiness, irritation in the throat especially when swallowing. Link throat [sore, scratchy]. Thr. ♉ ♀ [♂].

THROAT CHAKRA (Thr): (See Chakras and Etheric Web/ Body).

Consciousness: This is the creative, communication centre, which vitalises lower mind. Eventually the transmuted forces of the sexual sacral centre, flow up and out through it.

Ray and Astrology energies: The primary ray is the 3rd of Intelligence, which flows via Saturn and the Earth. Ray 7 is starting to flow through it with greater frequency. Because it is the communication centre, Gemini (the 3rd sign) and Mercury are related. So are Venus and Taurus because of their rulership over the neck.

Body rulership: This 16-petal lotus enters the spine at the base of the neck, between C7 and T1, anchoring in the thyroid gland. It vitalises the brainstem, the cerebellum, metabolism, the airways - respiration , the bronchial tree, the gastrointestinal tract, and lymphatic system.

Diseases: Psychological troubles due to mental hyper-activity or manipulation. Trouble in all organs and systems it rules, including the ears.

Thromboembolic Pulmonary Hypertension: (See Pulmonary Embolism). It is a form of Pulmonary Embolism/ Hypertension.

Thrombophlebitis - see Phlebitis.

Thrombosis: The forming of a blood clot, either in an artery or vein. Link heart/ artery/ or blood flow [and clot]. Hrt. ♌☉/ ♃ ♌♒ / ♒ ♅ ♇ [♄/♃)].

(1) King George VI of England (14 Dec 1895, 03:05, Sandringham, Eng). He died in his sleep of coronary thrombosis. ♃ ♌℞ [□♄].

Thrush - see Candida, Vaginal Thrush.

Thumb: The short thick digit of the hand. Thr. ♊ ☿ .

Thymus Gland: An endocrine gland located in the upper chest behind the breast-bone. It is the physical body anchorage of the heart chakra. Its prime functions in conjunction with the heart chakra is vitalisation and immunity - it produces *thymosin* and *thymulin* that stimulate disease fighting T-cells. This gland shrinks with aging. But it is re-stimulated in adults who are developing inclusive love - the awakening heart chakra re-stimulates the gland. The thymus is ruled by Gemini, [1] and is related to Leo. Hrt. ♊, ♌.

Thyroid Gland: (See Hypothyroidism, Hyperthyroidism, Iodine Deficiency). This endocrine gland is located at the base of the throat and is the anchorage of the throat chakra.

It is said to be "the keystone of the endocrine system.. the controller of metabolism.. the great catalyst of energy in the body." [2]

---

1   Bailey, Alice: Esoteric Astrology, 367.
2   Bailey, Alice: The Soul and its Mechanism, 46.

Thyroxine increases the rate of cellular metabolism. Problems with this gland can cause symptoms such as irritability, fatigue, weight loss or gain. Saturn is a ruler of the throat chakra which vitalises the thyroid, so is a substitute ruler. Thr. ♉ ♀ (♄).

- Thyroid Cancer: Link the thyroid [to the cancer formula]. ♉ ♀ [(♋ ☽ > ♄ ♇) > ♃ ☉].
(1) Hoimar von Ditfurth (15 Oct 1921, 22:30, Berlin, Ger). ♀ ♍ [(qd ☽ > □ ♇ ♋ 12) > ☽ ☍ ♃].

Tibia: The long, larger bone, in the inside lower leg. Base. ♒ ♅.

Ticks: Small wingless, bloodsucking insects, that cause Lyme disease. [♏ ♂ ♇].

Tics: (See Tourette's). Sudden, spontaneous, nerve and muscle twitches, movements, and sounds. Link the nervous system and / or muscles [and tics]. Ajna. ♊ ☿ / ♂ [♅].

Tinea, Athlete's Foot: A fungal infection that usually begins between the toes. Link feet [fungal /infection]. Base. ♓ ♆ ♃ [♋ ☽ , ♓ ♆ > ♂ ♅ ♆].
(1) Lindsay Lohan (2 Jul 1986, 04:40, Bronx, NY). ♆ ♑ [⚼ ☽].

Tinnitus: Ringing/ buzzing in the ears. It is usually caused by an underlying condition such as age-related hearing loss, an ear injury, or a problem with the circulatory system. Link ears [and ringing]. Ajna. ♊ ☿ [♅].
(1) Rachel Goswell (16 May 1971, 04:00, Fareham, Eng). A viral infection left Goswell with chronic tinnitus. ☿ ♈ [□ ♂ ♒; ♅ 6 ℞].
(2) William Shatner (22 Mar 1931, 04:00, Montreal, Quebec). ☿ [☌ ♅].

Tiredness: (See Chronic Fatigue). A feeling of constant tiredness. Thr. Spx [♄],

Tissue: Is formed from groups of cells. *Hard tissue* refers to bones, *soft tissue* to muscle, ligaments, tendons or connective tissue. These are ruled by Capricorn and Saturn. *Soft moist tissue* that excretes mucous, that lines some organs and body cavities - are ruled by Cancer and the Moon. Since these signs are polar-opposites, they can substitute for each other. ♋ ☽ / ♑ ♄.

Tobacco Addiction - see Nicotine.

Toes: One of the terminal members of the foot. Base. ♓ ♆.

Tongue: The fleshy muscular organ in the mouth used for tasting, licking, swallowing, and for speech. The tongue is an agent of creativity, "The tongue typifies the creative faculty, the third aspect." [1]. Thr. R3, ☿ ♉.

Tonic: A substance that stimulates well-being, invigorates, restores, or refreshes. Jupiter restores health and the Sun and Mars both have a tonic effect upon the body. ☉ ♂ ♃.

Tonsils: Lymphatic immune system glands - the two oval-shaped pads of tissue located each side of the back of the throat. Thr. ♉ ♀.

- Tonsillitis and Tonsillectomy: (See Quinsy). Tonsils that are infected and inflamed. Tonsillectomy was a once common surgical procedure to remove the tonsils. Link tonsils [and infected/ inflamed]. Thr. ♉ ♀ [♂ ♅ ♆/ ♂ ☉].

Tooth Ache: Pain in a tooth, caused by an infection. Link teeth [pain]. Thr. ♑ ♄ [♂].

Tooth Decay, Toothache - see Teeth.

1 Bailey, Alice: Light of the Soul, 80.

Torpid: Sluggish in functioning or acting. [♄].

Touch Sense: (See Senses). Faculty by which external objects are perceived through contact with the body and hands. The senses are part of the peripheral nervous system, which brings them generally under the rulership of Gemini and Mercury. Ajna. Thr. R3, ♊ ☿.

Tourette's Syndrome: Neurological disorder characterized by involuntary tics and sounds. Link the nerves/ sound [involuntary tics]. Ajna. ♊ ☿ (♀) [♅].
(1) Jim Eisenreich (18 Apr 1959, 16:19, St. Cloud, MN). ☿ r12H [♀ ♊ mp ☿/♅].
(2) John Davidson (1 Jun 1971, 02:00, Galashiels, Scotland). ☿ [□♂♒12; ♂△♅℞].

Toxaemia, Pre-eclampsia: Occurs in pregnancy. The blood is poisoned by a bacterial infection, raising blood pressure. Saturn or Pluto may link in for 'pressure.' Link pregnant [blood > infection]. Hrt. Sac. ♋ ☽ [♂♃♒ > ♅♂♆].
(1) Laura Bush (4 Nov 1946, 18:00, Midland, TX), was admitted to hospital seven weeks before her due-date because of toxaemia. ☽ ♓ [□♅].

Toxins - see Poisons.

Trachea, the Windpipe: Airway leading from the larynx (voice box) to bronchi. Thr. ♊ ☿.

- Tracheotomy: An opening surgically created through the neck into the trachea (windpipe), in which a tube is inserted to provide an airway. throat [surgery]. ♉ ♀ [♂].

Trance: A state of semi-consciousness. Ajna. Spx. [♆].

Transfusion of Blood. A medical procedure in which donated blood is given through a tube placed in a vein. Gemini and Mercury govern transport. Link blood > and transfusion. Hrt. ♂♃♒ > ♊ ☿.

Transplant, Transport: An organ is removed from one person's body and surgically transplanted into another's. Transporting, moving from one place to another, comes under Gemini and Mercury. Link the organ involved: surgical > transplant. Organ > ♂♅ > ♊ ☿.
(1) Charlotte Valandrey (29 Nov 1968, 16:10, Paris, Fr). Valandrey had a first heart transplant in 2003, which was successful. ☉♐ > ⚹♂♅♃6. But after a second transplant in 2022, she died. ♃, dispositor of the ☉, [rules the 8H, ☌♇].
(2) Nathalie Rheims (27 Apr 1959, 14:10, Neuilly sur Seine, Fr). She had a kidney transplant. ♀ >(mp ♅12/ ☿♈). (See also Lupus - Selena Gomez).
(3) Larry Hagman (21 Sep 1931, 16:20, Fort Worth, TX). The actor made famous in the TV series Dallas, was a heavy drinker. He developed liver disease and had a successful liver transplant. ♃ > △♅♈ coruler 12H.

Trauma, Traumatised, Traumatises: The harm a terrible event can have on a person's psychology. Symptoms can include exhaustion, confusion, sadness, anxiety, agitation, numbness, dissociation and confusion. Trauma can affect a person's ability to cope or function normally. Link emotions [and trauma]. Spx. ♋ ☽ ♂ [♄♇].

Tremors: Nerve disorder that causes involuntary body shaking. Link nerves [and involuntary shakes]. Ajna. ♊ ☿ [♅].

Trench Fever - see Q Fever.

Trickery: The practice of deception. Thr. [☿♆].

Trigeminal Nerve: Cranial nerve providing sensation to the face. Ajna. ♈ ♊ ☿.

- Trigeminal Neuralgia: Chronic pain affecting the trigeminal nerve. Link nerves [and chronic/ pain]. Ajna. ♈ ♊ ☿ [♄/ ♂].

Triune Brain Theory: A theory presented by American neuroscientist Paul MacLean in the 60's. It divides the brain into three parts based on evolutionary development - the neocortex or thinking brain, the limbic or desire brain, and the reptilian or action brain. Aries, Taurus and Gemini are associated with each of these three parts.

1. *The neocortex.* It is the latest part of the brain to evolve and is concerned with advanced cognition, language and planning. It is the seat of curiosity and asks, "What can I learn?" Aries, the sign that rules exploration and pioneering is the natural ruler of the neocortex. It is ruled by the crown chakra. Cwn. ♈(☿).

2. *The Limbic System, the desire or emotional brain.* It emerged in the first mammals and in man is the seat of the desire nature. Taurus, the sign of desire rules this system. These are its parts: hypothalamus, thalamus, nucleus accumbens, olfactory bulb, amygdala and hippocampus. This centre is at the root of our emotional memories which links it to Cancer and the Moon. Thr. ♉ ♀ (♋ ☽).

3. *The Reptilian or instinctual brain.* This is the brainstem (pons, medulla oblongata) and cerebellum, the oldest part of the brain that dominated in reptiles. It controls breathing and balance, vital functions associated with Gemini. Thr. ♊ ☿ .

Tubal Pregnancy - see Ectopic Pregnancy.

Tuberculosis, TB: (See Pulmonary Tuberculosis). Bacterial infection that affects the lungs, also the brain, the kidneys or spine. [♅ ♂ ♆].

Tubes: Hollow cylinders that convey fluid or act as a passage. ♊ ☿ .

Tumours - Benign: (See Brain Tumour - Benign, Pituitary Tumour). Non-cancerous tumours that grow in one place. Most are benign and require no treatment. But they can be dangerous if they press on the brain or nerves or grow into cancer. An example of this type is an adenoma. Link cells [overbuilding]. ☉ ☽ [♃].

Tumours - Malignant - see Cancer, the Disease.

Twists, Distorts: Abnormal twisting of a body part. [♅ ♆].

Twitching, Tics: Nervous system disorder that causes involuntary muscle twitching (♅). Link nerves > muscles [twitching]. ♊ ☿ > ♂ [♅].

Typhoid Fever: Bacterial disease that attacks the intestines. Symptoms are a high fever and severe diarrhoea. The infection is spread through contaminated food, water or close contact. Link the intestines [and bacterial infection]. Spx. ♍ ☿ (♏ ♂ ♇) [♅ ♂ ♆].

These examples all died from the disease - an extra link for death has been added.

(1) Albert, Prince (26 Aug 1819, 06:00, Coburg, Ger). ☿ ♍℞ [□ ♂ > ☍ ♇].

(2) Georg Buchner (17 Oct 1813, 05:30, Goddelau, Ger). ♃ ♍ r6H [□ ♅ ♏ > qd ♇].

(3) Lucien Schnegg (19 Mar 1864, 01:00, Bordeaux, Fr). ☿ ♓ [□ ♅ > ⚹ ♇ ♉].

(4) Maximiliane Princess of Bavaria (21 Jul 1810, 23:00, Munich, Ger). ♀ ♍ [□ ♆ 8].

U

Ulcers: Sores that are slow to heal or keep returning, which can appear both on the inside and the outside of the body. Link the organ affected [ulcer - ♂ ☉, fire signs].

a. Duodenal peptic ulcers: in the upper small intestine. ♍ ☿ [♂ ☉, fire signs].

(1) James Joyce (2 Feb 1882, 06:00, Dublin, Ire). He had a perforated duodenal ulcer, which led to peritonitis, and he died. (See Peritonitis). ☿ [△ ♂ 6 > □ ♆ ♉ /♏ for death].

b. Foot ulcer: ♓ ♆ [♂ ☉, fire signs].

(1) Frida Kahlo (6 Jul 1907, 08:30, Coyoacan, MX). She had an ulcer on her right foot, from where gangrenous toes had been amputated in 1934. ♆ [⚹ ♂ ℞].

c. Oesophageal peptic ulcers. ♉ ♀, ♋ ☽ [♂ ☉, fire signs].

(1) Alvin Ailey (5 Jan 1931, 05:30, Rogers, TX). He had this type of ulcer. After a period of hospitalisation, he died from AIDS. ☽ ♋ 8 [♂ ♆ > ♆ ⚹ ☉].

d. Rectal ulcer: ♏ ♂ ♆ [♂ ☉, fire signs].

(1) Jack London (12 Jan 1876, 14:00, San Francisco, CA). He had several ailments towards the end of his relatively young life (died in 1916), including a rectal ulcer. ♆ ♉ /♏ 12H [□ ♅ ♌]. ♃ ♏ 6 [△ ♂].

c. Stomach peptic ulcers: in the stomach lining or small intestines. ♋ ☽ / ♍ ☿ [♂ ☉, fire signs].

(1) Jackie Onassis (28 Jul 1929, 14:30, Southampton, NY). In 1994, she was hospitalised with a bleeding stomach ulcer. This was in the year she took a job as an editor at Viking Press in NY. ☽ ♈ [□ ♆ ♋ coruler 12H].

(2) James Roosevelt (23 dec 1907, 02:45, New York, NY). His ulcer perforated and 2/3 of his stomach was removed. ☿ [□ ♂ r6H].

Ulna: One of the two bones (other is the radius) that make up the forearm. Thr. ♊ ☿.

Unconscious: Not conscious - unaware of activities in the external world. Depriving of consciousness is a 1st ray, Saturn, Pluto event. Neptune is associated, representing consciousness that has moved to another plane. Link conscious [and unconscious]. ☉ (☿) [♆ ♄ (♀)].

Unconventional Medicine, Treatment. Alternative medicines and therapies outside the western conservative standard practices. ♅.

Underactive: Abnormally low level of activity. [♄].

Underweight: A lessening in normal body weight. [♄].

Undeveloped Organ: An organ that does not mature as normal. [♄].

Unusual: Outside what is considered normal. [♅].

Unveiling and Veiling of Energies: This term is used in esoteric astrology (the astrology of the soul). Higher spiritual energies (which are fiery and electrical), are 'veiled' or blocked from entering the brains of people who are not yet ready to receive them. As spiritual disciplines are applied, these barriers are ‘unveiled’ or removed.

Uraemia, Kidney Failure: A dangerous condition - the final stage of chronic kidney disease. The kidneys no longer filter properly resulting in abnormally high levels of waste in the blood. Link the kidneys [chronic disease]. Pisces and Neptune may connect in for ‘filtering.’ R1. Base. ♎♀ [♄♇].

(1) Dimitry Pavlovich (6 Sep 1891, 08:55, Moscow, Russia). Russian royal who died of uraemia in 1942 or 1943. ♀♍/♓ [□♇8].

(2) Dorothy Bar-Adon (2 Aug 1907, 10:30, Philadelphia, PA). Died in 1950, from uraemia. It was still incurable at that time. ♀♋ [♆♋ mp ♀/♇].

(3) Margaret Woodrow Wilson (16 Apr 1886, 11:30, Gainesville, GA). The daughter of US President Woodrow Wilson. She died from uraemia in 1944. She was in India at the time. ☽♎ [☌♅ r8H, □♄♋12].

Uranium: Chemical element that is dangerous to health with long term exposure. Nuclear power station accidents poison the environment and people’s health. ♅♇.

URANUS. ♅.

Signs it rules: Uranus is the exoteric ruler of Aquarius, the esoteric ruler of Libra, and is the hierarchy ruler of Aries and Aquarius.

House it rules: The 11H.

Ray: Uranus carries the 7th ray of Ceremony, Order and Magic. Its force can crystallise and/or organise on the one hand - and can shatter, and cause wild and unpredictable effects on the other. Then, unexpectedly, produce a miracle outcome or healing. Uranus also carries R5, the ray of science, via Aquarius.

Body: Governs the sacral chakra, sex and sex attitudes; and corules the crown chakra in disciples. It is related to the heart chakra and blood circulation via the Aquarius-Leo relationship; and to the ajna due to its shared rule of nervous energy and nerve synapses. It rules the etheric body, DNA, the calves and ankles.

Disease: When afflicted, Uranus can represent potential trouble with nerves, blood quality, with blood flow; or with the lower legs and ankles (via Aquarius).

As the afflictor, Uranus represents the abnormal and bizarre, the shocking and shattering, conditions that strike suddenly, which are arrhythmic and that no longer conform to nature’s healthy design and pattern (spasms, cramps, asymmetry). The 7th ray force that Uranus carries, governs the atomic, cellular level of life and brings together life and matter to create life on earth. When this process goes awry, aberrant and aborted cells become virulent germs, bacterial infections and contagious diseases. Uranus is the prime representative of bacterial infections.

Psychology: The 7th Ray of Ceremony, Order and Magic that is carried by Uranus, gives the people it vitalises an amazing ability to manifest what they want, and talent in science. It urges them to let go of the past, to be free, to rebel, to experiment and to awaken to the new. When this energy is abused, there is chaos, destructive wildness, promiscuity and selfish individualism.

Urea, Uric Acid: Waste product of protein metabolism that is excreted via urine. ♄♂.

Ureter: Duct by which urine passes from the kidney to the bladder. Base. ♎ [1] ♀.

1 Heindel, Astro-Diagnosis, 21.

Urethra: Duct by which urine is conveyed out of the body from the bladder, and in men also conveys semen. Base. Sac. ♎, ♏.

Urine: Yellowish waste fluid made by the filtering process of the kidneys. Base. ♎♀.

- **Urinary Tract:** The body's drainage system for removing urine. Kidneys make urine, Scorpio removes it. Base. ♎♀ (♏♂♇).

- **Urinary Tract Infection, Cystitis:** A bacterial infection in the bladder/ in the urinary tract. Link the urinary tract [and infection]. Base. ♎♀ (♏♂♇) [♅☌♆].
(1) Carlos Menem (2 Jul 1930, 06:20, La Rioja, Argentina). ♀ [☐♂ ♉/♏].
(2) Jerry Lewis (16 Mar 1926, 12:15, Newark, NJ). ♀8 [☍♆].
(3) Terri Schiavo (3 Dec 1963, no time). ♀ [☌♂].
(4) Barbara Rare (30 Jun 1944, 14:04, Gisborne NZ). ☽♎12 [⚻♅]. ♀ [∠♂ r6H].
(5) Virginia Rappe (7 Jul 1891, no time). American actress of the silent screen died after having sex with a comedy super-star of the day, Fatty Arbuckle. An autopsy showed she died from cystitis. ♂♋ [☐♅♎].

- **Urine Hesitancy in Older Men:** Difficulty urinating due to an enlarged prostate. Link urine [and hesitancy/ older]. Jupiter may link in for the 'enlarged' problem. Base. ♎♀ [♑♄].

Uterus/ the Womb: Female organ in which offspring are conceived and gestate before they are birthed. Problems in the uterus are represented by afflictions to Cancer and the Moon. Sac. ♋☽.

- **Uterine Cancer:** (See Cancer). Link the uterus to the cancer formula: Sac. ♋☽[(♋☽ >♄♇) > ♃☉].
(1) Ann Dunham (29 Nov 1942, 08:34, Sedgwick, KS). Mother of US President Barack Obama, died of the disease in 1995. ☽ [♇8 mp ☽/♃♋].
(2) Eva Peron (7 May 1919, 05:00, Buenos Aires, Argentina). The first lady of Argentina died of the disease in 1952. ☽ [(☌♄, ∠♇ r8H) > ☐☉].
(3) Lois Rodden (22 May 1928, 00:27, Lang, Saskatchewan, Canada). Canadian-American astrologer. In 1973, she had surgery for cervical and uterine cancer - and later for other cancers over the years. ☽♋ r6H [(☌♇♋) > ♇∠☉].
(4) Sylvia-Jo Schlueter (26 Sep 1937, 05:42, Rock Island, IL). Another astrologer, she was diagnosed with uterine cancer in 2000. Treatment was not recommended as it had metastasised. She died in 2001. ☽ [♄ mp ☽/♃♑].

- **Uterine Fibroids, Tumours:** Fibroids are muscular tumours that grow in the wall of the uterus. They are noncancerous. Link the uterus [benign tumour]. Sac. ♋☽ [♋☽ > ♃].
(1) Condoleeza Rice (14 Nov 1954, 11:30, Birmingham, AL). In 2004, she had surgery to alleviate symptoms of benign fibroid tumours. ☽♋6 [wide conjunct - ♅♋☌♃6].

Uvula: Fleshy hanging ball back of throat, which prevents food or liquid from going up the nose. Thr. ♉♀.

V

Vaccine: A biological preparation which provides immunity to a particular infectious disease. ♅.

Vagina: Female reproductive canal involved in sex, menstruation, pregnancy, childbirth. Sac. ♏ ♀ ♂.

- Vaginal Thrush: A yeast infection of the vagina and vulva. Link vagina [fungal]. ♏ ♀ ♂ [♋ ☽, ♓ ♆].

(1) Charlotte Crosby (17 May 1990, no time). In 2020, the English TV personality and reality star, revealed she was suffering from a bad case of thrush. She is susceptible with: ♀ ♈ 1 [□ ♆ ♑]. ♂ ♓ [⚹ ♆ ♑].

- Vaginitis: A bacterial infection of the vagina, itching and pain caused by an infection. Link vagina [and infection/ inflammation, pain]. ♏ ♀ ♂ [♂ ♅ ♆/ ♂ ☉].

(1) Pauline Borghese (20 Oct 1780, 22:30, Ajaccio, Fr). The sister of Napoleon I. She was reportedly morally lax, and "loved luxury and fornication." She "suffered from continual vaginal distress and illness due to overuse." [1] ♂ [□ ♅ 12, ☌ ♆ ♎].

Vagus Nerve: Also called the '10th cranial nerve' and the 'wandering nerve'. It runs from the brain through the face and thorax to the abdomen. It allows the brain to monitor and receive information about several of the body's different functions.

This nerve has a special function when the crown chakra opens at a spiritually advanced stage. The higher energies entering via the crown are distributed to the rest of the body via the vagus. [2] The vagus is also involved (again at a spiritually advanced stage), when kundalini fire rises from the base chakra to the crown. [3] Ajna. ♊ ☿.

Valves: They control the direction of fluid flows in the body. ♅.

Vans Deferens: A male duct which conveys sperm from the testicle to the urethra. Sac. ♏ ♂ ♇.

Varicose Veins: Gnarled, enlarged veins. Link veins/ blood vessels [and gnarled]. Hrt. ♀/ ♒ ♅ [♄].

Vascular System - see Cardiovascular System.

- Vascular Dementia: (See Dementia). A form of dementia which is caused by small strokes - sometimes such strokes can pass unnoticed. Parts of the brain die because they do not get enough blood. This affects intelligence/ consciousness. Planets for the intelligence (☿ ♀), or consciousness (☉), may connect in. Link the brain [stroke > hardening, death]. Cwn. ♈ ♂, ☽ ♋ [♂ ♅ > ♄ ♇].

(1) Andrew Sachs (7 Apr 1930, 09:00, Berlin-Mitte, Ger). German-British writer and actor died from this disease. ☿ ♈ coruler 12H [disposited by ♂ r6H > ☿ □ ♇ ♋ 1].

1 Astro.com
2 Bailey, Alice: Esoteric Healing, 122.
3 Bailey, Alice: Esoteric Healing, 335-336.

(2) Carl Gardner (29 Apr 1928, 11:00, Tyler, TX). The R&B singer developed this disease and died from its effects. ♀♈ [disposited by ♂8 > ♀□♇♋12].

(3) Margaret Thatcher (13 Oct 1925, 09:00, Grantham, Eng). The British PM was renowned for her razor-like intellect and power-house memory. But that declined due to this disease. A series of strokes led to the death of brain tissue and impairment of consciousness/ intelligence. ♂♎/♈ [□♇♋8].

Veins: Blood circulation tubes carrying oxygen-depleted blood back towards the heart. Hrt. ♀♒♅♆.

Vena Cava: A large vein carrying deoxygenated blood into the heart. Hrt. ♀, ♒♅♆.

Venereal Disease - see Sexually Transmitted Disease.

Venous system: The network of veins that work to deliver deoxygenated blood back to the heart. Hrt. ♀, ♒♅♆.

VENUS. ♀.

Signs it rules: Venus is the exoteric ruler of Taurus and Libra, it is the esoteric ruler of Gemini, and is the hierarchy ruler of Capricorn.

Houses it rules: The 2H and 7H.

Rays: Its personal force is the 5th ray of Science and Concrete Mind. It also carries R3 of Intelligence via its sign Libra, and R4 via Taurus.

Body: Venus governs the ajna and throat chakras, the pituitary and thyroid glands, the nervous system (with Mercury), the venous system, the kidneys and the bladder - the urinary tract (sharing this with Mars and Pluto). It assists digestion with its management of insulin and balancing of glucose levels. Venus co-governs sex and female sex glands, and shares rulership of the menstrual cycle with the Moon.

Disease: When afflicted, Venus can indicate trouble with balance and the nervous system via the ajna chakra, with the throat via Taurus, and with the urine tract via Libra. As the afflictor, it can represent corruption, weakening of tissue, prolapses, desire cravings and behaviours that result in physical disease.

Psychology: Venus represents a desire for pleasure and love, which can manifest as a love of sweet foods if this desire is thwarted. Venus rules the ajna chakra, which is related to our mental development. When it is afflicted, the 5th ray force it carries can indicate mental trouble - an unhealthy detachment and isolation from people and life, narcissism and the debasing of love and sex. Working positively, the 5th ray via Venus gives the ability to think accurately and to reason logically and clearly.

Venus indicates where our thought life needs beautifying, where we should endeavour to think and speak with intelligent love and to radiate soul wisdom - which it also represents.

Vermin: Wild animals (eg. rodents), parasitic worms or insects believed to be harmful to crops, farm animals, to game, or which carry disease. [♏♂♇, 6H].

Vertebrae: (See Spine). The bones forming the backbone. Although the Sun and Saturn generally rule the spine, stretches of vertebrae are specifically ruled by the sign governing their region: Cervical neck bones (C1 - C7), ♉♀. Thoracic or dorsal (T1-T12), ♌☉. Lumbar L1 - L5 (♎♀). Sacrum (S1–S5), (♐♃). Tailbone, coccyx (♐♃).

- Vertebrae Degeneration: Gradual loss of normal structure and function of the spine over time. Base. ♌☉ [♄ (♇)].

Vertigo: Internal spinning sensation that upsets balance. It is commonly caused by an inner ear problem. Link the ears [spinning/ imbalance]. Ajna. ♊ ☿ [♅/ ♎].

(1) Jim Hodgson (8 Sep 1947, 01:55, Hawkwell, Eng). The victim of a road-rage attack in 2021, in which the temporal bone in his skull was fractured. He suffered seriously from vertigo just after it happened. Over time, it became less acute. ☿ 3H of transport [□ ♅ ♊ 12].

(2) Les Paul (9 Jun 1915, 02:00, Waukesha, WI). The American musician had several operations for Meniere's syndrome, a vertigo-inducing ear disorder. ☿ ♋ r6H [☽ □ ♅ ♒].

(3) Louisa May Alcott (29 Nov 1832, 00:30, Germantown, PA). The author suffered from vertigo and other maladies for many years. ☿ [⚹ ☽ 6 fluid in the ear, ☽ ☌ ♅ ♒].

Vestibular System, the Balance System in the Body: It includes fluid canals and crystals in the inner ear, which process the sensory information involved with balance and eye movements. Ajna. ♎ ♀.

Violate, Violent: Eruptive force, using force to hurt or attack. [♂ ♅].

VIRGO. ♍.

Rulers: The exoteric ruler is Mercury. The esoteric ruler is the Moon unveiling Vulcan. (The Moon represents the body, while Vulcan represents the purification of the body which begins when we step onto the Path of Spiritual Development). The hierarchy ruler of Virgo is Jupiter.

Rays: Virgo carries R2 of Wisdom and R6 of Devotion and Idealism. It also carries R4 via Mercury and the Moon, and R1 via Vulcan. Virgo's energy is practical, technical, discriminatory and intelligent.

Body: Virgo is related to the solar plexus chakra, and digestion through its rulership of the intestines.

Disease: When planets are afflicted in Virgo, or when Virgo rules the 6H, it indicates trouble with the intestines, and/ or with the lymphatic system, governed by its opposite sign Pisces. As an afflictor, Virgo promotes criticalness, worry, fretfulness, peevishness, all of which can lead to niggling problems with the bowels.

Psychology: Negative Virgo is critical, nit-picking, complaining. Positively, it teaches us to be meticulous and discriminatory, and in time to start choosing higher and finer ways of being, doing and expressing. Eventually this leads to the birth of the Christ spirit (love and wisdom) in the heart - the higher keynote of Virgo is, 'Christ in you, the hope of glory.'

Virile: Having strength, energy, and a strong sex drive. Sac. ♂.

Virus: An infectious disease. Viruses are of the nature of Neptune, subtle and stealthy, hiding until they replicate enormously prior to flooding the body. [♆ (♂ ♅)].

Viscera: The soft internal organs of the body. ♋ ☽.

Viscous: Being thick, sticky. [♄>♃].

Vision - see Sight.

Vitality, Vitalise: Vitality is the energy of life, and good vitality is essential for life, for good health and immunity.

> When vitality is great and the life force has free and unimpeded circulation, germs cannot find a lodging and there will not be the risk of infection. [1]

1 Bailey, Alice: Esoteric Healing, 321,

The primary representative of vitality is the Sun. Mars "vitalises, purifies and stimulates all aspects and organisms in the body, via the blood stream." [1] Hrt. ☉♂.

Vitamins: Organic compounds essential for normal growth and nutrition. ☉♃.

Vitiligo: A disease that usually starts in childhood, which causes the loss of skin colour. The immune system attacks melanocytes cells, which give the skin colour. Self-hatred underlies autoimmune diseases - in this case, dislike of the appearance.

The Moon and Saturn make the complexion paler, but Saturn can also darken skin. Link appearance/ skin [immune attack > pale]. Base. Asc, 1H / ♑♄ (♋) [♂ > ☽♄].

(1) Lauren Elyse (29 Apr 1991, 08:51, Chicago, IL). At the early age of 5, she developed vitiligo in her knees. By 20, it had spread to her face. Asc [⚼ ☽]. ☿ ruler Asc ♊ [□♂ > ⚻☽].

(2)Michael Jackson (29 Aug 1958, 19:33, Gary, IN). Hating his face, his colour, he underwent extensive cosmetic surgeries to change his appearance. Asc [☌☽1, ☽□♄ > ♄⚻♂]. Mars for the immune attack and surgery.

(3) Rigo Tovar (29 Mar 1946, 12:45, Matamoros, MX). A Mexican singer. Asc ♋ [☌♂1 > ☌♄12].

(4) Tamar Braxton (17 Mar 1977, 00:45, Severn, MD). An American singer. ♃6, ruler Asc [□☽♂ > ♂qd ♄].

(5) Winnie Harlow (27 July 1994, no time). She was diagnosed with vitiligo at age four. A zero Aries rising chart is used, and the Moon is conjunct that point. Asc [☌☽♈].

Vocal Cords: Two bands of muscle within the larynx (voice box), which vibrate to produce the voice. Thr. ♉♀ (♊☿).

Voice: The sound produced in a person's larynx (voice box) and uttered through the mouth. ♉☿.

- Voice Box - see Larynx.

- Voice Loss (of): (See Laryngitis). A temporary loss of voice can be caused by an infection, or straining the voice to talk or sing. Permanent loss of voice can be caused by medical conditions that impair vocal cord nerves. Link vocal cords / the voice [infection/ strain > loss]. Thr. ♉♀ / ☿♊ [♂♅♆ > ♄♇].

(1) Aureliano Pertile (9 Nov 1885, 11:20, Montagnana, Italy). A singer, he lost his voice at age 17. Eight years later his voice was sufficiently improved and he returned to opera. ☿♐ [Tsq. □♂ > ☍♇♊]. ♀♑12 [Tsq. □♅ > ☍♄♋6].

(2) Connie Francis (12 Dec 1937, 07:28, Newark, NJ). After an operation in 1977 to correct postnasal drip, the songstress lost her voice for four years. ☿♑1 r6H [∠♂ > ♄ disposits ☿].

Vomit: Forcefully expel the stomach's contents out of the mouth. Link stomach contents [and vomit]. Spx. ♋☽ [♂♅]

- Vomit, Choked On: Choking on one's own vomit. Add to the formula, rulers for death if the subject dies. Link stomach contents [vomit > choked]. Spx. ♋☽ [♂♅ > ♏♇].

(1) Bon Scott (9 Jul 1946, 23:20, Forfar, Scotland). The lead vocalist of the hard rock band AC/DC, went on an all-night drinking binge. Later he choked on his own vomit and died. ☽♏8 [♂♍ r8H, mp ☽/♅].

1 Bailey, Alice: Esoteric Astrology, 211.

VULCAN. ↓.

Signs it rules: Esoteric ruler of Taurus and Virgo, hierarchy ruler of Taurus.

This 'undiscovered' planet is known to occultists. It is the closest planet to the Sun, orbiting very close to the fiery star. Vulcan is not an exoteric or traditional ruler of a sign. It does not rule or develop the personality nature. It influences consciousness when we begin to develop spiritually.

Ray: Vulcan carries the 1st ray and represents the will of God.

Body: More research is required.

Disease: More research is required.

Psychology: When active in the life of aspirants, those who have recently stepped onto the Path of Spiritual Development, Vulcan is felt as the urge to apply personal disciplines and to purify the life. Via Taurus, purification of desire and the sex life; via the Moon, the urge to purify the emotions; via Virgo, purification at all levels - health, the emotions and thought life. Vulcan rules the crown chakra in disciples and initiates. When operational at this level, it manifests as higher spiritual will, the 'will of God' in manifestation.

Vulva: The outer part of the female genitals. Sac. ♏ ♂ ♀.

W

Waist: Part of the body below the ribs and above the hips. ♎♀.

Warts: Small, fleshy bump on the skin caused by human papilloma virus. Warts are traditionally ruled by Saturn. Base [♄].

Water Retention: - see Oedema.

Water, Watery: The symbol of the astral or emotional plane is water—fluid, stormy, reflecting all impressions. Hence, water problems in the body like oedema, occur under water sign, or Moon, Neptune afflictions. [1] ♋☽,♓♆.

Wasting Away: To become thinner and weaker because of illness or lack of food. [♄♆].

Weakens, Weakness (in the body): To cause to become less strong. Ray 4 [2] (carried by the Moon), and ray 6 [3] (carried by Pisces and Neptune), weaken. Pisces and Neptune dilute and dissolve boundaries, thereby weakening. [♓♆, ☽].

Weight: The body's relative mass (Saturn). ♄.

Wheezing: Breathing with a whistling or rattling sound in the chest. It can be caused by an obstruction in the airways, airway muscles becoming spastic in response to an allergen, the airway lining being inflamed and narrowed, mucous or a foreign object physically blocking airflow. Link breathing [and whistling]. Thr. ♊☿ [♂♅].

Whiplash: The head suddenly moves backward then whips forward, causing a neck vertebrae injury. Saturn for vertebrae may link in. Link neck/ head [whip, fracture, injury]. Thr. ♉♀/ ♈♂ [♂♅].

(1) James Huberty (11 Oct 1942, 00:11, Canton, OH). Debilitating car wrecks left him with whiplash ♀♎/♈ [☌♂]; and tremors ☿ [⚻♅♊].

(2) Jennifer Grey (26 Mar 1960, no time). A whiplash injury ripped off the ligaments at the back of her neck, leaving her with long-term headaches and shoulder pain. ♂ head [☍♅].

(3) Lynn Rodden (14 Mar 1951, 23:11, Palo Alto, CA). Between 1972 and 1982 she had four whiplash car accidents with mild concussions, leading to endless headaches. ♂♈ [□♅].

White Blood Cells: (See Cells, Tissue, T-Cells). They are immune system cells. Produced in bone marrow, they are stored in blood and lymph tissue. When called upon, they race forth to defend the body. All body cells are ruled by the 3rd ray of matter, carried by Cancer, Libra, Capricorn, the Earth and Saturn. Hrt. ♋☽.

White-collar Crime: A nonviolent crime, based on deceit and fraud. Some forms of this are: embezzlement, theft, identity theft, Ponzi Schemes, online scamming. The personality is greedy and predatory, and preys on the vulnerability, weakness or naivety of people.

---

1 Bailey, Alice: The Rays and the Initiations, 581.
2 Bailey, Alice; Esoteric Healing, 301.
3 Bailey, Alice; Esoteric Healing, 303.

Mercury is the thief; Neptune rules fraud; Saturn carrying R3, is intelligently cunning and avaricious; Pluto and Scorpio rule predators; and Taurus is the primary sign of greed. Link the self, the 2nd/ 8th houses of money [greedy, predatory, thieving]. R3. Thr. ☉, Asc, 2/8H [♉, ☿ ♆ ♄ ♇].

Ponzi Schemes.

These three men were convicted for running Ponzi Schemes - a fraudulent system that pays profits to earlier investors, from funds extracted from later investors.

(1) Bernie Madoff (29 Apr 1938, 13:50, New York, NY). American businessman whose Ponzi scheme is considered to be the largest financial fraud in U.S. history. ☉ ♉ [☌ ☽ ♉ , ☽ ⚼ ♆♍1 r8H]. Asc ♌ [☉ ♉]. Asc [⚼ ♄8].

(2) Charles Ponzi (3 Mar 1882, 23:15, Lugo, Italy). Italian swindler and con artist, after whom Ponzi schemes are named. ☉♓5 (speculation, gambling) [⚹ ♆♉; ♆∠♂8]. ☿ r8H [□ ♃ ♇ ♉].

(3) Dieter Behring (27 Apr 1955, 05:00, Solothurn, Switzerland). A devious Swiss financier. Asc [☍♆; ♆⚼♂ r8H]. ♂ is in the 2H of personal money. He siphoned other people's money into his personal bank account.

Whooping Cough: Contagious bacterial disease affecting the airways. It is characterized by convulsive, hacking coughs followed by a whoop as the body struggles to breathe. It is a serious disease because it can lead to pneumonia, brain damage and sometimes death. Link throat/ airways [bacterial disease > cough]. Thr. ♉ ♀, ☿ ♊ [♂ ♅ ♆ > ♂ ♅].

These 3 examples who lived in Gresham PA, all died of the disease.

(1) Astro.com 7022 (24 Feb 1932, 06:30). ☿ ♓ [☌ ♂ coruler 8H > ∠ ♅ coruler 12H].

(2) Astro.com 7027 (10 Mar 1932, 18:25). ♀ ☽ ♉8 [∠♂♓6].

(3) Astro.com 8321 (16 Feb 1939, 23:50). ☿ r8H [mp ♂ r6H/ ♅ ♉/♏].

Will to Live, to Survive, to Exist: The instinct to survive when life is threatened. A ray 1, Pluto response, embedded in the animal nature, in the base chakra. It is the most powerful instinct in the animal body. Base. R1, ♇.

Wind: (See Colic). Caused by air swallowed by a baby when feeding, crying or yawning. Symptoms are squirming or crying during a feed. It can cause colic. Spx [☿].

Windpipe - see Trachea.

Wither: Slowly disappear, lose weight, become thin and weak. Saturn is the prime significator of this problem. Link to the planet/ organ affected. [♄ ♆].

(1) Bob Dole (22 Jul 1923, 00:10, Russell, KS). The American politician suffered a withered right arm (♊ ☿), as the result of a war injury. ☿ [(☌ ♂ for war), ☿ mp ♆/♇].

(2) Kaiser Wilhelm II (27 Jan 1859, 15:00, Potsdam, Ger). The German aristocrat had a difficult birth, leaving him with a withered arm, which he always tried to conceal. Link birth > arm [wither]. ☽ ♏ for birth [∠ ☿ ♑6 disposited by ♄].

Womb - see Uterus.

Women. Adult female human beings. ♋ ☽.

Workaholic: Person who compulsively (♇), works (♍, 6H), excessively hard and long hours (♄). ☉ Asc [♍ ☿, 6H, ♄].

(1) Eunice Shriver (10 Jul 1921, 11:00, Brookline, MA). Asc [☌ ♄ ♍].

(2) Melanie Chisholm (12 Jan 1974, 21:32, Widnes, Eng). A member of the Spice Girl group, she described herself as a workaholic. Asc [☌ ☽ ♄ ♍].

(3) Ron Howard (1 Mar 1954, 9:03, Duncan, OK). Howard considers himself a workaholic. ☉ ☿ r6H [△ ♄ r10H].

Worms: Intestinal worms are one of the main types of parasites in humans, living and breeding mostly in the bowel. The most common worm is the threadworm. Link the bowel [and worms]. Spx. ♏♂♆ (♍ ☿) [♏♂♆].

(1) Una Chiodini (21 Nov 1936,10:58, Chicago, IL). She was an American numerologist, palmist and astrologer. In 1965, she became so physically run down, she said "the body began to shut down, bringing on a case of worms". Astro.com. ♅ ♉/♏ [⚻ ♂ ♎8].

Worry: Cause to feel anxious or troubled. Thr. Spx [♄].

Wounds: Injuries to living tissue caused by a cut, blow, or other impact. [♂].

Wrinkles: Creases, folds, or ridges in the skin. Base. ♄.

Wrist: The joint between the hand and arm. Thr. ♊ ☿ .

- **Wrist Fracture**: A broken bone in the wrist joint. Link wrist [and fracture]. Thr. ♊ ☿ [♂ ♅].

(1) Joe Namath (31 May 1943, 21:00, Beaver Falls, PA). The American football great had many fractures during his career. ☿ 6℞ [☌ ♅ ♊].

(2) Mike Connors (15 Aug 1925, 14:50, Fresno, CA). American actor suffered a wrist fracture and other injuries from doing his own movie action-stunt. ☿ ℞ coruler 6 [☌ ♂].

(3) Robert Stack (13 Jan 1919, 16:40, Los Angeles, CA). The movie actor was a top polo player but was forced to retire after fracturing his right wrist three times. ☿ ♑6 [disposited by ♄ (bones) ♄ ☍ ♂ ♅].

X

X-Ray: An image of the internal composition of the body. ♅.

Xeroderma: Excessively dry skin. Link skin [dry]. ♑ ♄ (♋ ☽) [♄].

Xerostomia: Dry mouth. Link mouth [dry]. ♉ ♀ [♄].

Y

Yaws: A chronic bacterial infection that most often affects children in tropical regions of Africa, Asia and Latin America. A berry-like sore spreads, as the infection attacks the skin, bone and cartilage. It can disfigure and disable. Link skin and bones [infection/ sore] Base. ♑ ♄ (♋ ☽) [♅ ♂ ♆].

Yeast Infection: A fungal infection. Candida and Thrush are synonymous terms. See Candida.

Yellow Fever: Viral infection spread by mosquitos, which can damage the liver (hence the yellowing of skin), and other internal organs. It can be fatal in severe cases. Link the liver [parasite > infection/ fever]. Spx. ♃ (♋ ☽) [♏ ♂ ♇ > ♂ ♅ ♆].

These men died from the disease.

(1) Benajamin Bache (12 Aug 1769, no time), an American journalist. ♃ ♏ [⚹ ♂ ♆ ♍].

(2) Louis Faidherbe (15 Jan 1857, 16:00, Saint-Louis, Senegal). ♃ r6H [mp ♂/♇].

(3) Paul-Louis Simond (30 Jul 1858, 11:00, Beaufort-sur-Gervanne, Fr). ♃ r6H [♇ mp ♃8 / ☽ ♆ ♓6].

(4) Seisaku Noguchi (24 Nov 1876, 11:30, Sekiwaki, Japan). ♃ [∠ ♂ ♎8, qd ♇].

Z

Zika Virus: Spread by mosquitos, the disease spreads in tropical areas with large mosquito populations. While affected people can have mild or no symptoms, an infection during pregnancy can cause a miscarriage, and infants to be born with serious congenital malformations. For instances concerning babies, link pregnancy [infection > serious malformation] Sac. ♋ ☽ [♆ ♂ ♅ > ♄ ♇, ♅].

Zoonosis: An infectious disease that has jumped from a nonhuman animal to humans. [♂ ♅ ♆].

Final Words

"The Science of the Centres is yet in its infancy, as is the Science of the Rays and the Science of Astrology. But much is being learned and developed along these three lines and when the present barriers are down and true scientific investigation is instituted along these lines, a new era will begin for the human being. These three sciences will constitute the three major departments of the Science of Psychology in the New Age, plus the contributions of modern psychology and the insight into the nature of man (particularly the physical nature) which it has so wonderfully developed." Master Djwhal Khul. [1]

---

1   Bailey, Esoteric Psychology, vol. II, p479-480.

—

Bibliography

Bailey, Alice A.
   A Treatise of Cosmic Fire, (11th printing 1977).
   A Treatise on White Magic, (13th printing 1974).
   Discipleship in the New Age II, (5th printing 1979).
   Education in the New Age (6th printing 1971).
   Esoteric Astrology, (11th printing 1975).
   Esoteric Healing, (8th printing 1977).
   Esoteric Psychology I, (9th printing 1979).
   Esoteric Psychology II, (9th printing 1979).
   From Intellect to Intuition, (6th printing 1965).
   Letters on Occult Meditation, (13th printing 1979).
   The Destiny of the Nations, (5th printing 1974).
   The Externalisation of the Hierarchy, (7th printing 1982).
   The Light of the Soul (9th printing, 1972).
   The Rays and the Initiations, (5th printing 1976).
   The Soul and its Mechanism, (5th printing 1971).

Bills, Rex, E. The Rulership Book (2007 printing).

Blavatsky, H. P. Collected Writings, vol IV. Theosophical Society CD Rom.

Cornell, H. L. The Encyclopaedia of Medical Astrology (3rd edition 1972).

Cramer, Diane, L. Dictionary of Medical Astrology (2003).

Daath, Heinrich. Medical Astrology, (Cosimo printing 2005).

Hay, Louise. Heal Your Body. 1982.

Heindel, Max. Astro-Diagnosis or a Guide to Healing, (9th Edition, 1976).

Hodgson, Leoni.
   Astrology of Spirit, Soul & Body. Amazon, Ingram's, 2018.
   Journey of the Soul (7th revised printing). Amazon, Ingram's, 2018.
   Medical Astrology. Amazon, Ingram's, 2018.

Jansky, Robert. Modern Medical Astrology (2nd revision 1978).

Made in United States
North Haven, CT
11 May 2024

52408329R00098